Anonymous

Norfolk Records:

Preserved in the Public Record Office, London: Volume II.

Anonymous

Norfolk Records:
Preserved in the Public Record Office, London: Volume II.

ISBN/EAN: 9783744783385

Printed in Europe, USA, Canada, Australia, Japan

Cover: Foto ©Suzi / pixelio.de

More available books at **www.hansebooks.com**

Norfolk Records:

BEING AN

INDEX TO FOUR SERIES OF NORFOLK INQUISITIONS,

The Tower Series, The Chancery or
Rolls Series, The Exchequer Series, The Wards
and Liveries or Court of Wards Series,

PRESERVED

IN THE PUBLIC RECORD OFFICE, LONDON.

Volume II.

EDITED BY

WALTER RYE.

Norwich:

PRINTED FOR THE NORFOLK AND NORWICH ARCHÆOLOGICAL SOCIETY
BY AGAS H. GOOSE, RAMPANT HORSE STREET.

1892.

NOTICE.

Mr. Walter Rye having kindly offered the following Index of Norfolk Inquisitions to the Norfolk and Norwich Archæological Society, the Committee has decided to print it as a continuation of the Calendar of *Norfolk Records*, by Mr. Walford Selby, issued to the Members in 1886. That Volume was called Volume I., and was to have been followed by another also compiled by him. His lamented death, however, brought his work to an unexpected termination.

PREFACE.

THE four series of Inquisitions to the Norfolk entries to which I print a collected index in this volume, consist of :—

(1) The Tower Series, of which very inaccurate calendars, giving the names and localities only, were printed by the Government many years ago, in four volumes folio, abounding in errors, arising chiefly from the compilation of the calendars being entrusted to men who had no special knowledge of the place-names of each county, and who, therefore, made very many natural mistakes in reading them.

(2) The Chancery, or, as it is sometimes called, The Rolls Series, which is really only a continuation of the last; but the calendar to which remained unprinted until the late Mr. Selby printed it for our Society, in his "Norfolk Records" (1886).

(3) The Exchequer Series; calendars of which were first printed in the 10th Report of the Deputy Keeper, from which Mr. Selby reprinted them in the volume just mentioned.

(4) The Wards and Liveries, or, as it is sometimes called, The Court of Wards Series, the list—we can hardly call it an index—of which was first printed by Mr. Selby in the same volume.

Besides these there is the series belonging to the Duchy of
Lancaster, which contains some relating to Norfolk, but the people
named in them are not, with a few exceptions, of the same class
as those in the other series.

However useful it was to have printed calendars of Nos. 2 and 4,
there was still the great drawback that No. 1 was only alphabetically
and not lexicographically arranged, and that No. 3 was not arranged
in index form at all, but under the names of the different escheators,
and that much of No. 4 was not arranged at all.   Consequently,
before one could find out what inquisitions there were relating to
any one family, one had to search—

(1) One, or rather four, printed volumes of calendar in No. 1,
with four of fairly good lexicographical index.

(2) One alphabetical list.

(3) One mass of absolutely unindexed matter.

(4) One alphabetical list, and some more wholly unindexed matter.

Or, in all, no less than eight searches had to be made, two of
them being very long and troublesome.

Finding it absolutely necessary to have for my own use in my
edition of the *Norfolk Visitations*, which I am about to issue for
the Harleian Society, to have a more consultable work, I have
arranged the scattered entries in the following pages, so one
opening shows all the entries relating to one family, and the exact
reference needed to write for the document—for example, in
writing for an Exchequer inquisition, it is unluckily necessary to
give the escheator's name, as a guide to the bundle in which it is
to be found.

A somewhat lengthy apprenticeship to the study of Norfolk
surnames, has enabled me to correct many errors of the various
calendarers, who having no special knowledge of Norfolk surnames,
have often made sad hashes of them; *i.a.*, reading Candewell for
Caudewell, Carnell for Carvell, Divileston for Durleston, Hervle
for Kervile, Bonycher for Bouycher, and Hepham for Hexham.

Other readings can often be guessed at, *e.g.*, Blyant is probably Bryant, and Brodoocke, Broderick.

Mis-spellings I have tried to bring back to their proper places, *e.g.*, Genison should be Jennison, Jillet should be Gillett, but in every case I have put cross references to the original or corrected entry.

In the groupings, I have throughout adopted the natural or usually adopted spelling, the archaic spelling with "y" being altered by me throughout to "i," wherever the spelling has not become quite fixed otherwise, as in Wynne, &c.

Thus "Barncy" and "Burney" will be found under Berney, Bullen under Boleyn, Gurling under Girling, Skarburgh under Scarburgh, Skarlet under Scarlet, Hubart and Hubbard under Hobart, and Hoogan and Huggon under Hogan. By the way, the aristocratic-sounding surname of Gurdon now turns out to come, not from Scotch Gordon, but from Gording or Gourding.

While working out so many surnames, the *variorum* readings have suggested several derivations for well-known Norfolk names, for example, Caley is, no doubt, the Norman de Cailly; Mealing, de Meauling; Money, le Moigne; Limmer, Lomnour; Nunn, de Noion; Pecke, de Pecche; Pratt, de Pratis; and Rowse, de Rous.

"Well-beloved" is probably the "Bienamour" we find here, and Heylett the diminutive of Hale or Heyle, while Ropkyn seems similarly Roperkyn; and our well-known Norfolk surname of Riches is Richards or Richers.

The interchange of initials is noteworthy; Powditch is clearly Bowditch, and Twyer, Dwyer. Both of these would, of course, be missed by a searcher who looked for them under their proper initials, as would Nevette by a searcher for Knevett.

The double names, which seem in most cases trade-names tacked on to patronymics, are interesting, and a complete list of them should be made out, as it might help many an aspiring Smith or Baker out of his genealogical mire. Among them are Ladd, alias Baker; Lomb, alias Baker; and Warren, alias Baker. Some of these aliases, however, are *variorum* readings, as Kendall, alias Tindall; Cremer, alias Skrme; Sparke, alias Parker.

The result of a careful study of these lists is very instructive. They give an accurate idea as to whether a family really was of the greater gentry in the old days or not; for if a family held any quantity of land worth having, its name must be found here.

Searchers should note that from Richard I. to Henry VI. the printed folio calendars of the Chancery Series give the names of the places at which the dead men held land, and the "Calendarium Genealogicum," which covers the reigns of Henry III. and Edward I., gives the actual words of the finding as to the heir; so that for the first two reigns the country student, who has not the chance of looking up the manuscript, can, by combining the facts in the two calendars, practically get the substance of the inquisition, or something like it.

WALTER RYE.

NORFOLK INQUISITIONS.

Abergavenny, Edward, Earl of; Tower, 16 Edw. IV., No. 66 (4, p. 378a).

Ablotte—Richard Ablotte; Ch., 4 and 5 P. and M., pt. 1, No. 118.

Adamson—John Adamson; W. and L., 18-20 Eliz., vol. 18, p. 9; Ch., 19 Eliz., pt. 2, No. 55.

Aguillon—Robert Aguillon; Tower, 14 Edw. I., No. 16 (1, p. 89b).

Albiniaco, de—Isabel de Albiniaco; Tower, 12 Edw. I., No. 34 (1, p. 84b).

Isabella de Albiniaco; Tower, 10 Edw. II., No. 72 (1, p. 285a).

Alden—J. Henry Alden; Ch. Misc., 14 Jas. I., pt. 6, No. 120.

Aldham—John Aldham; Ch., 10 Chas. I., pt. 3, No. 26.

Aldred—Roger Aldred; Exch., 34-35 Hen. VIII. (Robt. Downys, Esch.), No. 36.

Aldrich or Aldreche—Thomas Aldreche, sen.; Exch., 33-34 Hen. VIII. (Thos. Halse, Esch.), No. 7.

Thomas Aldreche; Ch., 34 Hen. VIII., No. 37.

John Aldreche; W. and L., 6 Chas. I., bund. 48, No. 122, and Ch., 6 Chas. I., pt. 3, No. 77.

Richard Aldreche; Ch. Misc., 5 Jas. I., pt. 6, No. 103.

Allcocke—John Allcocke; W. and L., 23 and 24 Eliz., vol. 20, p. 108, and Ch., 23 Eliz., pt. 2, No. 112, W. and L.

Allen or Alleyn—Robert Aleyn; Tower, 6 Edw. IV., No. 11 (4, p. 333b).

John Aleyn; Tower, 20 Edw. IV., No. 21 (4, p. 399b).

Thomas Aleyn, Gent.; Exch., 20-21 Hen. VIII. (Henry Rychers, Esch.), No. 15.

Allen or Alleyn—Thomas Allen; Ch., 21 Hen. VIII., No. 138; and Ch., v.o. Eliz., bund. 1, No. 205.

Thomas Allen; W. and L., 15 and 16 Eliz., vol. 14, p. 83; and Ch., 15 Eliz., No. 143.

Nicholas Allen; Ch., 2 Chas. I., pt. 2, No. 40.

Henry Allen; Ch., 1 and 2 P. and M., pt. 2, No. 51.

Robert Allen; Ch. Misc., 18 Chas. I., pt. 16, No. 24.

Aleyns—Christiana Aleyns, wid. of Geoffrey; Tower, 5 Hen. IV., No. 5 (3, p. 294a).

Allington—William Allington; Ch., 1 Hen. VII., No. 80.

William Alyngton; Exch., 1-2 Hen. VII. (Gregory Lovell, Esch.), No. 5.

John Alyngton, Esq.; Exch., 1 Eliz. (James Bigott, Esch.), No. 27.

John Alyngton; Ch., 1 Eliz., pt. 3, No. 134.

Alpe—Edward Alpe; W. and L., 7 and 8 Jas. I., bund. 3, No. 109; 8 Jas. I., bund. 15, No. 151; and Ch., 8 Jas. I., pt. 2, No. 138.

Alverd—Thomas Alverd, Esq.; Exch., 34-35 Hen. VIII. (Robert Downys, Esch.), No. 45.

Ambley—Galfr. de Ambley; Tower S., 29 Hen. III., No. 32.

Amys—Christopher Amys; W. and L., 5 and 6 Edw. VI., vol. 6, p. 109; Ch., 6 Edw. VI., pt. 2, No. 50; Ch., 1 Jas. I., pt. 13, No. 55; Ch., 21 Jas. I., pt. 2, No. 139; W. and L., 21 Jas. I., bundle 36, No. 163.

Andrewes—Stephen Andrewes; W. and L., 6 Eliz., bund. 9, No. 22, and Ch., 6 Eliz., pt. 1, No. 144.

Edward Andrewes; Ch. Misc., 8 Chas. I., pt. 81, No. 90.

Anguish—Edward Anguish; Ch. Misc., 14 Jas. I., pt. 6, No. 122.

Richard Anguish; W. and L., 4 Chas. I., bund. 45, No. 26; Ch., 4 Chas. I., pt. 2, No. 4; and Ch., 4 Chas. I., pt. 24, No. 157.

Anketel—Nicholas Anketel; Tower S., 14 Rich. II., No. 72 (3, p. 128a).

Antingham—Bartholomew de Antingham; Tower S., 16 Edw. I., No. 36 (1, p. 96b).

Antingham—Bartholomew de Antingham; Tower S., 17 Edw. I., No. 10 (1, p. 98b).

Bartholomew de Antingham; Tower S., 39 Edw. III. (2nd Nos.) No. 18 (2, p. 272a).

Appleton—William Appulton, Esq.; Exch., 32-33 Hen. VIII. (John Tasburgh, Esch.), No. 22.

Appleyard—William Appleyard; Tower S., 15 Rich. II., pt. 1, No. 77 (3, p. 140a).

William Appleyard; Tower S., 7 Hen. V., No. 6 (4, p. 47b).

Nicholas Appleyard, Knt.; Ch., 10 Hen. VIII., No. 13, and Exch., 9 and 10 Hen. VIII. (Henry Russell, Esch.), No. 14.

John Appelyerd; Ch., 14 Hen. VII., No. 124.

John Applyard; Exch., 13-14 Hen. VII. (Philip Tilney, Esch.), No. 10.

Roger Applyard; Exch., 21-22 Hen. VIII. (Anthony Thwaytys, Esch.), No. 5.

Roger Applyerd; Ch., 21 Hen. VIII., No. 7.

Thomas Applyard, Esq.; Exch., 2-3 Edw. VI. (John Flowerdew, Esch.), No. 16; W. and L., 3 Edw. VI., vol. 3, p. 87; and Ch., 3 Edw. VI., pt. 1, No. 112.

Argentine, de—Giles de Argenteyn; Tower S., 11 Edw. I., No. 19.

John de Argenteyn; Tower S., 12 Edw. II., No. 43 (1, p. 291a).

Armiger—William Armiger; W. and L., 6 Jas. I., bund. 11, No. 153, and Ch., 7 Jas. I., pt. 1, No. 148.

Armstead—William Armstead; Ch., 16 Chas. I., pt. 3, Nos. 93 and 112.

Arnold—William Arnold, Sen., Gent.; Exch., 14-15 Hen. VIII. (John Brampton, Esch.), No. 4; and Ch., 15 Hen. VIII., No. 102.

Arundel, Earl of—Richard, Earl of Arundel; Tower S., 21 Rich. II., No. 2 (3, p. 213a; and see 3, p. 224a and b).

Thomas, Earl of Arundel; 4 Hen. V., No. 54 (4, p. 26b).

John, Earl of Arundel; 13 Hen. VI., No. 37 (4, p. 161b).

Beatrix, Countess of Arundel; 18 Hen. VI., No. 28 (4, p. 197b).

Humfrey, s. and h. of John, late Count of Arundel; 16 Hen. VI. (4, p. 113a).

Arundel—John Arundel; Tower S., 9 Hen. V., No. 20 (4, p. 60b).
  ,,   ,,   Tower S., 7 Hen. VI., No. 25 (4, p. 120).
  Joan Arundell; Exch., 14-15 Hen. VIII. (John Brampton,
    Esch.), No. 1 ; and Exch., 15-16 Hen. VIII. (Christopher
    Harman, Esch.), No. 15.

Ashfield—Robert Ashfelde; Tower S., 3 Hen. IV., No. 11 (3, p. 280).
  John Ashfeld; Ch., 15 Hen. VII., No. 30.
  George Aysshefeld; Exch., 9-10 Hen. VIII. (Henry Russell,
    Esch.), No. 7.
  Margery Asshefeld; Exch., 15-16 Hen. VIII. (Christopher
    Harman, Esch.), No. 6.
  Robert Asshefelde; Exch., 4-5 Edw. VI. (John Tirrell,
    Esch.), No. 15.

Aslak—Richard Aslak; W. and L., 15 and 16 Edw. VI., vol. 6, p. 96,
    and Ch., 7 Edw. VI., pt. 1, No. 46.

Astley—Thomas Astley; Ch., 16 Hen. VII., No. 76.
  ,,   ,,   Ch., 36 Jas., No. 102.
  Sir Francis Astley; W. and L., 15 (?) Chas. I., bund. 61,
    No. 156, and Ch., 15 Chas. I., pt. 3, No. 92.
  Thomas Astley; W. and L., 15 Jas. I., bund. 35, No. 219.
  ,,   ,,   Ch., 20 Jas. I., pt. 2, No. 140.
  Isaac Astley; Ch., 41 Eliz., pt. 1, No. 44.

Asty—Thomas Asty, Gent.; Ch. Misc., 11 Chas. I., pt. 22, No. 32.

Athill—James Athell; Ch., 40 Eliz., pt. 2, No. 35; W. and L., 43
    and 44 Eliz., vol. 26, p. 102 ; Ch., 42 Eliz., pt. 2, No.
    25 ; Ch., 42 Eliz., pt. 2, No. 100.
  John Athell; W. and L., 41 and 42 Eliz., vol. 24, p. No. 115.
  James Athell, yeoman; Ch. Misc., 1 Chas. I., pt. 5, No. 71.
  Roger Athell, Gent. ; Ch. Misc., 12 Chas. I., pt. 31, No. 108.

Athol, Countess of—Elizabeth, Countess of Athol; 49 Edw. III.,
    pt. 1, No. 4 (2, p. 337b).

Athow—Elizabeth Athow; W. and L., 9 Chas. I., bund. 53, No. 221.
  Thomas Athow ; W. and L., 7 Chas. I., bund. 62, No. 322.
  Robert Athow ; Ch., 9 Chas. I., pt. 1, No. 31 ; Ch., 11 Eliz.,
    9 Chas. I., pt. 1, No. 99.
  Thomas Athaue ; Ch., 15 Chas. I., pt. 3, No. 39.

Atte Lath. See **Lath.**

Atmere—Robert Atmere; Misc. Ch., 8 Jas. I., pt. 6, No. 107.

Atwoods. See **Woods.**

Aubyn—Reginald Aubyn; Tower S., 23 Edw. III., pt. 2, No. 117 (2, p. 148a).

Audley—Hugh de Audele, Comes Glouces.; Tower S. (2, p. 137a), 21 Edw. III. (1st Nov.), No. 59 (2, p. 137b).

    John Awdeley, Knt.; Exch., 22-23 Hen. VIII. (Edmund Clere, Esch.), No. 5.

    John Awdeley; Exch., 27-28 Hen. VIII. (Thomas Woodehouse, Esch.), No. 9.

    Thomas Audley; Ch., 20 Jas. I., pt. 1, No. 34; Ch., 19 Jas. I., pt. 1, No. 4; W. and L., 19 Jas. I., bund. 33, No. 147; W. and L., 20 Jas. I., bund. 35, No. 183.

Aunterons (?)—John Aunterons; Tower S., 46 Edw. III., pt. 1, No. 2 (2, p. 315a).

    John Anterons; Tower S., App., 46 Edw. III., No. 10 (4, p. 454a).

Austen—John Austen; W. and L., 4 Chas. I., bund. 46, No. 136, and Ch., 4 Chas. I., pt. 2, No. 45.

Avenel—John Avenel; Tower S., 33 Edw. III., pt. 1, No. 15 (2, p. 212a). John Avenell; Tower S., 6 Rich. II., No. 6 (3, p. 45b).

Avilers, de—Bartholomew de Avilers; Tower S., 4 Edw. I., No. 70 (1, p. 60).

Avys—William Avys; Ch., v.o. Eliz., bund. 3, No. 245.

Aylmer—Alexander Aylemer, Esq.; Exch., 4-5 Edw. VI. (John Tirrell, Esch.), No. 1.

    Alexander Aylmer; Ch., 5 Edw. VI., pt. 2, No. 40.

Bachecroft. See **Beachcroft.**

Bachelor. See **Batchelor.**

Bacon (? also see **Beacon**)—Margerie, ux. Edward Bacon; 27 Edw. III. (1st Nos.), No. 28 (2, p. 181b).

    Robert Bacon (felo); Tower S., 45 Edw. III. (2nd Nos.), No. 30 (2, p. 313b); and see 46 Edw. III. (2nd Nos.), No. 57a; and 47 (2nd Nos.), 12 and 40; and 51 Edw. III. (2nd Nos.), No. 52.

    Robert Bacon of Dickleburgh, action with King; Tower S., 15 Rich. II., pt. 2, No. 184 (3, p. 151a).

Bacon—Bartholomew Bacon and Johana ux.; Tower S., 15 Rich. II., pt. 1, No. 10 (3, p. 133a).

John Bacon; Tower S., 18 Edw. IV., No. 16 (4, p. 388a).

Thomas Bacon; Exch., 1-2 Hen. VII. (Gregory Lovell, Esch.), No. 1.

Thomas Bacon (? Bilton); Ch., 1 Hen. VII., No. 96.

Richard Bacon; Ch., 33 Hen. VIII., No. 45.

John Bacon; Exch., 3-4 Hen. VIII. (Anthony Hansart, Esch.), No. 3.

Richard Bacon, Gent.; Exch., 32-33 Hen. VIII. (John Tasburgh, Esch.), No. 4.

Edmund Bacon, Esq.; Exch., 1 Mary to 1 and 2 Philip and Mary (Edmund Wright, Esch.), No. 15.

John Bacon, Gent.; Exch., 1 Eliz. (James Bigott, Esch.), No. 8.

Robert Bacon; W. and L., 1-3 Eliz., vol. 8, p. 80.

    ,,   ,,   Ch., 2 Eliz., pt. 2, No. 36.

Baquevil Bacon; W. and L., 11 Chas. I., bund. 56, No. 220; Ch., 11 Chas. I., pt. 1, No. 19; and Ch., 17 Chas. I., pt. 3, No. 26.

Lady Dorothy Bacon; W. and L., 8 Chas. I., bund. 56, No. 44; and Ch., 11 Chas. I., pt. 2, No. 27.

Nathaniel Bacon, Knt.; Ch., 11 Chas. I., pt. 2, No. 154; and Ch., 17 Chas. I., pt. 3, No. 57.

Bagecroft. See **Beachcroft.**

Bagge—Simon Bagge; Ch., v.o. Eliz., bund. 3, No. 132.

Baispoll. See **Baspoole.**

Baker (and see **Lamb als. Baker**; and see **Warren als. Baker.**)

William Baker; Ch., 10 Hen. VII., No. 57.

    ,,   ,,   Exch., 7 Edw. VI. to 1 Mary (John Spencer, Esch.), No. 4.

William Baker; Ch., 7 Edw. VI., pt. 1, No. 49.

Edward Baker; Exch., 1 Mary to 1 and 2 Philip and Mary (Edmund Wright, Esch.), No. 5.

Edward Baker; Ch., 1 and 2 P. and M., pt. 2, No. 53.

Balaam—Robert Balam; Ch., 15 Eliz., No. 144.

Charles Balam; Ch., 34 Eliz., pt. 2, No. 54.

Baldry—George Baldrye; Exch., 31-32 Hen. VIII. (William Andrews, Esch.), No. 11.

Richard Baldry; Exch., 37-38 Hen. VIII. (John Spencer, Esch.), No. 22.

Ball—John Balle; Ch., 34 Hen. VIII., pt. 2, No. 53.

Balliol—John de Balliolo; Tower S., 8 Edw. II., No. 30 (1, p. 257a).

Bancroft—Thomas Bancroft; W. and L., 12 Chas. I., bund. 57, No. 90; and Ch., 12 Chas. I., pt. 3, No. 112.

Baniard. See **Baynard**.

Banting—William Banting; Ch., 39 Eliz., pt. 2, No. 48.

Bardolf—William Bardulf; Tower S., 4 Edward I., No. 51, and 18 Edw. I., No. 29 (1, p. 102a).

Juliana de Bardolf; Tower S., 23 Edw. I., No. 129 (1, p. 127a).

Hugh Bardolf; Tower S., 32 Edw. I., No. 64 (1, p. 191b).

Robert Bardolf; Tower S., 33 Edw. I., No. 21.

Isabelle Bardolf, wife of Hugh; Tower S., 17 Edw. II., No. 39 (1, p. 308a).

Thomas Bardolf and Agnes ux.; Tower S., 3 Edw. III. (1st Nos.), No. 66 (2, p. 24a).

John Bardolf; Tower S., 45 Edw. III. (1st Nos.), No. 7 (2, p. 308a).

William de Bardolf; Tower S., 9 Rich. II., No. 11 (3, p. 74a).

William de Bardolf; Tower S., 13 Rich. II., No. 6 (3, p. 112a).

Lady Johanna Bardolf; Tower S., 25 Hen. VI., No. 29-30 (4, p. 234a).

Bardwell. See **Berdwell**.

Barker—Thomas Barker; Misc. Ch., 15 Chas. I., pt. 31, No. 172.

Barnaby—Katherine Barnabe; Exch., 26-27 Hen. VIII. (Philip Bedingfeld, Esch.), No. 5.

Barnack—John Barnack; Tower S., 11 Hen. IV., No. 17 (3, p. 328a).

Maria Barnack; Tower S., 9 Hen. V., No. 32a (4, p. 58b).

Barnard—Richard Barnard; W. and L., 35 Hen. VIII., vol. 1, p. 75.

Robert Barnard; Exch., 3-4 Hen. VIII. (Anthony Hansart, Esch.), No. 14.

Robert Barnard; W. and L., 2-5 Jas. I., vol. 30, p. 6; and Ch., 4 Jas. I., pt. 2, No. 45.

Barnard—Edward Barnard ; Ch., 18 Jas. I., pt. 2, No. 68.

    Also see **Bearnard.**

Barnardiston—Thomas Barnardyston, Knt. ; Exch., 34-35 Hen. VIII. (Robert Downys, Esch.), No. 20.

Barnwell—Stephen Barnewell ; Ch., 2 Chas. I., pt. 3, No. 163.

Barney. See **Berney.**

Barrett—John Barrett ; Ch., 9 Hen. VII., No. 4.

    Henry Barrett ; Ch., 37 Eliz., pt. 2, No. 15.

    Thomas Barrett; W. and L., 9 and 10 Jas. I., bund. 4, No. 13 ; and Ch., 10 Jas. I., pt. 1, No. 9.

    Jane Barrett ; Ch., 17 Jas. I., pt. 3, No. 53.

Barsham—Nicholas Barsham ; Exch., 2-3 Edw. VI. (John Flowerdew, Esch.), No. 10, and W. and L., 3-5 Edw. VI., vol. 5, p. 23.

    Nicholas Barsham ; Ch., 306, pt. 1, No. 108.

Baspoole—Robert Baspoole ; W. and L., 1-3 Jas. I., vol. 27, p. 13, and Ch., 2 Jas. I., pt. 2, No. 98.

    John Baspoole ; Ch., 13 Jas. I., pt. 1, No. 10.

    Robert Baspoole ; Ch. Misc., 21 Jas. I., pt. 5, No. 59.

    John Baspoole ; Ch. Misc., 8 Jas. I., pt. 6, No. 109.

    John Baspoole ; W. and L., 13 Jas. I., bund. 22, No. 200.

    Henry Baspoole ; W. and L., 2 Chas. I., pt. 3, No. 117.

Basset—Ralph Basset ; Tower S., 14 Rich. II., No. 9 (3, p. 124b), and Tower S., 14 Rich. II., No. 85 (3, p. 128b).

    Johanna Basset, wife of Ralph ; Tower S., 4 Hen. IV., No. 38 (3, p. 286b).

Batchelor—Thomas Batchelor; Ch., 17 Jas. I., pt. 3, No. 29.

    ,,   ,,   W. and L., 17 Jas. I., bund. 28, No. 108.

Bate—Anthony Bate ; W. and L., 20 Eliz., vol. 19, p. 16 ; and Ch., 20 Eliz., pt. 2, No. 33.

Bateman—Anthony Bateman ; W. and L., 22 Jas. I., bund. 41, No. 31 ; and Ch., 22 Jas. I., pt. 2, No. 38.

    Thomas Bateman ; Ch., 2 and 3 P. and M., No. 49.

    John Bateman; Ch., 11 Jas. I., pt. 3, No. 126 ; Ch. Misc., 10 Jas. I., pt. 6, No. 132 ; W. and L., 11 Jas. I., bund. 18, No. 138.

    Constance Bateman ; Ch., 2 Chas. I., pt. 3, No. 178.

    Thomas Bateman ; Ch., 16 Jas. I., pt. 1, No. 163.

Bates—Robert Bates; W. and L., 8 Chas. I., bund. 51, No. 64, and Ch., 8 Chas. I., pt. 2, No. 26.

Batesford—William Batesford; Tower S., 1 Hen. VI., No. 60 (4, p. 74b).

Bathonia, de—Alina de Batonia; Tower S., 2 Edw. I., No. 13.

John de Bathonie; Tower S., 19 Edw. I., No. 13 (1, p. 105a).

Bavaria—Matilda, ux. William, Duke of Bavaria; Tower S., 36 Edw. III. (1st pt.), No. 37 (2, p. 247a).

Baxter, Page als. See **Page**.

Baxter—Robert Baxter; Ch., 14 Eliz., No. 130.

Thomas Baxter; Ch., 37 Eliz., pt. 2, No. 80.

John Baxter: Ch., 42 Eliz., pt. 2, No 98.

Thomas Baxter; Misc. Ch., 12 Jas. I., pt. 6, No. 150.

Stephen Baxter; W. and L., 10 Chas. I., bund. 61, No. 160.

Thomas Baxter; Ch., 17 Chas. I., pt. 3, No. 14.

,, ,, W. and L., 1-6 Jas. I., bund. 2, No. 198; and Ch., 5 Jas. I., pt. 2, No. 13.

Thomas Baxter; 14 Jas. I., bund. 24, No. 168; and Ch., 14 Jas. I., pt. 3, No. 103.

Thomas Baxter; Ch. Misc., 4 Chas. I., pt. 25, No. 85.

Bayly—Robert Bayly; W. and L., 12 Jas. I., bund. 21, No. 73; and Ch., 12 Jas. I., pt. 1, No. 100, and pt. 2, No. 103.

Thomas Bayly; Ch., 17 Chas. I., pt. 3, No. 25.

Baynard—Fulco Baynard; Tower S., 33 Edw. I., No. 58.

Robert Baynard and Matilda his wife; Tower S., 4 Edw. III. (1st Nos.), No. 28 (2, p. 30b).

Robert Baynard and Matilda ux.; Tower S., 23 Edw. III. (1st Nos.), No. 7 (2, p. 148b).

Richard Banyarde; Exch., 34-5 Hen. VIII. (Richard Downys, Esch.), No. 46.

Richard Baniard; Ch., 35 Hen. VIII., No. 1.

Beauchamp. See **Bello Campo, de**.

Beachcroft—Thomas Beachcroft; Ch., 16 Hen. VII., No. 82.

Simon Beachcroft; Ch., v.o. Rich. III. to Hen. VII., No. 316.

William Bagecroft, Gent.; Exch., 9-10 Hen. VIII. (Henry Russell, Esch.), No. 1.

Beachcroft—Richard Bachecroft, Gent.; Exch., 3-4 Edw. VI. (Henry Minne, Esch.), No. 6.

Richard Bachecroft; Ch., 3 Edw. VI., pt. 1, No. 100.

Beacon—Cuthbert Beacon; W. and L., 9 Chas. I., bund. 53, No. 73; and Ch., 9 Chas. I., pt. 1, No. 36. [? See **Bacon**].

Beales—Richard Beales; Ch., v.o. Eliz., bund. 1, No. 176; and W. and L., 9-11 Eliz., vol. 11, p. 42; and Exch., 11 Eliz. (William Atwood, Esch.), No. 14.

Robert Beales; W. and L., 22 Jas. I., bund. 41, No. 127; and Ch., 1 Chas. I., pt. 2, No. 23.

Bealet (?)—Robert Bealet (? Beales); Ch., 17 Chas. I., pt. 3, No. 53.

Bealknap—Robert Bealknap; Tower S., 11 Rich. II., No. 116 (3, p. 99a).

Beardwell. See **Berdwell**.

Beaucham. See **Bello Campo, de**.

Beaufort, Duke of—Thomas, Duke of Beaufort; Exch., Tower S., 5 Hen. VI., No. 56 (4, p. 111b).

Beaufoy. See **Bella Fago, de**.

Beaumont or Bello Monte, de—Centia de Bello Monte; Tower S., 21 Edw. I., No. 49 (1, p. 114c).

William Beaumont; Tower S., 5 Edw. IV., No. 36 (4, p. 332b).

William Beaumont; Exch., 2-3 Hen. VIII. (Geo. Bokenham, Esch.), No. 7.

William Beaumont, Viscount; Ch., v.o. Hen. VIII., bund. 1, No. 41; and Ch., 1 Hen. VIII., No. 86.

Beaupre—Nicholas Beaupre; Exch., 5-6 Hen. VIII. (William Gryce, Esch.), No. 15.

Margaret Beaupre; Ch., 6 Hen. VIII., No. 70.

,, ,, Exch., 5-6 Hen. VIII. (William Gryce, Esch.), No. 2.

Edmund Beaupre; Ch., 10 Eliz., No. 60.

Edmund Beaupre, Esq.; Exch., 10 Eliz. (George Chettinge, Esch.), No. 2.

Beckham—John Bckham; Exch., 32-33 Hen. VIII. (John Tasburgh, Esch.), No. 7; Ch., 33 Hen. VIII., No. 184.

Richard Bekham; Ch., 22 Jas. I., pt. 5, No. 57.

Beckham—Walter Bekham; W. and L., 1-3 Eliz., vol. 8, p. 83; and
Ch., 3 Eliz., No. 160.

Walter Beckham; Exch., 3 Eliz. (Edmund Wright, Esch.),
No. 7.

Richard Beckham; W. and L., 11 Chas. I., bund. 56, No. 261.

Beckeswell. See **Bexwell.**

Beckswell. See **Bexwell.**

Bedford, Duke of—John, Duke of Bedford; Tower Rec., 14 Hen. VI.,
No. 36 (4, p. 168b).

Jasper, Duke of Bedford; Ch., v.o. Rich. III. to Hen.
VII., No. 281.

Bedingfield—Margaret Bedingfield; Tower Rec., 15 Edw. IV., No. 38
(4, p. 372a).

Robert de Bedingfield; Tower S., 2 Edw. II., No. 36.

Edmund Bedyngfeld, Knt.; Ch., 13 Hen. VII., No. 4.

Margaret Bedyngfeld; Exch., 6-7 Hen. VIII. (John Eston,
Esch.), No. 13; and Ch., 7 Hen. VIII., No. 77.

Thomas Bedyngfeld, Knt.; Exch., 30-31 Hen. VIII. (William
Woodhouse, Esch.), No. 9; & Ch., 31 Hen. VIII., No. 19.

Philip Bedyngfeld, Esq.; Exch., 34-35 Hen. VIII. (Robert
Downys, Esch.), No. 30.

John Bedyngfeld, Esq.; Exch., 37-38 Hen. VIII. (John
Spencer, Esch.), No. 5; and Ch., 38 Henry VIII., No. 35.

Francis Bedyngfeld, Esq.; Exch., 3-4 Edw. VI. (Henry
Minne, Esch.), No. 8.

Edmund Bedingfeld, Knt.; Exch., 7 Edw. VI. to 1 Mary
(John Spencer, Esch.), No. 15; and Ch., 7 Edw. VI., pt.
1, No. 51.

Anthony Bedingfeld, Esq.; Exch., 17-18 Eliz. (John Bacon,
Esch.), No. 8; Ch., 17 Eliz., pt. 1, No. 104; and W. and
L., 17 and 18 Eliz., vol. 17, p. 18.

Henry Bedingfeld, Knt.; Ch., 25 Eliz., pt. 1, No. 61.

Edmund Bedingfeld; Ch., 28 Eliz., pt. 1, No. 83.

Thomas Bedingfeld; Ch., 32 Eliz., pt. 1, No. 90.

Eustace Bedingfeld; Ch., 42 Eliz., pt. 2, No. 51; and W. and
L., 43 and 44 Eliz., vol. 26, p. 28.

Robert Bedingfeld; Ch., 44 Eliz., pt. 2, No. 173.

Bedingfield—Eustace Bedingfeld (quæ plura); Ch., 44 Eliz., pt. 2, No. 56.
Humphrey Bedingfeld, Esq.; Ch. Misc., 9 Jas. I., pt. 6, No. 127.
Philip Bedingfeld, Knt.; Ch., 5 Chas. I., pt. 2, No. 85.
Edmund Bedingfeld; Ch., 11 Chas. I., pt. 2, No. 105.

Beeles. See **Beales.**

Beke—Henry Beke; Ch., 14 Chas. I., pt. 3, No. 138; and W. and L.,
14 Chas. I., bund. 60, No. 311.

Belet—Margerie, ux. William Belet; Tower S., 1 Edw. II., No. 14.
Robert Belet; Tower S., App., Ed. II., No. 34 (4, p. 429b),
proof of age.
Ingelramus Belet and Lora ux.; Tower S., 6 Edw. II.,
No. 28 (1, p. 248a).

Belhus—Richard de Belhus; Tower S., 29 Edw. I., No. 55 (1, p. 169a).
Richard de Belhous; Tower, 33 Edw. III. (2nd Nos.),
No. 33 (2, p. 214b).
Richard Belhus; Tower, 10 Hen. VI., No. 22 (4, p. 135b).

Bell—Sir Edmund Bell (Edward?); W. and L., 6 James I., bund. 8,
No. 1; and Ch., 6 Jas. I., pt. 2, No. 133.
Sir Robert Bell; W. and L., 20 Eliz., vol. 19, p. 87; and
Ch., 20 Eliz., pt. 2, No. 28.
Sinolph Bell; W. and L., 13 Chas. I., bund. 62, No. 87; and
Ch., 15 Chas I., pt. 3, No. 27.

Bello Campo, de—Guy de Bello Campo; Tower, 34 Edw. III. (1st
Nos.), No. 27 (2, p. 219a).
Philippa, ux. Guy Bello Campo; Tower, 8 Ric. II., No.
7 (3, p. 67a).
Johanna, widow of Bello Campo; Tower, 14 Hen. VI.,
No. 35 (4, p. 166b).
Richard de Bello Campo, Earl of Warwick; Tower, 17
Hen. VI., No. 54 (4, p. 192b).
Henry de Bello Campo, Duke of Warwick; Tower, 24
Hen. VI., No. 43 (4, p. 230a).

Bellofago, de, or Beaufoy—Amicia q. f. ux. Galr'e de Bellofago;
Tower, 20 Edw. I., No. 33-4 (Citra Trentam), Old No.
96 (1, p. 111b.) (Portf. ⅓).
William Beauson (Beaufoy) and Alice his wife; Tower, 21
Edw. III. (1st Nos.), No. 10 (2, p. 134a).

Bellofago, de, or Beaufoy—William de Beaufowe; Tower, 23 Edw. III. (2nd pt.), No. 36 (2, p. 155b).

John Beaufoy; Tower, 3 Hen. VI., No. 6 (4, p. 82b).

Bendish—Elizabeth Bendishe; Ch., Exch., 2 and 3, 3 and 4, P. and M. (Ralph Shelton, Esch.), No. 2.

Edmund Bendish; Ch., 3-7 Jas. I., vol. 25, p. 68.

(Edward?) Bendish; Ch., 7 Jas. I., pt. 1, No. 192.

John Bendish; Ch., 40 Eliz., pt. 2, No. 60.

Bennett—John Bennett; W. and L., 15 and 16 Eliz., vol. 14, p. 66; and Ch., 14 Eliz., No. 131, and 16 Eliz., pt. 1, No. 71.

Robert Bennett; Ch., 34 Eliz., pt. 2, No. 32; and Ch., 36 Eliz., pt. 1, No. 21.

Henry Benett; Exch., 31-32 Hen. VIII. (William Andrews, Esch.), No. 15.

Bennington—John Bennington; Ch. Misc., 1 Chas., pt. 5, No. 70.

Benstead—Edward Bensted; Ch., 11 Hen. VIII., No. 56.

Edward Bensted, Knt.; Exch., 10-11 Hen. VIII. (Geoffrey Cobbe, Esch.), No. 5.

Benwell—Thomas Benwell; Ch. Misc., 4 Chas. I., pt. 27, No. 51.

Berdwell—Isabella, wife of John Berdewelle; Tower, 13 Hen. VI., No. 32 (4, p. 159b).

William Bardwell; Ch., 16 Hen. VII., No. 69; Ch., 2 Hen. VIII., No. 67.

William Berdewell; Exch., 1-2 Hen. VIII. (John Glemham, Esch.), No. 12.

Sir Thomas Berdewell; Ch., 15 Jas. I., pt. 1, No. 197.

Berkeley—Lady Jane Berkeley; W. and L., 19 Jas. I., bund. 33, No. 148.

Bernak—William de Bernak; Tower, App., 13 Edw. III., No. 6 (4, p. 441b).

William de Bernak; Tower, 13 Ed. III. (1st Nos.), No. 26, (2, p. 89b), and see 2nd Nos., No. 27.

Hugh Bernak; Tower, 15 Edw. III. (1st Nos.), No. 12 (2, p. 98a).

Alice Bernak, ux. William; Tower, 15 Edw. III. (1st Nos.), No. 41 (2, p. 100a).

Bernak—Hugh Bernak, fil. William ; Tower, 15 Edw. III. (2nd Nos.),
No. 5 (2, p. 101a).

John de Bernak ; Tower, 20 Edw. III. (1st Nos.), No. 49
(2, p. 130a).

William Bernake, fil. John ; Tower, 39 Edw. III. (1st pt.),
No. 7 (2, p. 270a).

Bernard—Robert Bernard ; Ch., 4 Hen. VIII., No. 24.

John Bernard ; W. and L., 15 Chas. I., bund. 62, No. 122 ;
and Ch., 15 Chas. I., pt. 4, No. 48.

Berney—John de Berneye ; Tower, 30 Edw. III. (2nd Nos.), No. 51
(2, p. 201a), and 32 Edw. III. (2nd Nos.), No. 90 (2, p.
210b).

John de Berney ; Tower, 38 Edw. III. (2nd Nos.), No. 43
(2, p. 269a).

John Berney ; Tower, 13 Edw. IV., No. 17 (4, p. 361b).

Robert Berney ; Exch., 3-4 Hen. VII. (Edward Clopton,
Esch.), No. 6.

James Berney ; Ch., 20 Hen. VIII., No. 162.

John Berney, Esq. ; Exch., 4 and 5, 5 and 6 P. and M.
(Andrew Revet, Esch.), No. 18.

John Berney ; Ch., 5 and 6 P. and M., pt. 1, No. 29.

Robert Berney, Esq. ; Exch., 1 Eliz. (James Bigott, Esch.),
No. 26.

John Berney (?) ; Ch., 1 Eliz., pt. 3, No. 126.

John Berney, Esq. ; Exch., 1 Eliz. (James Bigott, Esch.),
No. 28 ; and Ch., 1 Eliz., pt. 3, No. 126.

Henry Berney ; Ch., 26-29 Eliz., vol. 26, p. 96.

,,   ,,   Ch., 27 Eliz., pt. 1, No. 10.

Francis Berney ; Ch., 36 Eliz., pt. 2, No. 110.

,,   ,,   Ch., 41 Eliz., pt. 1, No. 47.

Martin Berney ; Ch., 42 Eliz., pt. 2, No. 86.

Thomas Berney ; W. and L., 14 Jas. I., bund. 24, No. 75.

Thomas Berney, Knt.; Ch., 15 Jas. I., pt. 1, No. 197.

John Berney of Redham ; Ch., 22 Hen. VII., No. 51.

Henry Berney ; W. and L., 15 Chas. I., bund. 61,
No. 155.

See also **Burney.**

Bert—Miles Bert; W. and L., 17 Chas. I., bund. 65, No. 22; and Ch., 18 Chas. I., pt. 1, No. 8.

Berwick—John de Berewyk; Tower, 6 Edw. II., No. 43 (1, p. 250a).

Besevile—Richard Besevile, fil. William; Tower, 40 Edw. III. (1st pt.), No. 9 (2, p. 274a).

Bexwell, als. Schordiche—John Bexwell als. Schordiche; W. and L., 33 Hen. VIII. and 1 Edw. VI., bund. 1a, No. 33.

Richard Bexwell; Ch., 5 Hen. VIII., No. 48.

John Bexwell; Exch., 37-38 Hen. VIII. (John Spencer, Esch.), No. 2.

John Beckswell als. Shordycke; Ch., v.o. Hen. VIII. bund. 3, No. 292.

Humphrey Beckswell; W. and L., 11 and 12 Eliz., vol. 12, p. 28; and Ch., Eliz., No. 70.

Humphrey Beckswell, Gent.; Exch., 12 Eliz. (John Bull, Esch.), No. 2.

Beyvill—William de Beyvill; Tower, 13 Edw. II., No. 19 (1, p. 293a).

Bezill—Almaric de Bezill; Tower, 1 Edw. I., No. 20 (1, p. 49b).

Bidun—Matilda Bydun, als. John; Tower, 39 Hen. III., No. 10 (1, p. 13).

John de Bedun (vide **Rockeford**).

Bienamour—Richard Bienamour; Exch., 5-6 Hen. VII. (John Falstof, Esch.), No. 6.

Bigod—Roger le Bigod; Tower, 54 Hen. III., No. 25 (1, p. 34), No. 85.

John de Bigod; Tower, 33 Edw. I., No. 76.

Ralph Bigod; Tower, 9 Edw. II., No. 58 (1, p. 173b).

Roger Bigot; Tower, 36 Edw. III., pt. 1, No. 15 (2, p. 246b).

William Bygot; Tower, 49 Edw. III., pt. 1, No. 7 (2, p. 338a).

Walter Bygod; Tower, 4 Rich. II., No. 13 (3, p. 29a).

Roger Bygot; Tower, 10 Rich. II., No. 59 (3, p. 89b).

Billesby—Elizabeth Byllesby; Exch., 31-32 Hen. VIII. (William Andrews, Esch.), No. 18.

Billingforth—James Billingforth; Tower, 17 Edw. IV., No. 28 (4, p. 383b).

Billingay—Alice de Billinggeye; Tower, 28 Edw. I., No. 27.

Walter de Billingleye; Tower, 34 Edw. I., No. 32.

Billingay—John de Billingeye ; Tower, 1 Edw. III. (1st Nos.), No. 66
(2, p. 4a).

Birkham—Frank Birkham ; Ch., 22 Eliz., pt. 2, No. 63.

Bishop—John Bishop ; Ch., 14 Hen. VII., No. 91.

John Busshop ; Exch., 13-14 Hen. VII. (Philip Tilney,
Esch.), No. 11.

William Bisshop ; Exch., 30-31 Hen. VIII. (William
Woodhouse, Esch.), No. 3.

William Bishop ; Ch., 13 Chas. I., pt. 1, No. 173.

Bitson—Edward Bitson, Clerk ; Ch., 32 Hen. VIII., No. —

Bitton (?)—Thomas Bitton (Bacon ?) ; Ch., Hen. VII., No. 96.

Blackborne—Henry Blackborne ; Exch., 17 Jas. I., bund. 29, No. 61 ;
and Ch., 17 Jas. I., pt. 3, No. 81.

Bladwell—Giles Bladwell ; W. and L., 1-6 Jas. I., bund. 2, No. 119 ;
and Ch., 5 Jas. I., pt. 1, No. 92.

Blake—Simon Blake ; Exch., 5-6 Henry VII. (John Falstolf, Esch.),
No. 9.

Simon Blake ; Ch., 5 Hen. VII., No. 82.

Jasper Blake ; 1 Edw. VI., vol. 3, p. 6 ; and Ch., 1 Edw. VI.,
pt. 2, No. 21.

Jasper Blake, Gent. ; Ch. Misc., 12 Jas. I., pt. 6, No. 139.

Blakeman—Robert Blakeman, Gent. ; Exch., 15-16 Hen. VIII.
(Christopher Harman, Esch.), No. 7.

Blenerhasset or Bleverhasset—John Blenerhasset ; Exch., 2-3 Hen.
VIII. (George Bokenham, Esch.), No. 1.

Thomas Blenerhayset, Esq. ; Exch., 22-23 Hen. VIII.
(Edmund Clere, Esch.), No. 2.

George Blenerhaysett, Esq. ; Exch., 35-36 Hen. VIII.
(Anthony Thwaytes, Esch.), No. 1.

George Blenerhasset ; W. and L., 36 Hen. VIII., vol. 1, p.
137 ; and Ch., 36 Hen. VIII., No. 13.

John Blenerhasset ; Ch., 16 Hen. VII., No. 79.

,, ,, Ch., 3 Hen. VIII., No. 77.

Thomas Blenerhasset, Knt. ; Ch., 23 Hen. VIII., No. 9.

Blofield—Thomas Blofield ; W. and L., 15 Chas. I., bund. 62, No.
137 ; and Ch., 15 Chas. I., pt. 4, No. 60.

Blomefield—John Blomefield ; Ch., 9 Chas. I., pt. 1, No. 16.

Blomeville—William de Blumville; Tower, 4 Edw. I., No. 54 (1, p. 58).

William Blomvyll, fil. Richard; Tower, App., 10 Hen. VI., No. 1 (4, p. 471a).

Richard Blomevyle; Exch., 5-6 Hen. VI. 2 (John Falstolf, Esch.), No. 11.

Richard Blomevyle; Ch., 6 Hen. VII., No. 91.

Ralph Blomevyle; Ch., 7 Hen. VIII., No. 74.

Ralph Blomeville; Exch., 6-7 Hen. VIII. (John Eston, Esch.), No. 19.

Edward Blomeville, Esq.; Exch., 11 Eliz. (Wm. Attwood, Esch.), No. 5.

Edward Blomeville; Ch., 11 Eliz., No. 102.

John Blomefield; Ch., 9 Chas. I., pt. 1, No. 16.

Blower—Agnes Blower; Exch., 21-22 Hen. VIII. (Anthony Thwaytys, Esch.), No. 8.

Henry Blower; Ch., v.o. Hen. VIII., bundle 2, No. 111.

Blund, le—Robert le Blund; Tower, 47 Hen. III., No. 19.

William le Blund; Tower, 48 Hen. III., No. 25.

Blundeville—Edward Blundeville; W. and L., 9-11 Eliz., vol. 11, p. 93.

Thomas Blundeville; Ch., 4 Jas. I., pt. 2, No. 31.

Thomas Blundeville; Ch., 5 Chas. I., pt. 2, No. 31, and W. and L., 4 Chas. I., bund. 47, No 102.

Blyth—John Blyth; Tower, 20 Ric. II., No. 75 (3, p. 210b).

Bocking—John and Cecilia Bocking; Tower, 17 Edw. IV., No. 67 (4, p. 387b).

Richard Bokyng; Exch., 34-5 Hen. VIII. (Robt. Downys, Esch.), No. 9; W. and L., 35 Hen. VIII., vol. 1, pt. 13; Ch., 35 Hen. VIII., No. 88.

Bodham—John de Bodham (proof of age); Tower, App., 4 Edw. III., No. 6 (4, p. 438a).

William de Bodham; Tower, 45 Hen. III., No. 491, p. 21.

Bohun—John de Bohoun; Tower, 10 Edward II., No. 70 (1, p. 283b).

Humfrey de Bohun; Tower, 37 Edw. III. (1st pt.), No. 10 (2, p. 259b).

Humfrey de Bohun, Comes Hereford; Tower, 46 Edw. III. (1st No.), No. 10 (2, p. 314a).

Bois, de. See **Boys**; **Bosco, de.**

Bokenham—Edward Bukenham: Tower, 20 Edw. IV., No. 27 (4, p. 399b).

George Bokyngham, Esq.; Exch., 15-16 Hen. VIII. (Christopher Harman, Esch.), No. 11.

George Bokenham; Ch., 16 Hen. VIII., No. 68.

Thomas Bokenham; Ch., 28 Hen. VIII., No. 28.

Thomas Bokenham, Esq.; Exch., 27-28 Hen. VIII. (Thos. Woodehouse, Esch.), No. 4.

Margaret Bokenham; Exch., 29-30 Hen. VIII. (John Plandon, Esch.), No. 3.

Catharine Buckenham, widow, a lunatic; W. and L., 6 Jas. I., bundle 11, No. 129; and Ch., 6 Jas. I., pt. 2, No. 42.

Bokkyng. See **Bocking.**

Bole—John Bole, Gent.; Exch., 33-34 Hen. VIII. (Thos. Halse, Esch.), No. 4 (? **Bolt**).

Boleyn—Geoffrey Boleyn; Tower, 3 Edw. IV., No. 21 (4, p. 321a).

Anne Boleyn vel Bolane; Tower, 2 Ric. III., No. 23 (4, p. 420a).

Thomas Bolleyn, Knt.; Exch., 30-31 Hen. VIII. (Wm. Wodehouse, Esch.), No. 4.

Robert Bullen; Ch. Misc., 18 Chas. I., pt. 16, No. 69.

Bolte—Stephen Bolte; W. and L., 33 Hen. VIII., vol. 2, p. 169; Ch., 38 Hen. VIII., No. 27; and Exch., 37-38 Hen. VIII. (John Spencer, Esch.), No. 19.

Bolter—William Bolter; Ch., 4 Hen. VII., No. 42.

Richard Bolter, Gent.; Exch., 37-38 Hen. VIII. (John Spencer, Esch.), No. 10.

Richard Bolter; W. and L., 37 Hen. VIII., vol. 2, p. 40, and Ch., 37 Hen. VIII., No. 48.

Robert Bolter; W. and L., 15 and 16 Eliz., vol. 14, p. 66; and Ch., 16 Eliz., pt. 1, No. 68.

Bolton—Thomas Bolton; Ch., 26 Hen. VIII., No. 52.

Francis Bolton; Ch., 36 Eliz., pt. 2, No. 8.

Bond—John Bonde; Exch., 7-8 Eliz. (Geo. Waller, Esch.), No. 8.

Boning—Thomas Boning; Ch., 4 and 5 P. and M., pt. 3, No. 6.

Bordeleys. See **Burdeleys.**

Borham—Henry de Borham; Tower, 5 Edw. I., No. 3 (1, p. 61).

Borough (see **Burgh?**)—Katherine Borowghe or Boroughe; W. and L., 1 Edw. VI., vol. 3, p. 38; and Ch., 1 Edw. VI., pt. 2, No. 15.

Bosco, de (see **Boys**)—Robert de Bosco; Tower, 27 Edw. I., No. 31 (1, p. 149c).

Robert de Bosco; Tower, 5 Edw. II., No. 49 (1, p. 246b).

Bosoun—William Bosoun; Tower, 2 Hen. VI., No. 33 (4, p. 80a).

Boston—Thomas Boston; 27-28 Hen. VIII. (Thos. Woodehouse, Esch.), No. 10.

Botecourte—Thomas de Botecourte; Tower, 16 Edw. II., No. 56 (1, p. 304a).

Botevileyn. See **Butevelyn.**

Botiller (see **Butler**)—Richard le Botiler; wer, 38 Hen. III., No. 32 (1, p. 9).

Theobald le Botiler; Tower, 33 Hen. III., No. 49 and 52 (1, p. 6).

Joh³. ux. John Boteler; Tower, 45 Edw. III. (1st Nos.), No. 203 (2, p. 307b).

Andrew Botiller; Tower, 9 Hen. VI., No. 3 (4, p. 128a).

Booth or Bothe—Philip Bothe, Knt.; Exch., 31-32 Hen. VIII. (Wm. Andrewes, Esch.), No. 6.

Boucher—Anne Bouegcher; Exch., 11-12 Hen. VIII. (Philip Bernard, Esch.), No. 5.

Boure, Atte—John Atte Boure; Tower, 7 Hen. IV., No. 17 (3, p. 304b).

Roger Boure; Tower, 25 Hen. VI., No. 2 (4, p. 281a).

Bourne—John Bourne; W. and L., 11 and 12 Eliz., vol. 12, p. 73; and Ch., 12 Eliz., No. 75.

Bouslinge (Benslinge?)—Robert Bouslinge; Ch., 3 and 4 P. and M., pt. 1, No. 79.

Bowyer—George Bowyer; Ch., 28 Eliz., pt. 2, No. 88.

Bowditch. See **Powditch.**

Boyland—Richard de Boyland; Tower, 24 Edw. I., No. 60 (1, p. 129; and Ch., 1, p. 33b).

Boys (see **Bosco, de**)—Robert du Boys; Tower, 8 Edw. III. (1st Nos.), No. 41 (2, p. 60a).

James Boys; Ch., 6 Hen. VIII., No. 59.

William Boys; Ch., 22 Eliz., pt. 2, No. 56.

Boys—William Boise ; W. and L., 23 and 24 Eliz., vol. 20, p. 131.

    James Boyse; Exch., 5-6 Hen. VIII. (William Gryce, Esch.),
        No. 12.

Boyton—William de Boyton ; Tower, 38 Edw. I., No. 106 (1, p. 117b).

    William de Boyton ; Tower, 19 Edw. II., No. 84 (1, p. 327a).

    Osbert de Boyton ; Tower, 19 Edw. III. (1st Nos.), No. 18
        (2, p. 123a).

Bradbury—Thomas Bradbury ; W. and L., 8 and 9 Jas. I., bund. 5,
        No. 255 ; and Ch., 9 Jas. I., pt. 1, No. 122.

Bradenham—Henry de Bradenham ; Tower, 32 Edw. I., No. 189 (1,
        p. 195).

Bradford—Nicholas Bradford; W. and L., 6 Chas. I., bund. 49, No.
        184.

    John Bradford ; W. and L., 17 Chas. I., bund. 28, No. 90 ;
        and Ch., v.o. 17 Jas. I., No. 33.

Brampton—Thomas de Brampton ; Tower, 54 Hen. III., No. 5.

    John Brampton, Esq. ; Exch., 27-28 Hen. VIII. (Thos.
        Woodehouse, Esch.), No. 14.

    John Brampton ; Ch., 28 Hen. VIII., No. 57.

    Edward Brampton ; Ch. Misc., 1 Chas. I., pt. 5, No. 76.

Branche—Robert Branche ; Ch., 19 Hen. VII., No. 29.

Brandeston, de—Hugh de Braundeston ; Tower, 27 Edw. I., No. 33.

Brandon—Robert Brandon, Knt. ; Exch., 15-16 Hen. VIII.
        (Christopher Harman, Esch.), No. 17.

    Sir Robt. Brandon ; Ch., 10 Hen. VIII., No. 64.

Branthwayte—Miles Branthwayte ; W. and L., 13 Jas. I., bund. 22,
        No. 260 ; and Ch., 17 Jas. I., pt. 3, Nos. 31, 41, and 43.

    Arthur Branthwayte ; Misc. Ch., 21 Chas. I., pt. 32, Nos.
        117-133.

    Miles Branthwaite ; W. and L, 17 Jas. I., bund. 29, No. 66.

Brend—Catherine Brende ; W. and L., 1-3 Jas. I., vol. 27, p. 156 ;
        and Ch., 3 Jas. I., pt. 1, No. 84.

Breton—Henry de Breton ; 41 Edw. III. (1st Nos.), No. 7 (2, p.
        285b).

Brewes, de—Robert de Brewes ; Tower, 4 Edw. I., No. 4 (1, p. 57a).

    Alice de Breues ; Tower, 29 Edw. I., No. 52.

    Egidius de Brewosa ; Tower, 4 Edw. II., No. 40.

Brewes, de—Marie, ux. William Brewosa; Tower, 19 Edw. II., No. 90
(1, p. 327b).

Robert Brewosa, son and heir of Giles; Tower, 19 Edw. II.,
No. 95 (1, p. 328b.)

Katherine Breux; Tower, 3 Ric. II., No. 14 (3, p. 20b).

Thomas Brewes; Tower, 22 Edw. IV., No. 50 (4, p. 411b).

William Brewes; Exch., 5-6 Hen. VII. (John Falstolf,
Esch.), No. 7.

William Brewse; Exch., 13-14 Hen. VII. (Philip Tilney,
Esch.), No. 1.

Robert Brews, Esq.; Exch., 5-6 Hen. VIII. (Wm. Gryce,
Esch.), No. 6.

Thomas Brews, Esq.; Exch., 6-7 Hen. VIII. (John Eston,
Esch.), No. 17.

William Brewese; Exch., 9-10 Hen. VII. (James Braybroke,
Esch.), No. 14.

William Brewese; Ch., 10 Hen. VII., No. 60.

Robert Brewese; Ch., 6 Hen. VIII., No. 24.

Sir John Brewes; W. and L., 26-29 Eliz., vol. 21, p. 116.

John Brewes, Knt.; Ch., 27 Eliz., pt. 1, No. 98.

Thomas Brewes; Ch., 36 Eliz., pt. 2, No. 116.

William Brewes; Ch., 42 Eliz., pt. 2, No. 127.

Brewster—Thomas Brewster; Ch., 33 Eliz., pt. 1, No. 9.

Thomas Brewster; Ch., 17 Jas. I., pt. 3, No. 3.

Brigge—Thomas Brygge; Exch., 9-10 Hen. VII. (James Braybroke,
Esch.), No. 12.

Thomas Brygge; Ch., 10 Hen. VII., No. 45.

James Brigge; W. and L., 6 Eliz., bund. 9, No. 62.

James Brigge; Ch., 6 Eliz., pt. 2, No. 146.

John Brigge; Ch., 14 Eliz., No. 70.

Briggs—Everard Brigges; Ch., 4 Hen. VIII., No. 50.

Everard Brigges; Ch., 20 Hen. VIII., No. 55.

Eborard Brigges; Exch., 3 1 Hen. VIII. (Anthy. Hansart,
Esch.), No. 9.

Thomas Briggis, Esq.; Exch., 34-35 Hen. VIII. (Robt.
Downys, Esch.), No. 7.

Thomas Briggis; Ch., 35 Hen. VIII., No. 36.

Briggs—John Brigges, Gent.; Exch., 2-3 Edw. VI. (John Flowerdew, Esch.), No. 11.

John Brigges; Ch., 3 Edw. VI., pt. 1, No. 111.

Edward Brigges; Ch., 6 Eliz., pt. 2, No. 147.

Edward Brygges; W. and L., 6 Eliz., bund. 9, No. 58.

George Brygges; Ch., 41 Eliz., pt. 2, No. 43.

Bright—Thomas Bright; Ch., 3 Chas. I., pt. 2, No. 57.

Thomas Bright, sen.; Ch., 43 Eliz., pt. 2, No. 57.

Brightiff or Brightive—John Brightive; 13-14 Hen. VII. (Philip Tilney, Esch.), No. 8.

John Brightiff; Ch., 11 and 12 Hen. VII., No. 81.

Briston—John Briston; Tower, App., 8 Edw. IV., No. 1 (4, p. 476a).

Ralph Briston; Ch., 1 Hen. VII., No. 102.

Ralph Briston; Exch., 1-2 Hen. VII. (Gregory Lovell, Esch.), No. 14.

Brodooke (?)—Simon Brodooke, Gent.; Exch., 1-3 Eliz. (Wm. Drake, Esch.), No. 5.

Broghton (see Broughton)—John Broghton; 19 Edw. IV., No. 46 (4, p. 395b).

Broke—Edward Broke; Tower, 4 Edw. IV., No. 26 (4, p. 324b).

John Broke, Gent.; Exch., 7-8 Eliz. (Geo. Waller, Esch.), No. 5.

Nicholas Broke; Ch., 36 Eliz., pt. 2, No. 101, and 40 Eliz., pt. 2, No. 61.

Brokedish, de—Galf. de Brokedish; Tower, 34 Edw. I., No. 35 (1, p. 206b).

Stephen de Brokedish; Tower, 32 Edw. III. (1st Nos.), No. 6 (2, p. 205b).

Brokesby—Bartholomew Brokysby, Sen., Esq.; Exch., 15-16 Hen. VIII. (Christopher Harman, Esch.), No. 9.

Brome—Roger de Brom; Tower, 32 Edw. I., No. 62 (1, p. 190a).

James Brome; Exch., 1-2 Hen. VIII. (John Glenham, Esch.), No. 12.

James Brome; Ch., v.o. Hen. VIII., bund. 1, No. 57.

Brooke—Edward Brooke, Esq.; Exch., 32-33 Hen. VIII. (John Tasburgh, Esch.), No. 49.

Brooksby (see **Brokesby**)—Maria, wife of Thomas de Brotherton; 36
    Edw. III., 2nd pt., No. 9 (2, p. 252b).

Broughton—John Broghton; Tower, 19 Edw. IV., No. 46 (4, p. 395b).
    John Broughton; Exch., 4-5 Hen. VII. (John Rodon, Esch.),
      No. 1.
    John Broughton; Ch., 5 Hen. VII., No. 141.
    Robert Broughton, Knt.; Ch. 22 Hen. VII., No. 28.
    John Broughton; Ch., 10 Hen. VIII., No. 32.
    John Broughton, Esq.; Exch., 9-10 Hen. VIII. (Henry
      Russell, Esch.), No. 8.

Brounflete—Johanna Brounflete; Tower, 12 Hen.VI., No.43 (4, p. 157a).

Broun or Brown—John Brown; Tower, 17 Edw. III. (1st Nos.), No.
    4 (2, p. 108b).
    Hugh Brown; Tower, 18 Edw. III. (2nd Nos.), No. 63 (2, p.
      121a).
    Philip, fil. John Browne; Tower, 26 Edw. III. (1st Nos.), No.
      18 (2, p. 173a).
    Nicholas Browne; Tower, 30 Hen. VI., No. 1 (4, p. 250a).
    Simon Browne; W. and L., 2 Edw. VI., vol. 3, p. 100; and
      Ch., 2 Edw. VI., pt. 2, No. 39.
    Anne Browne; Ch., 4 and 8 P. and M., pt. 1, No. 116.
    Anne Brown; Exch., 4 and 5, 5 and 6 Philip and Mary
      (Andrew Revet, Esch.), No. 26.
    Robert Browne; Exch., 1-3 Eliz. (Wm. Drake, Esch.), No. 11.
    William Browne; W. and L., 7 and 8 Jas. I., pt. 2, No. 9.
    Henry Browne; W. and L., 22 Jas. I., bund. 57, No. 261.
    Anthony Browne, Knt.; Ch. Misc., 4 Chas. I., pt. 25, No. 22.
    Thomas Browne; W. and L., 12 Chas. I., bund. 57, No. 276;
      and Ch., 12 Jas. I., pt. 3, No. 136.
    Henry Browne; Ch., 12 Chas. I., pt. 3, No. 75.

Bryant (?)—Anne Blyant (Bryant?); Ch., 14 Hen. VIII., No. 52.

Buckskyn—Peter de Buckeskyn; see Tower, 7 Edw. III. (2nd Nos.)
    No. 15 (?, p. 56b).

Bukenham. See **Bokenham.**

Bullen. See **Boleyn.**

Bulwer—Roger Bulwer; Exch., 5-6 Hen. VIII. (Wm. Gryce, Esch.),
    No. 11.

Bulwer—Roger Bulwer; Ch., 6 Hen. VIII., No. 80.

John Bulwer; Ch., 1 Eliz., pt. 1, No. 136.

John Bulwer; Exch., 1 Eliz. (James Bigott, Esch.), No. 33.

Robert Bulwer; W. and L., 14 Jas. I., bund. 23, No. 86.

Roger Bulwer; W. and L., 15 Jas. I., bund. 24, No. 76.

Edward Bulwer; W. and L., 6 Chas. I., bund. 49, No. 170, and Ch., 7 Chas. I., pt. 3, No. 77.

Richard Bulwer; W. and L., 13 Chas. I., bund. 59, No. 156; Ch., 13 Chas. I., pt. 1, No. 201; and Misc. Ch., 15 Chas. I., pt. 31, No. 35.

Bumpstead—Robert Bumpstead, Gent.; Exch., 8-9 Eliz. (Thos. Dereham, Esch.), No. 4.

Buning or Bunting—Thos. Buning; Ch., v.o. 1 and 2 Jas. I., No. 22; and W. and L., 3 Jas. I., bund. 6, No. 56.

Richard Bunting; Ch., 44 Eliz., pt. 2, No. 73; and W. and L., 43 and 44 Eliz., vol. 26, p. 237.

John Buning; Ch., 3 and 4 P. and M., pt. 1, No. 76.

Burdeleys—Galfr. de Burdeleys; Tower, 48 Hen. III., No. 31.

John de Burdeleys; Tower, 11 Edw. I., No. 21 (1, p. 78a).

Margaret, wife of John Burdeleys; Tower, 8 Edw. III. (1st Nos.), No. 31 (2, p. 59b).

John de Burdeleys; Tower, 21 Edw. III. (1st Nos.), No. 46 (2, p. 135a).

Matilda, wife of John Bordeleys; Tower, 35 Edw. III. (1st Nos.), No. 33 (2, p. 229b).

Bures—Robert Bures; Exch., 15-16 Hen. VIII. (Christopher Harman, Esch.), No. 2.

Burges—Robert Burges; W. and L., 6 Chas. I., bund. 49, No. 66; 6 Chas. I., bund. 48, No. 110; Ch., Chas. I., pt. 3, No. 21; and Ch., 7 Chas. I., pt. 3, No. 22.

Burgh, de—Elizabeth de Burgo; Tower, 34 Edw. III. (1st Nos.), No. 83 (2, p. 222b).

William de Burgh; Tower, 12 Ric. II., No. 94 (3, p. 107b).

Burgoin. See **Burgony.**

Burguillon, de—William de Burguillun; Tower, 3 Edw. I., No. 62.

Robert de Burguillun; Tower, Edw. I., No. 136 (1, p. 172a).

Burguillon, de—Robert de Burguillon; Tower, 15 Edw. II., No. 39 (1, p. 299b.)

Sarah de Burguillon; Tower, 16 Edw. II., No. 46b. (1, p. 303b).

Hugh Burgoloun; Tower, 23 Edw. III. (1st Nos.), No. 44 (2, p. 149a).

Burgony—Richard Burgony; Ch., v.o. Eliz., bund. 3, No. 312.

Burlingham—Christopher Burlingham; Ch., 17 Jas. I., pt. 3, No. 90.

Burman—John Burman; Ch. Misc., 22 Jas. I., pt. 5, No. 63; W. and L., 9 Jas. I., pt. 1, No. 132.

Burnell—Philip Burnell; Tower, 22 Edw. I., No. 45 (p. 1, 20a).

Edward Burnell and also his wife; Tower, 9 Edw. II., No. 67 (1, p. 274a).

Alice, ux. Edward Burnel; Tower, 37 Edw. III. (1st pt.), No. 14 (2, p. 260a).

Nicholas Burnell; Tower, 6 Ric. II., No. 20 (3, p. 466).

Burney (see **Berney**)—John Burney; Ch., 1 Eliz., pt. 3, No. 126.

Burradge—Richard Burradge; Ch. Misc., 16 Chas. I., pt. 31, No. 187.

Bursham (see **Barsham**)—W. and L., p. 25.

Burton—William de Buxton; Tower, 49 Edw. III. (1st pt.), No. 18 (2, p. 338b).

Richard Burton; Ch., v.o. Eliz., bund. 3, No. 291.

Burward—John Burward; Exch., 10-17 Eliz. (John Dowbes, Esch.), No. 1.

Bury—Thomas Bury; Exch., 29-30 Hen. VIII. (John Plandon, Esch.), No. 11.

Bussey—William Bussey; Ch., 13 Chas. I., pt. 1, No. 173.

Butecourt. See **Botecourte.**

Butiler. See **Botiler.**

Butler—Robert Butler; Misc. Ch., 13 Chas. I., pt. 1, No. 173.

Buteveleyn—William Buteveleyn (fatuus), 30 Hen. VI., No. 4 (4, p. 250b).

Butt or Butts—William Butte, Knt.; Exch., 37-38 Hen. VIII. (John Spencer, Esch.), No. 23.

William Butt; W. and L., 17 Jas. I., bund. 63, No. 160.

William Buttes, Knt.; Ch., 37 Hen. VIII., No. 50.

William Buttes, Knt.; Ch., 26 Eliz., pt. 1, No. 172.

Butt or Buttes—William Buttes; Ch., 2 Chas. I., pt. 2, No. 143.

Buxton—Robert Buxton; W. and L., 6 Jas. I., bund. 10, No. 203;
   Ch., 6 Jas. I., pt. 2, No. 137 ; W. and L., 8 and 9 Jas. I.,
   bund. 5, No. 68; and Ch., 9 Jas. I., pt. 1, No. 176.

   Francis Buxton; Ch. Misc., 15 Jas. I., pt. 6, No. 140.

Cage—Elizabeth Cage; W. and L., 18 Jas. I., bund. 30, No. 179.

   Elizabeth Cage; Ch., 18 Jas. I., pt. 2, No. 92.

Cailly de—Thomas de Cailly and Margaret his wife; Tower, 10 Edw.
   II., No. 63 (1, p. 281b).

   Thomas le Cailly; Tower, 17 Edw. II., No. 44 (1, p. 308b).

   Johanne ux. Adam Cailly; Tower, 19 Edw. II., No. 66 (1, p.
   326a).

   Thomas de Caylly; Ada de Clifton, cousin and heiress, proof
   of age, App., 2 Edw. III., No. 13 (4, p. 437a).

   John Caly ; Exch., 34-35 Hen. VIII. (Robt. Downys, Esch.),
   No. 34.

Caldewell. See Candewell?

Calibut—Francis Calybut, Sen.; Exch., 8-9 Hen. VIII. (John Stede,
   Esch.), No. 10.

   Francis Calibut; Ch., 9 Hen. VIII., No. 125.

   John Callibut, Esq.; Exch., 2 & 3, 3 & 4 Philip and Mary
   (Ralph Shelton, Esch.), No. 4.

   John Calebutt; Ch., 2 and 3 Philip and Mary, pt. 2, No. 52.

   Bridget Callybutt; Ch., 7 Eliz., No. 140.

   John Calybut; W. and L., 11 and 12 Eliz., vol. 12, p. 74.

   John Calybutt, Esq.; Ch., 12 Eliz., No. 66.

Calthorp—William de Calthorp; Tower, 33 Edward III. (1st Nos.),
   No. 20 (2, p. 212a).

   William Calthorp; Tower, 9 Hen. V., No. 52 (4, p. 61a).

   William fil. John Calthorpe; Tower, 9 Hen. VI., No. 66
   (4, p. 134b), proof of age.

   William Calthorpe, Knt.; Exch., 10-11 Hen. VII. (Richd.
   Hungerford, Esch.), No. 3.

   William Calthrop, Knt. ; Ch., 10 Hen. VII., No. 11.

   William Calthorpe ; Ch., 22 Hen. VIII., No. 64.

   Francis Calthorp, Knt. ; W. and L., 35 Hen. VIII., vol. 1,
   p. 83.

Calthorp—Francis Calthorp, Knt.; Ch., 35 Hen. VIII., No. 22.

Francis Calthorp, Knt.; Exch., 34-35 Hen. VIII. (Robert Downys, Esch.), No. 48.

William Calthorpe, Esq.; Exch., 21-22 Hen. VIII. (Anthony Thwaytys, Esch.), No. 7.

Philip Calthorp, Knt.; Exch., 26-27 Hen. VIII. (Philip Bedingfield, Esch.), No. 1.

Christopher Calthorp; W. and L., 1 Edw. VI., vol. 3, p. 7.

Christopher Caltrop; Ch., 1 Edw. VI., pt. 2, No. 20.

Philip Calthorp; Exch., 2-3 Edw. VI. (John Flowerdew, Esch.), No. 5.

James Calthorpe; Ch., 1 Eliz., pt. 1, No. 125.

Christopher Calthrope; Ch., 4 Eliz., No. 72.

Christopher Calthropp, Esq.; Ch., 10 Eliz., No. 63.

Christopher Callthorpe; Ch., 17 Eliz., pt. 1, No. 110.

Christopher Calthorpe; W. and L., 17 and 18 Eliz., vol. 16, p. 13.

Christopher Calthorpe; W. and L., 17 and 18 Eliz., vol. 17, p. 2.

Christopher Calthorpe; Ch., 18 Eliz., pt. 2, No. 52.

Martin Calthorpe, Knt.; Ch., 36 Eliz., pt. 2, No. 74.

Martin Calthorpe; W. and L., 14 Jas. I., bund. 28, No. 165.

Sir James Calthorpe; W. and L., 14 Jas. I., bund. 29, No. 275.

Martin Calthorp; Ch., 16 Jas. I., pt. 1, No. 144.

James Calthorpe; Ch., 18 Jas. I., pt. 2, No. 140.

Christopher Calthorpe; W. and L., 1 Chas. I., bund. 41, No. 122a.

Christopher Calthorpe; Ch., 1 Chas. I., pt. 2, No. 20.

Henry Calthorpe, Knt.; Ch., 13 Chas. I., pt. 4, No. 160.

Calverley—John de Calverley; Tower, 35 Edw. III. (1st Nos.), No. 48 (2, p. 230b).

Camoys—Ralph Cameys, sen.; Tower, 3 Hen. III., Nos. 2 and 3 (vol. 1, p. 1).

Rad. de Cameys; Tower, 5 Edw. I., No. 1 (vol. 1, p. 61).

Thomas de Camoys; Tower, 9 Hen. V., No. 29 (4, p. 58b).

Canceller—Henry Canceller; W. and L., 1-3 Eliz., vol. 8, p. 66.

Robert Chanceller; W. and L., 1-3 Eliz., vol. 8, p. 116.

Canceller—Robert Canceler; Ch., 2 Eliz., pt. 2, No. 32.

Henry Canceller; Ch., 2 Eliz., pt. 2, No. 33.

Candewell (Caudewell ?)—John Candewell; Exch., 3-4 Hen. VIII. (Anthony Hansart, Esch.), No. 6.

Canham—Simon Canham; Ch., 26 Eliz., pt. 1, No. 161.

Cannon—Robert Cannon, sen.; Ch., 22 Eliz., part 2, No. 61.

Robert Cannon; Ch., 26 Eliz., pt. 1, No. 133.

Robert Cannon; Ch., 33 Eliz., pt. 1, No. 16.

Robert Canon; Ch., 38 Eliz., pt. 2, No. 10.

Capell—William Capell, Knt.; Exch., 6-7 Hen. VIII. (John Eston, Esch.), No. 23.

William Capell, Knt.; Ch., 7 Hen. VIII., No. 5.

Capps—Etheldreda Cappis; Exch., 33-34 Hen. VIII. (Thomas Halse, Esch.), No. 2.

Etheldred Cappys; Ch., 34 Hen. VIII., No. 48.

Carbonel—Robert Carbonel and Margaret his wife; Tower, 21 Richard II., No., 14 (3, 215b).

John Carbonel; Tower, 5 Hen. IV., No. 47 (proof of age), 3, p. 298b.

Richard Carbonel; Tower, 9 Hen. VI., No. 23 (4, p. 129a.)

Carew—John Carewe, Esq.; Exch., 15-16 Hen. VIII. (Christopher Harman, Esch.), No. 9.

John Carewe, Esq.; Exch., 15-16 Hen. VIII. (Christopher Harman, Esch.), No. 10.

Roger Carewe; Ch., 33 Eliz., pt. 2, No. 62.

Carill or Caryll—Thomas Carell, Esq.; Exch., 11 Eliz. (Wm. Attwood, Esch.), No. 9.

Thomas Carrell; W. and L., 9-11 Eliz., vol. 11, p. 35.

Dorothy Cawyll (? Caryll); Ch., 12 Eliz., No. 71.

Dorothy Carill; W. and L., 11 and 12 Eliz., vol. 12, p. 4.

Carlton—Robert Carleton; Ch., 13 Chas. I., pt. 1, No. 192.

Robert Carleton; Ch., 11 Elizabeth, No. 100.

Robert Carleton; W. and L., 13 Chas. I., bund. 59, No. 149.

Carnell (error for **Carvell** or **Kervill**, q.v.)

Carr—Andrew Carr, Clerk; Misc. Ch., 2 Chas. I., pt. 26, No. 127.

Carsey—Robert Carsey; Misc. Ch., 17 Jas. I., pt. 31, No. 87.

Carter—William Carter; Ch., 29 Eliz., pt. 1, No. 207.

Carter—Richard Carter; Ch., 43 Eliz., pt. 2, No. 19.

William Carter; W. and L., 20 Jas. I., bund. 41, No. 62.

William Carter; Ch., 1 Chas. I., pt. 2, No. 1.

William Carter; Ch., 2 Chas. I., pt. 3, No. 54.

Cartwright—Peter Cartwright; Ch., 40 Eliz., pt. 2, No. 149.

John Cartwright; Ch., 9 Jas. I., pt. 2, No. 23.

John Cartwright; W. and L., 9 and 10 Jas. I., bund. 4, No. 130.

Carvell. See **Kerville.**

Castell—Hugh de Castell; Tower, 30 Edw. III. (2nd Nos.), No. 62 (2, p. 201b).

Leonard Castell; Ch., 5 Hen. VIII., No. 47.

Roger Castell; Ch., 23 Eliz., pt. 2, No. 99.

John Castle; Ch., 35 Eliz., pt. 2, No. 96.

Nicholas Castell; W. and L., 2-5 Jas. I., vol. 30, p. 51.

Nicholas Castell, Esq.; Ch., 4 Jas. I., pt. 2, No. 106.

Caston—John de Caston; Tower, 50 Edw. III. (2nd Nos.), No. 50 (2, p. 358a).

Castre—Simon de Castre; Tower, 1 Ric. II. (1st Nos.), No. 14 (3, p. 5a).

Cateson—Robert Cateson; Ch., 16 Hen. VII., No. 75.

Catfield—Roger de Catfeld; Tower, 1 Ric. II. (1st Nos.), No. 11 (3, p. 1b).

Cath, le (see **Kett?**)—Margery, ux. Henry le Cath; Tower, 19 Edw. II., No. 29 (1, p. 324b), (*s.v.* **Fastolf**).

Catlin—Richard Catelin, Esq.; Exch., 2 and 3, 3 and 4 Philip and Mary (Ralph Shelton, Esch.), No. 7.

Richard Catlyn; Ch., 3 and 4 Philip and Mary, pt. 2, No. 122.

Caton—Thomas Caton; W. and L., 6 Eliz., bund. 9, No. 74.

Thomas Caton; Ch., 6 Eliz., No. 150.

Thomas Caton; Ch., 26 Eliz., pt. 1, No. 159.

Henry Caton; Misc. Ch., 6 Chas. I., pt. 32, No. 139.

Henry Caton; Misc. Ch., 16 Chas. I., pt. 30, No. 49.

Cator—Elizabeth Cator; Tower, 20 Edw. IV., No. 20 (4, p. 399a).

Caudewell. See **Candewell** and **Kankewell?**

Cause—Richard Cause; Tower, 19 Edw. IV., No 49 (4, p. 395b).

Richard Cause; Ch., 10 Hen. VII., No. 124.

Cause—Richard Cause; Exch., 10-11 Hen. VII. (Richard Hungerford, Esch.), No. 6.

Cavendish—Alice, ux. John Cavendish; Tower, 6 Hen. VI., No. 37 (4, p. 113b).

Beatrix Cavendish; Tower, 15 Hen. VI., No. 44 (4, p. 176b).

Richard Caundisshe, Knt.; Exch., 8-9 Hen. VIII. (John Stede, Esch.), No. 2.

Thomas Cavendish, Esq.; Exch., 15-16 Hen. VIII. (Christopher Harman, Esch.), No. 13.

Richard Caundish, Knt.; Exch., 1 Mary to 1 and 2 Philip and Mary (Edmund Wright, Esch.), No. 14.

Chadwick—Robert Chadwicke; Ch., 34 Eliz., pt. 2, No. 34.

Chalvers—John Chalvers; Tower, 11 Rich. II., No. 127 (3, p. 99b).

Chamberlain—Robert Chamberlayne, Knt. (attained); Ch., v.o. Rich. III. and Hen. VII., No. 118.

Lady Elizabeth Chamberleyn; Ch., 9 Hen. VIII., No. 116.

Elizabeth Chamberleyn; Exch., 8-9 Hen. VIII. (John Stede, Esch.), No. 5.

Edward Chamberleyn, Knt.; Exch., 32-33 Hen. VIII. (John Tasburgh, Esch.), No. 14.

Edward Chamberleyne, Knt.; Ch., 33 Hen. VIII., No. 11.

Ralph Chamberleyn; Ch., 14 Hen. VIII., No. 125.

Leonard Chamberlaine; Ch., 4 Eliz., No. 80.

George Chamberleyn; W. and L., 5-7 Eliz., vol. 10, p. 101.

George Chamberlaine; Ch., 7 Eliz., No. 139.

George Chamberleyn, Esq.; Exch., 7-8 Eliz. (Geo. Waller, Esch.), No. 3.

Edward Chamberlyne; W. and L., 14 Jas. I., bund. 24, No. 68.

Edward Chamberleyne; W. and L., 15 Jas. I., bund. 25, No. 108.

Edward Chamberleyne; Ch., 15 Jas. I., pt. 2, No. 63.

Edward Chamberlyne; Ch., 15 Jas. I., pt. 1, No. 201.

John Chamberlayne; Ch., 21 Jas. I., pt. 1, No. 112.

John Chamberlayne; Ch., 22 Jas. I., pt. 2, No. 35.

John Chamberlain; W. and L., Jas. I., bund. 38, No. 110.

Reginald Chamberlayne; W. and L., 18 Jas. I., bund. 30, No. 168.

John Chamberlayne; W. and L., 22 Jas. I., bund. 37, No. 166.

Chambers—Reginald Chambers; Ch., 18 Jas. I., pt. 2, No. 78.

Chancellor. See **Canceller.**

Chambre, de la or **del**—Johanna, ux. Gilbert de la Chaumbre ; Tower,
49 Edw. III. (1st pt.), No. 38 (2, p. 341a).

Edmund del Chambre; Tower, 12 Hen. IV., No. 17 (3, p. 332a).

John de la Chambre ; Tower, 26 Hen. VI., No. 6 (4, p. 234b).

Chapman—John Chapman; Exch., 10-11 Hen. VII. (Richd. Hungerford, Esch.), No. 7.

Alexander Chapman ; Ch., 1-3 P. and M., vol. 7, p. 35.

Alexander Chapman; Ch., 2 and 3 P. and M., pt. 2, No. 53.

Alexander Chapman ; Ch., 5 and 6 P. and M., pt. 1, .No. 23.

Alexander Chapman; Exch., 4 and 5, 5 and 6 P. and M.
(Andrew Revet, Esch.), No. 15.

Charles—Joh*. Charles ; Tower, 33 Edw. I., No. 54.

Edward Charles ; Tower, 3 Edw. III. (1st Nos.), No. 40 (2,
p. 22b).

Robert Charles ; Tower, 2 Hen. IV., No. 23 (3, p. 373a).

Thomas Charles ; Tower, 7 Hen. V., No. 25 (4, p. 40a).

Chervill. See **Kervill.**

Cheveley—Henry Chevely, *alias* Chevery ; Ch., 2 Chas. I., pt. 2, No.
41.

Church—George Churche ; W. and L., 20 Jas. I., bund. 35, No. 2.

George Churche ; Ch., 20 Jas. I., pt. 1, No. 42.

Clare—Richard de Clare ; Tower, 47 Hen. III., No. 34 (1, p. 24 and 25).

Gilbert de Clare ; Tower, 24 Edw. I., No. 107, (1, p. 131b).

Gilbert de Clare ; Tower, 8 Edw. II., No. 68 (1, p. 265a
and 269b).

Clarence, Duke of—Lionel, Duke of Clarence ; Tower, 43 Edw. III.
(1st Nos.), No. 23 (2, p. 294b).

Clarke. See **Clerk.**

Claxton—William Claxton, Gent. ; Exch., 31-32 Hen. VIII. (Wm.
Andrews, Esch.), No. 1.

John Claxton ; Exch., 2-3 Edw. VI. (John Flowerdew, Esch.),
No. 1.

Edward Claxton ; W. and L., 29 and 30 Eliz., vol. 22, p. 44.

Edward Claxton ; Ch., 30 Eliz., pt. 1, No. 60.

Nicholas Claxton ; W. and L., 21 Jas. I., bund. 39, No. 149.

Claxton—Nicholas Clayton ; Ch., 22 Jas. I., pt. 1, No. 16.

 Owen Claxton, Gent. ; Misc. Ch., 3 Chas. I., pt. 24, No. 141.

Claydon. See **Cleydon.**

Clere—Edmund Clere ; Tower, 2 Edw. III., 1st Nos., No. 41 (2, p. 15a).

 Isabella, wife of Edmund Clere ; Tower, App., Edw. III., No. 9 (4, p. 437a).

 Robert Clere ; Tower, 7 Hen. V., No. 19 (4, p. 47b).

 William Clere ; Tower, 7 Hen. VI., No. 33 (4, p. 120b).

 Edmund Clere ; Exch., 4-5 Hen. VII. (John Rodon, Esch.), No. 5.

 Edmund Clere, Esq. ; Ch., 4 Hen. VII., No. 84.

 Elizabeth Clere, widow ; Ch., 9 Hen. VII., No. 47.

 Robert Clere, Knt. ; Ch., 30 Hen. VIII., No. 4.

 Robert Clere, Knt. ; Exch., 29-30 Hen. VIII. (John Plandon, Exch.), No. 5.

 Lady Alice Clere ; Exch., 29-30 Hen. VIII. (John Plandon, Esch.), No. 4.

 Thomas Clere, Knt. ; W. and L., 5 and 6 Edw. VI., vol. 6, p. 126.

 Thomas Clere, Knt. ; Exch., 7 Edw. VI., to 1 Mary (John Spencer, Esch.), No. 8.

 John Clere, Knt. ; Exch., 4 and 5, 5 and 6 Philip and Mary (Andrew Revet, Esch.), No. 21.

 Charles Clere ; Ch., 14 Eliz., pt. 2, No. 119.

 John Clere, Knt. ; Ch., 4 and 5 Ph. and Mary, pt. 1, No. 123.

 John Clere ; Ch., 4 and 5 Ph. and Mary, pt. 1, No. 120.

 Edward Clere ; W. and L., 8 Jas. I., bund. 13, No. 16.

 Edward Cleere, Knt. ; Ch., 9 Jas. I., pt. 1, No. 169.

 Francis Clere ; W. and L., 14 Jas. I., bund. 25, No. 172.

 Francis Clere ; Ch., 15 Jas. I., pt. 2, No. 150.

 Thomas Cleere ; W. and L., 18 Jas. I., bund. 29, No. 271.

 Thomas Cleere ; Ch., 18 Jas. I., pt. 2, No. 159.

 Sir Henry Cleere ; W. and L., 13 Chas. I., bund. 59, No. 161.

 Henry Clere, Bart. ; 13 Chas. I., pt. 1, No. 48.

 Charles Clere, Esq. ; Misc. Ch., 16 Chas. I., pt. 34, No. 6.

 Charles Clere, Esq. ; Misc. Ch., 16 Chas. I., pt. 30, No. 46.

Clerebeke—Thomas Clerebeke, Gent.; Exch., 18-19 Hen. VIII. (Wm. Gryce, Esch.), No. 5.

Clerk or Clark—John Clerk; Tower, 47 Edw. III. (1st Nos.), No. 8 (2, p. 327a).

John Clarke; Exch., 2 and 3, 3 and 4 Philip and Mary (Ralph Shelton, Esch.), No. 9.

Thomas Clarke; Ch., 2 Edw. VI., pt. 2, No. 37.

Thomas Clerke; W. and L., 2 Edw. VI., vol. 4, p. 38.

Thomas Clarke (Clere?), Knt.; Ch., 7 Edw. VI., pt. 1, No. 43.

John Clerke; W. and L., 16 and 17 Eliz., vol. 15, p. 20.

John Clarke; Ch., 16 Eliz., pt. 1, No. 65.

John Clerke; Exch., 16-17 Eliz. (John Dowles, Esch.), No. 6.

Henry Clarke; Ch., 2 Chas. I., pt. 3, No. 81.

John Clarke; Ch., 3 Chas. I., pt. 2, No. 72.

Clarke, Taylor; alias John Taylour—Exch., 7 Edw. VI., 1 Mary (John Spencer, Esch.), No. 3; and Ch., 1 Mary, pt. 1, No. 94.

Cleydon—William de Cleydon, and Aleanore his wife; Tower, 4 Edw. III. (1st Nos.), No. 19 (2, p. 30a).

Stephen Claydon, Gent.; Exch., 2-3 Edw. VI. (John Flowerdew, Esch.), No. 12.

Stephen Cleydon; Ch., 3 Edw. VI., pt. 1, No. 115.

Stephen Cleydon; W. and L., 3-5 Edw. VI., vol. 5, p. 2.

Clifton—Ada de Clifton (proof of age); Tower, App., 2 Edw. III., No. 13 (4, p. 437a).

Adam de Clyfton; Tower, 40 Edw. III. (1st Nos.), No. 14 (2, p. 279b).

John de Clifton; Tower, 50 Edw. III. (2nd Nos.), No. 42 (2, p. 357b).

John de Clifton; Tower, 7 Ric. II., No. 162 (3, p. 66a).

Elizabeth, ux. John de Clifton; Tower, 12 Ric. II., No. 16 (3, p. 100b.)

Constantine de Clifton; Tower, 19 Ric. II., No. 13 (3, p. 189a).

Adam de Clifton; Tower, 13 Hen. IV., No. 29 (3, p. 336a).

John de Clifton (proof of age); Tower, 8 Hen. V., No. 121 (4, p. 56b).

Clifton—Margaret Clifton, ux. Constantine ; Tower, 11 Hen. VI., No. 46 (4, p. 152a).

    John Clifton ; Tower, 26 Hen. VI., No. 17 (4, p. 235b).

    Thomas Clifton ; Tower, 33 Hen. VI., No. 17 (4, p. 263a).

    Robert Clifton (proof of age) ; Tower, 2 Edw. IV., No. 32 (4, p. 320a).

    Robert Clifton; Tower, 9 and 10 Edw. IV., No. 51 (4, p. 350a).

    Robert Clyfton, Knt. ; Ch., 7 Hen. VII., No. 64.

    Thomas Clifton ; W. and L., 18-20 Eliz., vol. 18, p. 73.

    Henry Clifton, Esq. ; Ch. Misc., 19 Jas. I., pt. 31, No. 84.

    Thomas Clifton ; Ch., 20 Eliz., pt. 2, No. 36.

        ,,   ,,   W. and L., 19 Jas. I., bund. 32, No. 24.

    Thomas Clyfton ; Ch., 19 Jas. I., pt. 1, No. 104.

    Henry Clifton, Esq. (lunatic) ; Ch. Misc., 22 Chas. I., pt. 20, No. 183.

Clinton—William de Clinton ; Tower, 28 Edw. III. (1st Nos.), No. 59 (2, p. 188b).

Clippesby—William Clippesby ; Exch., 32-33 Hen. VIII. (John Tasburgh, Esch.), No. 3.

    William Clippysby ; Ch., 32 Hen. VIII., No. 94.

    John Clippesby ; W. and L., 37 Eliz., bund. 6, No. 20.

    John Clippesbye ; Ch., 1 Jas. I., pt. 1, No. 52.

Clopton—John Clopton, Esq. ; Exch., 33-34 Hen. VIII. (Thos. Halse, Esch.), No. 10.

Cobbe—William Cobbe ; Ch., 9 Henry VII., No. 1.

    Geoffrey Cobbe, Esq. ; Exch., 30-31 Hen. VIII. (Wm. Woodhouse, Esch.), No. 7.

    William Cobbe ; W. and L., 38 Hen. VIII. and 1 Edw. VI., bund. 1a, No. 116.

    Geoffrey Cobbe ; W. and L., 38 Hen. VIII. and 1 Edw. VI., bund. 1a, No. 103.

    Geoffrey Cobbe ; Ch., 1 Edw. VI., pt. 2, No. 10.

    William Cobbe ; Ch., 1 Edw. VI., pt. 2, No. 16.

    Sir William Cobbe ; W. and L., 5 Jas. I., bund. 8, No. 66.

    Geoffrey Cobbe ; W. and L., 20-24 Eliz., vol. 20, p. 244.

    Thomas Cobbe ; Ch., 22 Eliz., pt. 2, No. 48.

Cobbe—Geoffrey Cobbe; Ch., 23 Eliz., pt. 2, No. 102.

Francis Cobbe; Ch., 24 Eliz., pt. 1, No. 25.

Geoffrey Cobbe; Ch., 29 Eliz., pt. 1, No. 166.

Edward Cobbe; Ch., 29 Eliz., pt. 1, No. 181.

William Cobbe; Ch., 5 Jas. I., pt. 1, No. 155.

William Cobbe; W. and L., 9 Jas. I., bund. 14, No. 65.

William Cobbe; Ch., 10 Jas. I., pt. 1, No. 93.

Geoffrey Cobbe; W. and L., 21 Jas. I., bund. 37, No. 11.

Geoffrey Cobb; Ch., 21 Jas. I., pt. 1, No. 134.

Martin Cobb, Esq.; Ch. Misc., 18 Chas. I., pt. 16, No. 46.

Cobham—Ralph de Cobham; Tower, 20 Edw. III. (1st Nos.), No. 18 (2, p. 128b).

Anna, ux. Reginald Cobham; Tower, 32 Hen. VI., No. 26 (4, p. 259a).

John de Cobham; Tower, 1 Ric. II., No. 146b (3, p. 10a).

Cock—William Cock; W. and L., 18 Chas. I., bund. 66, No. 77.

William Cocke; Ch., 19 Chas. I., No. 27.

Cockerell—Katherine Cockerell; Tower, 10 Hen. VI., No. 25 (4, p. 135b).

Katherine, ux. John Cockerell; Tower, 6 Hen. VI., No. 53 (4, p. 119b).

Cockeshale or Coggeshall—John de Coggeshale; Tower, 13 Edw. II., No. 30 (1, p. 293b).

Elizabeth Cockesale; Exch., 4 and 5, 5 and 6 Philip and Mary, Andrew Revet, Esch., No. 9.

Cognye. See **Gogney**?

Coke—William Coke, Gent.; 37-38 Hen. VIII. (John Spencer, Esch.), No. 7.

Merieth Coke; Misc. Ch., 14 Chas. I., pt. 27, No. 168.

Cokefield—Thomas de Cokefeld; Tower, 30 Edw. III. (2nd Nos.), No. 42 (2, p. 200a).

Cokesey—Alice, ux. Hugh Cokesey; Tower, 38 and 39 Hen. VI., No. 49 (4, p. 287b).

Coket—John Coket; Tower, 2 Ric. III., No. 2 (4, p. 419a).

John Coket; Exch., 9-10 Hen. VII. (James Braybroke, Esch.), No. 3.

John Cokett, of Ampton; Ch., 10 Hen. VII., No. 44.

Coket—Edward Cokett; Exch., 32-33 Hen. VIII. (John Tasburgh, Esch.), No. 8.

Edward Cokett, Esq.; Exch., 32-33 Hen. VIII. (John Tasburgh, Esch.), No. 35.

John Coket; Ch., 8 Hen. VIII., No. 85.

Edward Cokett; Ch., 33 Hen. VIII., No. 190.

Thomas Cockett, Esq.; Misc. Ch., 5 Jas. I., pt. 6, No. 102.

Colby—Thomas Colby; Ch., 14 Jas. I., pt. 3, No. 27.

Thomas Colbye; W. and L., 14 Chas. I., bund. 20, No. 165.

Colett—Henry Colett; Ch., 21 Henry VII., No. 25.

Colfer—Richard Colferr; W. and L., 1 Jas. I., pt. 1, No. 41.

Richard Colfer; W. and L., 1 and 2 Jas. I., vol. 28, p. 141.

Colvile—Jno. de Colvile; 35 Edw. III. (1st Nos.), No. 51 (2, p. 230b).

Francis Colvyle; Ch., 9 Hen. VII., No. 33.

Anne Colvyle; Ch., 10 Hen. VII., No. 56.

Richard Colvyle; Ch., 18 Hen. VII., No. 88.

Richard Colvell; Ch., 16 Hen. VIII., No. 24.

Richard Colvile, Esq.; Exch., 16-17 Hen. VIII. (Thos. Germayn, Esch.), No. 4.

Richard Colvile; W. and L., 43 and 44 Eliz., vol. 26, p. 219.

Richard Colville; Ch., 44 Eliz., pt. 2, No. 49.

Sir Thomas Colville; W. and L., 10 Jas. I., bund. 15, No. 149.

Sir Thomas Colville; W. and L., 10 Jas. I., bund. 14, No. 69.

Thomas Colvile, Knt.; Ch., 10 Jas. I., pt. 1, No. 26.

Thomas Colvile, Knt.; Ch., 11 Jas. I., pt. 3, No. 129.

Compton—William Compton, Knt.; Exch., 20-21 Hen. VIII. (Henry Rychers, Esch.), No. 18.

William Compton, Knt.; Ch., 20 Hen. VIII., No. 53.

Comyn—Euphemia, ux. William de Comyn; Tower, 17 Edw. I., No. 13 (1, p. 99).

Edmund Comyn; Tower, 14 Edw. II., No. 25 (1, p. 295b).

Coney. See **Conney.**

Coningsby—William Conyngsby, Esq.; 31-32 Hen. VIII. (Wm. Andrews, Esch.), No. 16.

William Coningesby; Ch., 32 Henry VIII., No. 37.

Christopher Conysby; W. and L., 1 Edw. VI., vol. 3, p. 72.

Christopher Conyngesby; Ch., 1 Edw. VI., pt. 2, No. 9.

Conney or Coney—Robert Connye; Ch., 32 Eliz., pt. 1, No. 24.

    Humphrey Conney; Ch., 10 Eliz., No. 62.

    Robert Conney; Ch., 10 Eliz., No. 66.

Conyers—John Conyers; Ch., v.o. Ric. III. and Hen. VII., No. 29.

Constable—Thomas Constable; W. and L., 8 and 9 Jas. I., bund. 5, No. 260.

    Thomas Constable; Ch., 9 Jas. I., pt. 2, No. 31.

    Thomas Constable; Ch., 12 Jas. I., pt. 1, No. 90.

Coo—Jno. de Coo; Tower, 1 Ric. III., No. 14 (4, p. 413b).

Cooke—Robert Cooke; Ch., v.o. 3 Edw. VI., pt. 1, No. 46.

    Robert Cooke; Ch., 4 Eliz., No. 73.

    Thomas Cooke; Ch., 4 Eliz., No. 74.

    Martin Cooke; Ch., 40 Eliz., pt. 2, No. 48.

    Martin Cooke; W. and L., 43 and 44 Eliz., vol. 26, p. 225.

    Martin Cooke (melius inquirendum); Ch., 44 Eliz., pt. 2, No. 80.

    Richard Cooke; W. and L., 9 and 10 Jas. I., bund. 4, No. 24.

    Richard Cooke; Ch., 10 Jas. I., pt. 1, No. 34.

    Richard Cooke; W. and L., 10 Jas. I., bund. 22, No. 270.

    Richard Cooke; W. and L., 10 Jas. I., bund. 14, No. 24.

    Richard Cooke; Ch., 10 Jas. I., pt. 1, No. 118.

    Robert Cooke; Misc. Ch., 11 Jas. I., pt. 6, No. 99.

    Richard Cooke; Ch., 13 Jas. I., pt. 1, No. 89.

    Nicholas Cooke; Misc. Ch., 11 Chas. I., pt. 31, No. 101.

Cooper—George Cooper; Misc. Ch., 12 Chas. I., pt. 31, No. 106.

Copping—John Copping, Clerk; Esch., 37-38 Hen. VIII. (John Spencer, Esch.), No. 25.

    John Coppyng, Gent.; Exch., 1 Eliz. (James Bigott, Esch.), No. 19.

    John Coppinge; Ch., 19 Eliz., pt. 2, No. 50.

    John Coppynge; W. and L., 18-20 Eliz., vol. 18, p. 136.

    John Coppinge; Ch., 39 Eliz., pt. 2, No. 52.

    Stephen Coppinge; Ch., 42 Eliz., pt. 2, No. 74.

    Gregory (? George) Coppynge; Ch., 43 Eliz., pt. 2, No. 36.

    George Coppinge; W. and L., 43 and 44 Eliz., vol. 26, p. 108.

Coppinger—John Coppinger; Ch., 1 Eliz., pt. 3, No. 125.

Coppuldike—John Copildike; Ch., 7 Hen. VII., No. 42.

John Coppuldike; Ch., 36 Eliz., pt. 2, No. 13.

Corbett—Robert Corbet; Tower, 37 Hen. VI., No. 48 (4, p. 285a).

Richard Corbett, Knt.; Exch., 15-16 Hen. VIII. (Christopher Harman, Esch.), No. 3.

Roger Corbett, Esq.; Ch., 30 Hen. VIII., No. 122.

Roger Corbett, Esq.; 30-31 Hen. VIII. (William Woodhouse, Esch.), No. 2.

John Corbett, Sen.; 1 Eliz. (James Bigott, Esch.), No. 40.

John Corbett; Ch., 1 Eliz., pt. 1, No. 123.

Sir Miles Corbett; W. and L., 1-6 Jas. I., bund. 2, No. 146.

Miles Corbett, Knt.; Ch., 5 Jas. I., pt. 1, No. 129.

Thomas Corbett; Ch., 15 Jas. I., pt. 1, No. 177.

Thomas Corbett; W. and L., 15 Jas. I., bund. 26, No. 158.

John Corbett; W. and L., 4 Chas. I., bund. 45, No. 23.

John Corbett, Bart.; Ch., 4 Chas. I., pt. 2, No. 14.

Corbould—Jeremy Corbould; Ch., v.o. 11 Jas. I., No. 47.

Jeremiah Corbould; W. and L., 11 Jas. I., bund. 18, No. 135.

Corby—Robert de Corby; Tower, 39 Edw. III. (1st pt.), No. 9 (2, p. 270b).

Cornwallis—John Cornwales; Ch., 22 Hen. VII., No. 50.

William Cornewales; Ch., 12 Hen. VIII., No. 16.

John Cornwalys, Knt.; Ch., 36 Hen. VIII., No. 20.

Corsey—Robert Corsey; Ch., 17 Jas. I., pt. 3, No. 10.

Cote—Richard Cote; Ch., v.o. Ric. III. and Hen. VII., No. 194.

Cotton—Alice Cotton; Exch., 16-17 Hen. VIII. (Thos. Germayn, Esch.), No. 1.

Sigismund Cotton, Esq.; Exch., 34-35 Hen. VIII. (Robt. Downys, Esch.), No. 24.

Sigismund Cotwyn (?), Esq.; Exch., 34-35 Hen. VIII. (Robt. Downys, Esch.), No. 25.

Barber Cotton, Esq.; Misc. Ch., 12 Jas. I., pt. 6, No. 148.

Thomas Cotton; W. and L., 4 Chas. I., bund. 66, No. 15.

Bartholomew Cotton, Esq.; Ch., 10 Chas. I., pt. 3, No. 41.

Bartholomew Cotton; W. and L., 18 Chas. I., bund. 66, No. 10.

Bartholomew Cotton; Ch., 18 Chas I., pt. 1, No. 1.

Cotton—Thomas Cotton ; Ch., 18 Chas. I., pt. 1, No. 30.

Covill—Thomas Covill, Gent. ; Exch., 12 Eliz. (John Bull, Esch.), No. 1.

Cowper—Edmund Cowper ; W. and L., 9 Jas. I., bund. 16, No. 39.

Edward Cowper ; Ch., 11 Jas. I., pt. 3, No. 148.

Crane—John Crane ; Misc. Ch., v.o. Eliz., bund. 2, No. 185.

Richard Crane ; Misc. Ch., v.o. Eliz., bund. 3, No. 311.

John Crane ; Ch., 32 Eliz., pt. 1, No. 215.

John Crane ; W. and L., 22 Jas. I., bund. 49, No. 65.

John Crane ; Ch., 22 Jas. I., pt. 2, No. 128.

Crek, de—Jno. de Crek ; Tower, 17 Edw. I., No. 16 (1, p. 99a).

Cremer—John Cremer alias Skryme ; W. and L., 9 and 10 Jas. I., bund. 4, No. 147.

John Cremer alias Skryme ; Ch., 10 Jas. I., pt. 1, No. 183.

Cressingham, de—Jno. de Cressingham ; Tower, 6 Ric. II., No. 26 (3, p. 47b).

John de Cressingham ; Tower, 7 Ric. II., No. 162 (3, p. 66a).

Cressy, de—Reginald de Cressi ; Tower, 47 Hen. III., No. 19 (1, p. 22).

Hugh de Cressi ; Tower, 47 Hen. III., No. 28 (1, p. 23).

Isabella de Cressi ; Tower, 48 Hen. III., No. 23 (1, p. 27).

Crestener—Alexander Crestener ; Exch., 13-14 Hen. VII. (Philip Tilney, Esch.), No. 7.

Crickmer—William Crickmer ; W. and L., 11 Jas. I., bund. 18, No. 154.

Gawdy Crikmer ; Misc. Ch., 10 Jas. I., pt. 6, No. 126.

William Crackmer ; Ch., 11 Jas. I., pt. 3, No. 136.

Criketot, de—William de Cryketot ; Tower, 27 Edw. I., No. 47, p. 150a.

Croft—Anne Crofte, widow ; Ch., 6 Edw. VI., pt. 2, No. 52.

Thomas Crofte ; Ch., 1 and 2 Philip and Mary, pt. 2, No. 54.

Ann Croft, widow ; W. and L., 5 and 6 Eliz., vol. 6, p. 81.

Crofts—Elizabeth Croftys ; Exch., 11-12 Hen. VIII. (Philip Bernard, Esch.), No. 13.

Edmund Croftes, Esq. ; Exch., 4 and 5, 5 and 6 Philip and Mary (Andrew Revet, Esch.), No. 3.

John Croftes ; Exch., 4 and 5, 5 and 6 Philip and Mary (Andrew Revet, Esch.), No. 4.

Crofts—Alice Croftes; Exch., 4-5 Eliz. (Augustine Curtes, Esch.),
  Nos. 1 and 2.
  Thomas Croftes; W. and L., 15 Jas. I., bund. 24, No. 62.
  Thomas Croftes; Ch., 15 Jas. I., pt. 2, No. 64.
Cromwell—Matilda, widow of Ralph Cromwell, Sen.; Tower, 7 Hen.
  V., No. 72 (4, p. 45a).
Crow—Christopher Crowe; Esch., 20-21 Hen. VIII. (Henry Rychers,
  Esch.), No. 17.
  Christopher Croo; Ch., 21 Hen. VIII., No. 130.
  Thomas Crowe; Ch., 1 Eliz., pt. 1, No. 126.
  Christopher Crowe; W. and L., 10 Jas. I., bund. 16, No. 50.
  Christopher Crowe; Ch., 11 Jas. I., pt. 2, No. 46.
  John Crowe, Gent.; Misc. Ch., 15 Jas. I., pt. 6, No. 114.
  John Crow; Ch., 17 Jas. I., pt. 3, No. 11.
  John Crowe; Ch., 2 Chas. I., pt. 3, No. 83.
  Christopher Crowe; W. and L., 14 Chas. I., bund. 60,
  No. 332.
  Christopher Crowe; Ch., 14 Chas. I., pt. 3, No. 149.
  Roger Crowe; W. and L., 16 Chas. I., bund. 63, No. 81.
  Roger Crowe; Ch., 16 Chas. I., pt. 3, No. 26.
Cubitt—Thomas Cubitt, yeoman; Misc. Ch., 11 Jas. I., pt. 6, No. 128.
Curzon—William de Curtun(?); Tower, Hen. III., No. 204 (1,
  p. 461).
  William de Curzun; Tower, 1 Edw. II., No. 43 (1, p. 227).
  William de Curzon; Tower, 13 Edw. II., No. 12 (1, p. 292b).
  John Curzon and Margaret his wife; Tower, 20 Edw. II.,
  No. 46 (1, p. 333b).
  Margaret, ux. John fil' William Curzoun; Tower, 10
  Edw. III. (1st Nos.), No. 22 (2, p. 71a).
  Thomas Curson; Exch., 3-4 Hen. VIII. (Anthony Hansart,
  Esch.), No. 15.
  Thomas Curson; Ch., 4 Hen. VIII., No. 23.
  John Curson; W. and L., 38 Hen. VIII. and 1 Edw. VI.,
  bund. 1a, No. 118.
  John Curson; Ch., 1 Edw. VI., pt. 2, No. 11.
  William Curson; W. and L., 12-14 Eliz., vol. 13, p. 103.
  William Curson; Ch., 13 Eliz., pt. 2, No. 15.

Cusshyn—Edmund Cusshyn, Gent.; Exch., 4 and 5, 5 and 6 Philip and Mary (Andrew Rcvet, Esch.), No. 22.

Edward Cusshyn; Ch., 4 and 5 Philip and Mary, pt. 3, No. 5.

Edmund Cusshyng; W. and L., 15 and 16 Eliz., vol. 14, p. 97.

Edmund Cusshinge; Ch., 16 Eliz., pt. 1, No. 66.

Cutte—Richard Cute; Exch., 10-11 Hen. VII. (Richard Hungerford, Esch.), No. 4.

Richard Cutte; Ch., 11 and 12 Hen. VII., No. 42.

John Cutte, Knt.; Ch., 14 Hen. VIII., No. 14.

Dacre, Lord—Lord Fenys Dacre; Ch., 36 Hen. VIII., No. 187.

Lord Thomas Dacre; Ch., 1 Mary, pt. 1, No. 87.

Dade—John Dade; Ch., 11 and 12 Hen. VII., No. 16.

John Dade; Ch., 1 Hen. VIII., No. 53.

John Dade; Exch., 1-2 Hen. VIII. (John Glemham, Esch.), No. 2.

Richard Dade, Esq.; Exch., 27-28 Hen. VIII. (Thos. Woodehouse, Esch.), No. 11.

Richard Dade, Clerk; Ch., 28 Hen. VIII., No. 19.

Dagworth—Nicholas de Dagworth; Exch., 25 Edw. III. (1st Nos.), No. 33 (2, p. 169b).

Dallimond—Thomas Dallimond; W. and L., 1 and 5 Jas. I., vol. 29, p. 20.

Thomas Dallymond; Ch., 4 Jas. I., pt. 1, No. 20.

Daniell—Henry Daniel; Tower, 19 Edw. IV., No. 68 (4, p. 396a).

Henry Danyell, Clerk; Ch., 31 Hen. VIII., No. 75.

Henry Danyell, Clerk; Exch., 30-31 Hen. VIII. (William Woodhouse, Esch.), No. 11.

Thomas Danyell, Esq.; Exch., 9 Eliz. (Edmund Ashefeld, Esch.), No. 1.

Edmund Daniell, Esq.; Exch., 12 Eliz. (John Bull, Esch.), No. 4.

Robert Daniell; Ch., 13 Chas. I., pt. 1, No. 49.

Dannock—John Dannocke; W. and L., 17 and 18 Eliz., vol. 17, p. 31.

John Dannocke; Ch., 17 Eliz., pt. 1, No. 103.

Darby—John Darby; W. and L., 9 and 10 Jas. I., bund. 4, No. 23.

John Darbie; Ch., 10 Jas. I., pt. 1, No. 209.

John Darby; W. and L., 10 Jas. I., bund. 14, No. 68.

Darcy—John Darcy; Exch., 4-5 Hen. VII. (John Rodon, Esch.), No. 3.

Darell—Thomas Darrell, Esq.; Ch., 6 Hen. VII., No. 4.

  Thomas Darell; Ch., 21 Hen. VII., No. 100.

Daunce—Henry Daunce; Exch., 20-21 Hen. VIII. (Henry Rychers, Esch.), No. 10.

Davy—Robert Davy, Sen.; Exch., 37-38 Hen. VIII. (John Spencer, Esch.), No. 16.

  Robert Davy; Ch., 38 Hen. VIII., No. 36.

  George Davy; Ch., 1 Eliz., pt. 3, No. 133.

  Gregory Davye; Exch., 1 Eliz. (James Bigott, Esch.), No. 25.

  Thomas Davye; Exch., 9 Eliz. (Edmd. Ashefeld, Esch.), No. 3.

  Richard Davye; Exch., 16-17 Eliz. (John Dowbes, Esch.), No. 4.

  Stephen Davie; Exch., 16-17 Eliz. (John Dowbes, Esch.), No. 3.

  Richard Davye; Ch., 16 Eliz., pt. 1, No. 61.

  Stephen Davye; W. and L., 16 and 17 Eliz., vol. 15, p. 29.

  Stephen Davye; Ch., v.o. Eliz., bund. 1, No. 267.

  Henry Davye; W. and L., 17 Jas. I., bund. 35, No. 192.

  Henry Davye; Ch., 20 Jas. I., pt. 2, No. 134.

Dawbes—John Dawbes; Ch., 24 Eliz., pt. 1, No. 43.

Dawes—Jno. Dawes; Tower, 15 Edw. IV., No. 63 (4, p. 374a).

Dayrell. See **Darell.**

Deane—Edward Deane; Ch., 23 Eliz., pt. 2, No. 100.

  Oliver Deane; Exch., 1-3 Eliz. (William Drake, Esch.), No. 10.

Debenham—Gilbert Debenham; Tower, 21 Edw. IV., No. 48 (4, p. 407a).

  Gilbert Debenham; Ch., v.o. Ric. III. and Hen. VII., No. 155.

De Grey and Grey—Jno. de Grey; Tower, 56 Hen. III., No. 34.

  Henry de Grey; Tower, 2 Edw. II., No. 47.

  Richard de Grey; Tower, 9 Edw. III. (1st Nos.), No. 45 (2, p. 66b).

  Robert de Grey; Tower, 12 Ric. II., No. 24 (3, p. 101a).

  John Grey; Tower, 18 Hen. VI., No. 14 (4, p. 197a).

  Henry Grey; Tower, 28 Hen. VI., No. 30 (4, p. 245a).

De Grey and Grey—William Grey; Exch., 10-11 Hen. VII. (Rich. Hungerford, Esch.), No. 8.

    William Grey; Ch., 10 Hen. VII., No. 93.

    Humphrey Grey; Ch., 15 Hen. VII., No. 112.

    Thomas Grey (proof of age); Ch., 17 Hen. VII., No. 55.

    Henry Grey, Knt.; Ch., 11 and 12 Hen. VII., No. 92.

    John Grey, Knt.; Exch., 3-4 Hen. VIII. (Anthony Hansart, Esch.), No. 2.

    John Grey, Knt.; Exch., 10-11 Hen. VIII. (Geoffrey Cobbe, Esch.), No. 3.

    Elizabeth Grey; Exch., 27-28 Hen. VIII. (Thos. Woodehouse, Esch.), No. 13.

    Edmund de Grey; W. and L., 1 and 2 Edw. VI., vol. 4, p. 23.

    Edmund de Grey; Ch., 2 Edw. VI., pt. 2, No. 51.

    John de Grey; Ch., 1 Eliz., pt. 1, No. 131; and Exch., 1 Eliz. (Jas. Bigott, Esch.), No. 14.

    Thomas de Grey, alias Grey; Ch., 4 Eliz., No. 81.

    Thomas de Grey; Ch., 4 Eliz., No. 81.

    Thomas de Grey; Ch., 9 Eliz., No. 46.

    Thomas de Graye; Exch., 9 Eliz. (Edmund Ashefeld, Esch.), No. 10.

    Robert de Grey; Ch., 43 Eliz., pt. 2, No. 68.

    William de Gray, Knt.; Ch., 8 Chas. I., pt. 1, No. 66.

De la Hay. See **Dillahay.**

De la Mote. See **Mote, de le.**

De la Pole. See **Pole.**

De L'Isle. See **Insula, de.**

Dengayne. See **Engayne, de.**

Denny—Anthony Denny, Knt.; Exch., 3-4 Edw. VI., Hen. VI. (...... Minne, Esch.), No. 7.

    John Denny; W. and L., 1-6 Jas. I., bund. 2, No. 126.

    John Dennye, Esq.; Ch., 5 Jas. I., pt. 2, No. 135.

    Arthur Dennye; W. and L., 8 and 9 Jas. I., bund. 5, No. 291.

    Anthony Dennye; Ch., 9 Jas. I., pt. 1, No. 175.

    John Danney; W. and L., 13 Jas. I., bund. 22, No. 206.

    John Danny; Ch., 13 Jas. I., pt. 1, No. 125.

Denny—Firmin Denny; Ch., 21 Jas. I., pt. 2, No. 18.

Fermin Dennye; W. and L., 21 Jas. I., bund. 19, No. 40.

John Deny; Ch., 13 Chas. I., pt. 1, No. 185.

Sir William Denney (lunatic); W. and L., 17 Chas. I., bund. 65, No. 73.

William Denny, Knt. (lunatic); Ch., 17 Chas. I., pt. 3, No. 29.

Denys—Hugh Denys, Esq.; Exch., 3-4 Hen. VIII. (Anthony Hansart, Esch.), No. 13.

Hugh Denys; Ch., 4 Hen. VIII., No. 20.

Depden—Gregory Depden; 32-33 Hen. VIII. (John Tasburgh, Esch.), No. 21.

Derby. See **Darby.**

Dereham—Thomas Dereham, Esq.; Exch., 21-22 Hen. VIII. (Anthony Thwaytys, Esch.), No. 4.

Thomas Derham, Esq.; Exch., 2 and 3, 3 and 4 Philip and Mary (Ralph Shelton, Esch.), No. 8.

Thomas Derham; Ch., 2 and 3 Philip and Mary, pt. 2, No. 47.

Thomas Derham; Ch., 22 Hen. VIII., No. 36.

Thomas Dereham; W. and L., 19 Eliz., bund. 69, No. 90a.

Thomas Deareham; Ch., 19 Eliz., pt. 2, No. 49.

Robert Dereham; W. and L., 11 Jas. I., bund. 16, No. 51.

Robert Dercham; Ch., 11 Jas. I., pt. 2, No. 68.

Deschalers—Thomas Deschalers; Tower, 38 Edw. III. (1st pt.), No. 10 (2, p. 265b).

Despenser—John le Despenser; Tower, 49 Edw. III. (2nd pt.), No. 45 (2, p. 348b).

Dethick—John Dethyck; Exch., 1 Eliz. (James Bigott, Esch.), No. 29.

John Dethicke, Esq.; Ch., 1 Eliz., pt. 3, No. 135.

Edward Dethicke; Ch., 8 Eliz., No. 65.

Edmund Dethicke, Esq.; Exch., 8-9 Eliz. (Thos. Dercham, Esch.), No. 1.

Dewell—Thomas Dewell; Ch., 20 Hen. VIII., No. 58.

Dewing—Henry Dewynge; Misc. Ch., 15 Chas. I., pt. 31, No. 182.

Dey—John Dey; Ch., v.o. Eliz., bund. 3, No. 314.

Henry Day, Knt.; Misc. Ch., 11 Jas. I., pt. 6, No. 134.

John Dey; W. and L., 3 Chas. I., bund. 68, No. 28.

John Deye; Ch., 3 Chas. I., pt. 2, No. 21.

Dey—Robert Dey, Gent.; Misc. Ch., 3 Chas. I., pt. 24, No. 142.

 Robert Dey; Ch., 8 Chas. I., pt. 2, No. 47.

 Matthew Dey; Misc. Ch., 15 Chas. I., pt. 31, No. 111.

 Matthew Dey; W. and L., 18 Chas. I., bund. 65, No. 67.

 Matthew Dey; W. and L., 18 Chas. I., bund. 66, No. 68.

 Matthew Dey; W. and L., 19 Chas. I., bund. 66, No. 51.

 Matthew Dey; Ch., 18 Chas. I., pt. 1, No. 34.

 Matthew Dey; Ch., 18 Chas. I., pt. 1, No. 29.

 Matthew Dey; 19 Chas. I., No. 15.

 Cuthbert Dey, Gent.; Misc. Ch., 18 Chas. I., pt. 16, No. 52.

 Matthew Dey; Ch., 20 Chas. I., No. 20.

Diamond. See **Dimond.**

Digby—Simon Digby; Exch., 11-12 Hen. VIII. (Philip Bernard, Esch.), No. 1.

Dillahay—John Dillahay; W. and L., 18-20 Eliz., vol. 18, p. 6.

 John Dillahay; Ch., 19 Eliz., pt. 2, No. 56.

Dimond (see **Dymond**)—Tristram Dimond; Ch., 16 Jas. I., pt. 1, No. 26.

 Tristram Dimond alias Dyamond; 16 Jas. I., pt. 2, No. 124.

Discipline or Displin—Robert Displin; Misc. Ch., 16 Jas. I., pt. 6, No. 117.

Ditton—Thomas Ditton; Tower, 20 Edw. IV., No. 7 (4, p. 399a).

Divileston (Durleston?)—Thomas de Divileston; Tower, 18 Edw. I., No. 33.

Dix—William Dix; W. and L., 1 and 2 Jas. I., vol. 28, p. 152.

 William Dix; Ch., 2 Jas. I., pt. 2, No. 191.

 William Dixe; W. and L., 15 Chas. I., bund. 61, No. 123.

Dodd—Robert Dodd; Ch., 23 Eliz., pt. 2, No. 113.

 Thomas Dodd; Ch., 28 Eliz., No. 151.

Dodge—John Dodge; Ch., 40 Eliz., pt. 2, No. 42.

Dowe—Henry Dowe; Ch., 12 Jas. I., pt. 2, No. 94.

 Henry Dowe; W. and L., 12 Jas. I., bund. 18, No. 8.

Dowles—John Dowles; W. and L., 20-24 Eliz., vol. 20, p. 268.

Downe or Downes—Edward Down; Ch., v.o. Hen. VIII., bund. 3, No. 229.

 Edward Downes; W. and L., 35 Hen. VIII., vol. 1, p. 55.

 Edward Downes; Exch., 34-35 Hen. VIII. (Robt. Downys, Esch.), No. 4.

Downe or Downes—Thomas Downes, Gent.; Exch., 7 Edw. VI. to 1
Mary (John Spencer, Esch.), No. 2.

Thomas Downes; Ch., 1 Mary, pt. 1, No. 96.

James Downes, Esq.; Exch. 4 and 5, 5 and 6 Philip and
Mary (Andrew Revet, Esch.), No. 19.

James Downes; Ch., 4 and 5 Philip and Mary, pt. 3, No. 17.

Robert Downes; Ch., 37 Eliz., pt. 2, No. 67.

Robert Downes; W. and L., 9 Jas. 1, bund. 60, No. 273.

Robert Downes, Esq.; Ch., 14 Chas. I., pt. 3, No. 73.

Downing—Arthur Downing; Ch., 38 Eliz., pt. 1, No. 42.

Dowsing—Robert Dowsing; Misc. Ch., 13 Chas. I., pt. 33, No. 56.

John Dowsinge; W. and L., 13 Chas. I., bund. 60, No. 233.

John Dowsinge; Ch., 14 Chas. I., pt. 3, No. 30.

John Dowsinge; Misc. Ch., 14 Chas. I., pt. 27, No. 37.

Doyly—Henry Doylie; Ch., 39 Eliz., pt. 1, No. 41.

Edward Doyly; Ch., 11 Jas. I., pt. 2, No. 73.

Sir Henry Doylye; W. and L., 15 Jas. I., bund. 24, No. 80.

Henry Doylie, Knt.; Ch., 15 Jas. I., pt. 1, No. 202.

Charles Doyly, Gent.; Misc. Ch., 2 Chas. I., pt. 5, No. 72.

Edward Doyle, Esq.; Ch., 14 Chas. I., pt. 3, No. 119.

Edmund Doyly; W. and L., 14 Chas. I., bund. 61, No. 270.

Susanna Doyley; Ch., 16 Chas. I., pt. 3, No. 12.

Drake—William Drake; Ch., 19 Hen. VII., No. 23.

William Drake; Exch., 2-3 Edw. VI. (John Flowerdew,
Esch.), No. 13.

William Drake; Ch., 3 Edw. VI., pt. 1, No. 101.

William Drake; W. and L., 3-5 Edw. VI., vol. 5, p. 8.

William Drake; W. and L., 26-29 Eliz., vol. 21, p. 115.

Drew or Drue—Jno. Drewe; Tower, 11 Edw. IV., No. 23 (4, p. 352a).

John Drue; Tower (proof of age), 28 Hen. VI., No. 38
(4, p. 245b).

Jno. Drewe; Tower, 37 Hen. VI., No. 8 (4, p. 281a).

Driby—Simon de Dryby; Tower, 16 Edw. II., No. 39 (1, p. 302a).

Johanna de Driby; Tower, 3 Edw. III. (1st Nos.), No. 64
(2, p. 23b).

John de Dribi; Tower, 8 Edw. III. (1st Nos.), No. 32 (2,
p. 59b).

Driver—Robert Dryver; Exch., 4-5 Edw. VI. (John Tirrell, Esch.), No. 9.

Drury—Robert Drury, Knt.; Exch., 26-27 Hen. VIII. (Philip Bedingfeld, Esch.), No. 3.

Robert Drury; Ch., 27 Hen. VIII., No. 40.

Charles Drury; Ch., v.o. Hen. VIII., bund. 3, No. 225.

Charles Drury; Exch., 34-35 Hen. VIII. (Robt. Downys, Esch.), No. 28.

William Druryc, Knt.; Exch., 4 and 5, 5 and 6 Philip and Mary (Andrew Revet, Esch.), No. 1.

Robert Drury, Esq.; Exch., 4 and 5, 5 and 6 Philip and Mary (Andrew Revet, Esch.), No. 11.

Roger Druryc; Ch., 41 Eliz., pt. 1, No. 37.

Thomas Drewry; W. and L., 6 Jas. I., bund. 10, No. 176.

Thomas Drewryc; Ch., 6 Jas. I., pt. 2, No. 99.

Richard Drewry (lunatic); Ch., 7 Jas. I., pt. 1, No. 94.

Anthony Drury; Ch., 15 Jas. I., pt. 1, No. 200.

Anthony Drury; W. and L., 15 Jas. I., bund. 24, No. 69.

Robert Druryc; Ch., 22 Jas. I., pt. 2, No. 83.

Robert Druryc; W. and L., 22 Jas. I., bund. 41, No. 34.

William Drury, Knt.; Ch., 15 Chas. I., pt. 4, No. 20.

Anthony Drury; Ch., 16 Chas. I., pt. 3, No. 69.

Anthony Drury; W. and L., 16 Chas. I., bund. 63, No. 240.

Dry—Thomas Drye; Tower, 21 Edw. IV., No. 18 (4, p. 404b).

Duke—Margery Duke; Ch., 20 Hen. VIII., No. 117.

Margery Duke; Exch., 20-21 Hen. VIII. (Henry Rychers, Esch.), No. 3.

Edward Duke; Ch., 40 Eliz., pt. 2, No. 38.

George Duke, Esq.; Exch., 4-5 Edw. VI. (John Tirrell, Esch.), No. 11.

Hugh Duke; W. and L., 3-7 Jas. I., vol. 25, p. 64 (? See **Dyke**).

Dunckon—William Dunckon; Exch., 16-17 Eliz. (John Dowbes, Esch.), No. 2.

Dunham—John Dunham, Esq.; Exch., 16-17 Hen. VIII. (Thos. Germayn, Esch.), No. 2.

Dunster—Ann Dunster; W. and L., 6 Chas. I., bund. 48, No. 135.

Dunton—Robert de Dunton; Tower, 18 Edw. I., No. 111 (1, p. 104a).

Dunthorne—Thomas Dunthorne; Ch., v.o. Eliz., bund. 3, No. 181.

Durleston. See **Divileston?**

Durwarde—John Durwarde; 10 Hen. VII., No. 118.

Dusgate—John Dusgate; W. and L., 10 Jas. I., bund. 15, No. 72.

 John Dustgate; Ch., 10 Jas. I., pt. 2, No. 29.

Dyke (see **Duke?**)—Hugh Dyke; W. and L., 3-7 Jas. I., vol. 25, p. 64.

 Hugh Dyke; W. and L., 8 and 9 Jas. I., bund. 5, No. 247.

 Hugh Dyke; Ch., 7 Jas. I., pt. 1, No. 166.

 Hugh Dyke; Ch., 9 Jas. I., pt. 2, No. 14.

Dymond (See **Dimond**)—Tristram Dymond; 16 Jas. I., bund. 26, No. 78.

Dyne or Dynne—John Dynne; Ch., 80 Hen. VII., No. 48.

 Robert Dynne; Ch., 14 Hen. VII., No. 7.

 John Dyne; Ch., 21 Hen. VII., No. 41.

 Henry Dynne; Ch., Hen. VIII., No. 33.

 Henry Dynne, Gent.; Exch., 8-9 Hen. VIII. (John Stode, Esch.), No. 12.

Earlham de—Rad. de Erlcham; Tower, 24 Edw. I., No. 34 (1, p. 128a).

 John de Earlham; Tower, 20 Edw. III. (1st Nos.), No. 32 (2, p. 129b).

Echingham—Edward Echyngham, Knt.; Exch., 30-31 Hen. VIII. (William Woodhouse, Esch.), No. 13.

Edenham—Henry Edenhand(?); Tower, 12 Edw. IV., No. 25 (4, p. 357b).

Edgar—William Edgar; Exch., 1-3 Eliz. (William Drake, Esch.), No. 12.

Edward—Francis Edward; W. and L., 19 Jas. I., bund. 33, No. 161.

 John Edward; Ch., v.o. Hen. VIII., bund. 2, No. 111.

Edwards—Richard Edwards; Ch., 6 Eliz., No. 151.

 Richard Edwards; W. and L., 6 Eliz., bund. 9, No. 28.

 Robert Edwardes; Ch., 21 Eliz., pt. 2, No. 45.

 Robert Edwardes; W. and L., 20-24 Eliz., vol. 20, p. 15.

 Francis Edwardes; Ch., 19 Jas. I., pt. 1, No. 55.

Eldred—John Eldred; W. and L., 9 Chas. I., bund. 53, No. 58.

 John Eldred; Ch., 9 Chas. I., pt. 2, No. 46.

Ellis—Thomas Ellys, Gent.; Exch., 3-4 Edw. VI. (Henry Minne, Esch.), No. 4.

    John Elis; W. and L., 3-5 Edw. VI., vol. 5, p. 149.

    Thomas Ellys; Ch., 4 Edw. VI., pt. 2, No. 57.

    Thomas Ellys; Ch., 2 Eliz., pt. 2, No. 31.

Elmham—Robert Elmham; Tower, 17 Edw. IV., No. 68 (4, p. 387b).

Elwin—William Elwyn, Gent.; Exch., 10-11 Hen. VIII. (Geoffrey Cobbe, Esch.), No. 6.

    William Elwyn; Ch., 11 Hen. VIII., No. 122.

    Peter Elwyn; W. and L., 6 Jas. I., bund. 35, No. 212.

    Ela Elwyn, widow; Ch., 26 Hen. VIII., No. 65.

    Peter Elwyn; Ch., 20 Jas. I., pt. 2, No. 66.

Engayne, de—Jno. de Engayne; Tower, Edw. I., No. 46 (1, p. 135a).

Erpingham, de—Joha., wife of Thomas Erpingham; Tower, 3 Hen. VI., No. 19 (4, p. 83b).

    Sir Thomas Erpingham; Tower, 6 Hen. VI., No. 47 (4, p. 116b).

Eschalers. See **Deschalers.**

Essex, de—Thomas de Essex; Tower, 13 Edw. III. (1st Nos.), No. 20 (2, p. 89a).

    Thomas de Essex; Tower, 23 Edw. III. (pt. 2), No. 12 (2, p. 155a).

    Johanna, ux. Robert Essex; Tower, 6 Hen. V., No. 2 (4, p. 33b).

Eu, Comes de—Robert, Comes de Eu; Tower, 44 Edw. III. (2nd Nos.), No. 6 (2, p. 306a).

Everard—Henry Everard, Esq.; Exch., 32-33 Hen. VIII. (John Tasburgh, Esch.), No. 17.

    Henry Everard; Ch., 33 Hen. VIII., No. 97.

    John Everard; Exch., 7 Edw. VI. to 1 Mary (John Spencer, Esch.), No. 18.

    William Everarde; Ch., 4 and 5 Ph. and Mary, pt. 3, No. 16.

    William Everarde; Exch., 4 and 5, 5 and 6 Philip and Mary (Andrew Revet, Esch.), No. 16.

    Richard Everard; Exch., 1-3 Eliz. (William Drake, Esch.), No. 3.

    Richard Everarde; Ch., 41 Eliz., pt. 2, No. 69.

E

Everard—Edward Everard ; Ch., 43 Eliz., pt. 2, No. 96.

Evermuth, de—Walter de Evermuth ; Tower, 1 Edw. I., No. 33 (1, p. 50a).

Eyre. See **Leyre or Le Eyre ?**

Fairweather. See **Fayrewether.**

Fardin—William Fardin ; Ch., 43 Eliz., pt. 2, No. 12*.

Fastolf—John Fastolf ; Tower, 19 Edw. II., No. 29 (1, p. 324b).

    Hugh Fastolf ; Tower, 5 Hen. V., No. 49 (4, p. 30b).

    Matilda, wife of Hugh Fastolf ; Tower, 15 Hen. VI., No. 37 (4, p. 173b).

    John Fastolf ; Tower, 26 Hen. VI., No. 15 (4, p. 235a).

    John Falstolff ; Ch., 23 Hen. VII., No. —.

    John Falstalfe, Esq. ; Exch., 2-3 Edw. VI. (John Flowerdew, Esch.), No. 3.

Farror—Hamond Farror ; Ch., 13 Chas. I., pt. 1, No. 115.

Faukner—Juliana, ux. John Faukener ; Tower, 49 Edw. III. (1st pt.), No. 48 (2, p. 341b).

Fawcett—John Fawcett ; Ch., 2 Chas. I., pt. 3, No. 98.

    John Fawcett ; Ch., 2 Chas. I., pt. 2, No. 141.

    John Fawcett ; W. and L., 2 Chas. I., bund. 43, No. 167.

    William Fawcett ; W. and L., 3 Chas. I., bund. 44, No. 20.

    William Fawcett ; Ch., 3 Chas. I., pt. 2, No. 70.

    William Fawcett ; W. and L., 9 Chas. I., bund. 54, No. 123.

    Ann Fawcett ; W. and L., 9 Chas. I., bund. 53, No. 127.

    Anne Fawcett ; Ch., 9 Chas. I., pt. 1, No. 60.

Fayrewether—Simon Fayrewether ; W. and L., 10 Jas. I., bund. 18, No. 164.

    Symon Fayrewether ; Ch., 11 Jas. I., pt. 3, No. 118.

    Symon Fayrewether ; Ch., 11 Jas. I., pt. 3, No. 152.

    Simon Fayrewether ; W. and L., 11 Jas. I., bund. 18, No. 141.

Felbrigg—Roger, fil. Simon Felbrigg ; Tower, 28 Edw. III. (2nd Nos.), No. 40 (2, p. 190a).

Felmingham, de—William de Felmingham ; Tower, 40 Hen. III., No. 2 (1, p. 15) ; *id.* 42 Hen. III., No. 28.

    William de Felmingham ; Tower, 22 Edw. I. (missing).

    Gregory de Felmingham ; Tower, 14 Edw. II., No. 41 (1, p. 297a).

Feltham—Jno. fil. Thomas Feltham; Tower, 7 Ric. II., No. 35 (3, p. 59a).

Felton—William de Felton; Tower, 41 Edw. III. (1st Nos.), No. 23 (2, p. 286a).

Thomas de Felton; Tower, 4 Ric. II., No. 22 (3, p. 29b).

William Felton; Exch., 9-10 Hen. VII. (James Braybroke, Esch.), No. 5.

Edmund Felton, Esq.; Tower, 9-11 Hen. VIII. (Geoffrey Cobbe, Esch.), No. 1.

Thomas Felton; Tower, 34-35 Hen. VIII. (Robt. Downys, Esch.), No. 5.

Thomas Felton; Ch., 35 Hen. VIII., No. 106.

Edmund Felton; Exch., 34-35 Hen. VIII. (Robt. Downys, Esch.), No. 13.

Fenis (Fiennes or Fynes, *q.v.***)**—Thomas Fenis; Exch., 1 Mary to 1 and 2 Philip and Mary (Edmund Wright, Esch.), No. 10.

Joan Fenys, widow; Ch., 3 Hen. VII., No. 12.

Fenne—William Fenne; Ch., 40 Eliz., pt. 1, No. 66.

William Fenn (*quæ plura*); Ch., 43 Eliz., pt. 2, No. 2.

William Fenne; Ch., 14 Jas. I., pt. 3, No. 120.

William Fenn; W. and L., 14 Jas. I., bund. 23, No. 120.

William Fenn; W. and L., 14 Jas. I., bund. 24, No. 154.

William Fenn; Ch., 14 Jas. I., pt. 3, No. 41.

Simon Fenn; Ch., 15 Jas. I., pt. 1, No. 182.

Simon Fenn; W. and L., 15 Jas. I., bund. 25, No. 87.

William Fenne, Gent.; Misc. Ch., 16 Jas. I., pt. 6, No. 112.

Fermor—William Farmor, Knt.; Ch., 1 Eliz., pt. 3, No. 128.

Thomas Fermor; W. and L., 20 Jas. I., bund. 35, No. 189.

Thomas Farmor; Ch., 20 Jas. I., pt. 2, No. 128.

William Fermer, Esq.; Ch., 12 Chas. I., pt. 3, No. 129.

William Fermor; W. and L., 12 Chas. I., bund. 56, No. 260.

Ferrariis, de—Cecilia de Ferariis; Tower, 21 Edw. I., p. 49 (1, p. 114b).

Kath. de Ferrariis; Tower, 31 Hen. VI., No. 36 (4, p. 253b).

Field, atte—John atte Field; Tower, 10 Hen. IV., No. 8 (3, p. 321a).

Fincham—John Fyncham, Gent.; Ch., 11 and 12 Hen. VII., No. 20.

Fincham—John Fyncham; Exch., 20-21 Hen. VIII. (Henry Rychers, Esch.), No. 16.

    John Fyncheam; Ch., 21 Hen. VIII., No. 62.

    Simon Fincham, Gent.; Exch., 30-31 Hen. VIII. (Wm. Woodhouse, Esch.), No. 6.

    Ella Fyncham; Exch., 32-33 Hen. VIII. (John Tasburgh, Esch.), No. 47.

    John Fyncham, Jun.; Exch., 32-33 Hen. VIII. (John Tasburgh, Esch.), No. 19.

    John Fyncham; Ch., 33 Hen. VIII., No. 8.

    Thomas Fyncham; W. and L., 5 and 6 Edw. VI., vol. 6, p. 37.

    Thomas Fyncham; Ch., 6 Edw. VI., pt. 2, No. 47.

Findern—William Fyndern, Knt.; Exch., 8-9 Hen. VIII. (John Stede, Esch.), No. 9.

    Thomas Fyndern, Esq.; Exch., 15-16 Hen. VIII. (Christopher Harman, Esch.), No. 14.

Firmage—Henry Firmage, Gent.; Exch., 37-38 Hen. VIII. (John Spencer, Esch.), No. 21.

Fish—John Fysh; Exch., 9-10 Hen. VII. (James Braybroke, Esch.), No. 16.

    John Fysshe; Ch., 10 Hen. VII., No. 107.

Fisk—Ambrose Fiske; W. and L., 5 Jas. I., bund. 8, No. 84.

    Ambrose Fiske; Ch., v.o. 5 Jas. I., pt. 2, No. 79.

    William Fysk; Ch., 5 Chas. I., pt. 2, No. 11.

Fitz Lewes—Richard Fitz Lewes; Ch., 11 Chas. I., pt. 2, No. 23.

    Richard Fitz Lewes, Knt.; Ch., 21 Hen. VIII., No. 153.

    Richard Fitz Lewes, Knt.; Exch., 20-21 Hen. VI. (Hy. Richers, Esch.), No. 1.

Fitz Osbert—Roger fil. Pet. Fitz Osbert; Tower, 34 Edw. I., No. 58.

Fitz Ralph—Jno. Fitz Ralph; Tower, 18 Edw. IV., No. 27 (4, p. 388b).

Fitz Ranulph—Ralph fil. Ranulph; Tower, 54 Hen. III., No. 24 (1, p. 34).

Fitz Robert—Ran. Fitz Robert; Tower, 37 Hen. III., No. 66.

Fitz Symond—Robert Fitz Symond; Tower, 13 Edw. IV., No. 33 (4, p. 362a).

Fitz Walter—Robert le Fitz Wauter, sen.; Tower, 19 Edw. II., No. 99 (1, p. 329b).

Fitz Walter—John Fitz Walter; Tower, 35 Edw. III. (1st Nos.), No. 86 (2, p. 232a).

Walter Fitz Walter; Tower, 1 Rich. II., No. 55 (3, p. 65).

Walter Fitz Walter and Philippa ux.; Tower, 10 Rich. II., No. 15 (3, p. 82b).

Philippa, ux. Walter Fitz Walter; Tower, 10 Hen. VI., No. 45 (4, p. 137a).

Walter Fitz Walter; Tower, 10 Hen. VI., No. 46 (4, p. 138a).

Elizabeth, widow of Fitz Walter; Tower, 4 Edw. IV., No. 37 (4, p. 326a).

Fitz William—William Fitz William; Ch., 8 Hen. VIII., No. 27.

William Fitz William, Esq.; Exch., 8-9 Hen. VIII. (John Stede, Exch.), No. 14.

Flatman—Robert Flatman; Ch., 11 Jas. I., pt. 2, No. 70.

Robert Flatman; W. and L., 11 Jas. I., bund. 16, No. 55.

Thomas Flatman; W. and L., 17 Jas. I., bund. 29, No. 237.

Thomas Flatman; Ch., 18 Jas. I., pt. 2, No. 132.

Flint—Robert Flint; Ch., 34 Eliz., pt. 2, No. 77.

Robert Flynt; Misc. Ch., 12 Chas. I., pt. 31, No. 178.

Florence—William Florence; Tower, 40 Edw. III. (1st Nos.), No. 27 (2, p. 280a).

Florry or Florey—William Florry; W. and L., 1-3 Jas. I., vol. 27, p. 154.

William Florey; Ch., v.o. 1 and 2 Jas. I., No. 33.

Flower—Richard Flowre; Ch., 35 Hen. VIII., No. 71.

Flowerdew—John Flowerdew; W. and L., 5-7 Eliz., vol. 10, p. 114.

John Flowerdewe; Ch., 7 Eliz., No. 27.

Thomas Flowerdew; W. and L., 12-14 Eliz., vol. 13, p. 88.

Thomas Flowerdew; Ch., 13 Eliz., pt. 2, No. 13.

Edward Flowerdew; W. and L., 26-29 Eliz., vol. 21, p. 161.

Edward Flowredewe; Ch., 28 Eliz., pt. 2, No. 132.

John Flowerdew; W. and L., 29 and 30 Eliz., vol. 22, p. 67.

John Flowerdewe; Ch., 30 Eliz., pt. 2, No. 26.

Edward Flowerdew; W. and L., 39-42 Eliz., vol. 24, p. 169.

Edward Flowerdew; Ch., 42 Eliz., pt. 2, No. 85.

Thomas Flowerdew; Ch., 43 Eliz., pt. 2, No. 20*.

Foliot—Richard Folyet; Tower, 19 Edw. II., No. 22 (1, p. 324b).

Felmingham, de—Margerie de Foliot; Tower, 4 Edw. III. (1st Nos.),
No. 14 (2, p. 30a).

Folville—Roger Folvylle; Tower, 6 Ric. II., No. 40 (3, p. 48a).

Fogg—Thomas Foog; Ch., v.o. Hen. VIII., bund. 1, No. 201.

Forby—Hillary Forbye; Ch., 21 Eliz., pt. 2, No. 48.

Ford or Forthe—Robert Forde; Exch., 29-30 Henry VIII. (John
Plandon, Esch.), No. 1.

Robert Forde, alias Forthe; Exch., 32-33 Hen. VIII. (John
Tasburgh, Esch.), No. 37.

Forth—Robert Forth; Exch., 31-32 Hen. VIII. (William Andrewes,
Esch.), No. 4.

Thomas Forth; W. and L., 6 Chas. 1, bund. 52, No. 193.

Thomas Forth; Ch., 8 Chas. I., pt. 2, No. 49.

Thomas Forth; W. and L., 9 Chas. I., bund. 54, No. 39.

Thomas Forth; Ch., 10 Chas. I., pt. 3, No. 139.

Foster—Richard Foster; W. and L., 11 Jas. I., bund. 18, No. 133.

Richard Foster; Ch., v.o. 11 Jas. I., No. 43.

Foulsham—Robert Fowlsham; W. and L., 7 and 8 Jas. I., bund. 3,
No. 101.

Robert Foulsham; Ch., 8 Jas. I., pt. 2, No. 38.

Fountaine (see also **Funtaignes, de**)—Susanna Founteyne; W. and
L., 11 Jas. I., bund. 18, No. 142.

Susanna Fountaine; Ch., v.o. 11 Jas. I., No. 51.

John Fountayne, Esq.; Misc. Ch., 20 Jas. I., pt. 5, No. 69.

Susan Fountaine; W. and L., 3 Chas. I., bund. 45, No. 7.

Susanna Fowntayne; Ch., 4 Chas. I., pt. 4, No. 18.

Fowler—George Fowler; W. and L., 11 Jas. I., bund. 21, No. 82.

George Fowler; Ch., 12 Jas. I., pt. 2, No. 105.

Fox—Robert Foxe; Exch., 32-33 Hen. VIII. (John Tasburgh, Esch.),
No. 30.

Framingham—Edward Framyngham; Ch., 5 Chas. I., pt. 2, No. 13.

Francis—Thomas Frauncis; W. and L., 11 Jas. I., bund. 21, No. 47.

Thomas Frauncis; Ch., 13 Jas. I., pt. 1, No. 8.

Fraxinis, de—Roger fil. Roger de Fraxinis; Tower, 24 Edw. I.,
No. 92, 35 Edw. I., No. 79 (1, p. 222b).

Freelove—John Frelove; Exch., 11 Eliz. (William Attwood, Esch.),
No. 2.

Freeman—John Freman; W. and L., 17 Jas. I., bund. 29, No. 258.

John Freman; Ch., 18 Jas. I., pt. 2, No. 147.

Frere—Richard Frere; W. and L., 2 Chas. I., bund. 45, No. 21.

Richard Frere; Ch., 4 Chas. I., pt. 2, No. 2.

Richard Freere, Gent.; Misc. Ch., 13 Chas. I., pt. 31, No. 109.

Freeston or Freston—William Freeston; Exch., 4-5 Edw. VI. (John Tirrell, Esch.), No. 16.

Richard Freston; W. and L., 15 Jas. I., bund. 25, No. 74.

Richard Freston; Ch., 15 Jas. I., pt. 1, No. 179.

William Freston; W. and L., 2 Chas. I., bund. 19, No. 25.

William Freeston; Ch., 3 Chas. I., pt. 2, No. 82.

Frevill or Fryvill—Baldwin de Frevill; Tower, 17 Edw. I., No. 9.

Baldwin de Fryvill; Tower, 17 Edw. III. (1st Nos.), No. 37 (2, p. 109b).

Fryer—Robert Fryer; Exch., 4-5 Eliz. (Augustine Curtes, Esch.), No. 5.

Fulke—William Fulke; Ch., 36 Eliz., pt. 2, No. 43.

William Fulke; Ch., 38 Eliz., pt. 2, No. 14.

Fuller—Robert Fuller; W. and L., 1-3 Jas. I., bund. 6, No. 34.

Robert Fuller; Ch., 2 Jas. I., pt. 2, No. 180.

Fulmerston—Richard Fulmerston, Knt.; W. and L., 9-11 Eliz., vol. 11, p. 27.

Richard Fulmerston, Knt.; Ch., 9 Eliz., No. 45.

Richard Fulmerston; Exch., 9 Eliz. (Edmd. Ashefeld, Esch.), No. 15.

Funston—Thomas Funston; Ch., 17 Jas. I., pt. 2, No. 115.

Funtaignes, de (see **Fountaine ?**)—Galfr. de Funtaignes; Tower, 35 Edw. I., No. 22 (1, p. 15b).

Geoffrey Funteynes and Margery his wife; Tower, 9 Edw. II., No. 64 (1, p. 274c).

Fynes (see **Fenis ?**)—Thomas Fynes; 36 Hen. VIII., No. 187.

Gambon or Gambourn—William Gambon and Cecilia ux.; Ch., 17 Ric. II., No. 26 (3, p. 175a).

Richard fil. Richard Gambourn; Tower, 8 Hen. V., No. 52 (4, p. 49a).

John Gambon and Elena ux.; Tower, 12 Hen. VI., No. 29 (4, p. 154a).

Gangy (Gaugy?)—William Gangy; Tower, 49 Hen. III., No. 4 (1, p. 27); also temp. incert, Hen. III., No. 54.

Gardener—Joh. fil. Thomas Gardener; Tower, 1 Hen. IV., No. 8 (3, p. 272a).

Sir Robert Gardiner; W. and L., 19 Jas. I., bund. 36, No. 169.

Robert Gardiner; Ch., 21 Jas. I., pt. 2, No. 143.

Sir Robert Gardiner; W. and L., 22 Jas. I., bund. 41, No. 57.

Robert Gardiner; Ch., 1 Chas. I., pt. 2, No. 12.

Garneys—Richard Garneys; Exch., 6-7 Hen. VIII. (John Eston, Esch.), No. 9.

Richard Garneys; Ch., 7 Hen. VIII., No. 113.

John Garneys, Esq.; Exch., 16-17 Hen. VIII. (Thos. Germayn, Esch.), No. 3.

Thomas Garners, Esq.; Exch., 32-33 Hen. VIII. (John Tasburgh, Esch.), No. 27.

John Garneys, Gent.; Exch., 1 Mary to 1 and 2 Philip and Mary (Edmd. Wright, Esch.), No. 6.

John Garneys; Ch., 1 and 2 Ph. and Mary, No. 57.

Robert Garneise, Esq.; Exch., 1-3 Eliz. (Wm. Drake, Esch.), No. 1.

Thomas Garnyshe, Esq.; Exch., 9 Eliz. (Edmd. Ashefeld, Esch.), No. 11.

Thomas Garnyshe; Ch., 9 Eliz., No. 47.

Thomas Garnishe; Ch., 16 Eliz., pt. 1, No. 69.

Thomas Garnish; W. and L., 16 and 17 Eliz., vol. 15, p. 8.

Richard Garneys; Ch., 28 Eliz., No. 70.

Gascoigne—Bartholomew Gascoigne; W. and L., 12 Jas. I., bund. 30, No. 218.

Bartholomew Gascoigne; W. and L., 17 Jas. I., bund. 29, No. 64.

Bartholomew Gascoigne; Ch., 17 Jas. I., pt. 3, No. 8.

Bartholomew Gascoigne; Ch., 18 Jas. I., pt. 2, No. 62.

Bartholomew Gascoigne; Ch., 18 Jas. I., pt. 2, No. 125.

Bartholomew Gascoigne; W. and L., 18 Jas. I., bund. 31, No. 10.

Cotton Gascoigne, Gent.; Misc. Ch., 4 Chas. I., pt. 19, No. 65.

Gatele, de—Rad. de Gate[ley]; Tower, 36 Hen. III., No. 31a (1, p. 10).

Gatele, de—Rad. de Gatele; Tower, 15 Edw. I., No. 78.

Gaugy. See **Gangy**? or **Gawge**?

Gavell—Thomas Gavell; Ch., 6 Hen. VIII., No. 74.

Thomas Gavell, Gent.; Exch., 5-6 Hen. VIII. (Wm. Gryce, Esch.), No. 8.

Gawdy—Thomas Gawdy; Exch., 34-35 Hen. VIII. (Robt. Downys, Esch.), No. 38.

Thomas Gawdy; Ch., 3 and 4 Philip and Mary, pt. 2, No. 123.

Thomas Gawdye, Knt. ("Justiciarius ad placita"); Ch., 31 Eliz., pt. 2, No. 59.

Bassingbourn Gavdyn (? Gawdye); W. and L., 1-5 Jas. I., vol. 29, p. 21.

Bassingborne Gawdye, Knt.; Ch., 4 Jas. I., pt. 2, No. 9.

Sir Francis Gawdye; W. and L., 4 Jas. I., bund. 8, No. 2a.

Francis Gawdye, Knt.; Ch., 6 Jas. I., pt. 2, No. 136.

Clippesby Gawdye; W. and L., 18 Jas. I., bund. 29, No. 250.

Clipsby Gawdye, Knt.; Ch., 18 Jas. I., pt. 2, No. 149.

Sir Henry Gaudy; W. and L., 19 Jas. I., bund. 33, No. 184.

Henry Gawdye, Knt.; Ch., 19 Jas. I., pt. 1, No. 63.

Lady Frances Gawdye; W. and L., 20 Jas. I., bund. 36, No. 83.

Lady Frances Gawdye, widow; Ch., 20 Jas. I., pt. 2, No. 51.

Lady Mary Gawdye, widow; W. and L., 5 Chas. I., bund. 58, No. 272.

Bassingborn Gawdy; W. and L., 10 Chas. I., bund. 54, No. 7.

Bassingborn Gawdy; Ch., 10 Chas. I., pt. 3, No. 140.

Lady Mary Gawdye; Ch., 12 Chas. I., pt. 3, No. 68.

Robert Gawdy, Knt.; Ch., 16 Chas. I., pt. 31, No. 186.

Gawdron—John Gawdron; W. and L., 11 Chas. I., bund. 56, No. 197.

Thomas Gawdron; W. and L., 12 Chas. I., bund. 58, No. 218.

Thomas Gawdron; Ch., 12 Chas. I., pt. 3, No. 81.

Gawge—John Gawge, Exch.; 32-33 Hen. VIII. (John Tasburgh, Esch.), No. 26. See **Gangy** or **Gaugy**.

Gawsell—Richard Gawsell, Esq.; Exch., 30-31 Hen. VIII. (William Woodhouse, Esch.), No. 8.

Gawsell—Richard Gawsell; Ch., 8 Eliz., No. 66.

    Thomas Gawsell; Ch., 43 Eliz., pt. 2, No. 85.

    Mary Gawsell; W. and L., 17 Jas. I., bund. 28, No. 119.

    Mary Gawsell; Ch., 17 Jas. I., pt. 1, No. 98.

    Mary Gawsell; Ch., 17 Jas. I., pt. 3, No. 33.

Gayslee, de—Jno. de Gayslee; Tower, 33 Edw. III. (2nd Nos.), No. 43
    (2, p. 216a).

Gayton—Edmund Gayton; Ch., 20 Hen. VII., No. 123.

Gazelee. See **Gayslee.**

Gebon—Geo. Gebon; Tower, 20 Edw. IV., No. 13 (4, p. 399a).

Gedding—John and Robert Gedding; Exch., 9-10 Hen. VII. (James
    Braybroke, Esch.), No. 7.

    Robert Geddying; Ch., 10 Hen. VII., No. 153.

Gegge—Richard Gegge; Tower, 30 Hen. VI., No. 25 (4, p. 253a).

Genyson. See **Jennison.**

Gibbon (see **Gebon** ?)—Thomas Gibbon; Ch., 3 Jas. I., pt. 1, No. 143.

Gibbons (?)—Regd. Gybons; Exch., 1 Eliz. (James Bigott, Esch.), No. 3.

Gibson—Robert Gibson; W. and L., 5 Jas. I., bund. 5, No. 266.

    Robert Gybson; Ch., 9 Jas. I., pt. 2, No. 29.

Gilbert—Thomas Gilberte; W. and L., 16 Jas. I., bund. 26, No. 95.

    Thomas Gilbert; Ch., 16 Jas. I., pt. 2, No. 3.

    Thomas Gilbert; Ch., 16 Jas. I., pt. 2, No. 132.

Gillett—William Gillett; Ch., 22 Eliz., pt. 2, No. 69.

Gimmingham, de—Juln. de Gymmingham; Tower, 50 Hen. III., No. 18.

Girding—Robert Girdinge; Ch., v.o. Eliz., bund. 3, No. 133.

Girling—Thomas Gyrling, Gent.; Exch., 20-21 Hen. VIII. (Henry
    Rychers, Esch.), No. 9.

    William Girlyng; W. and L., 15 and 16 Eliz., vol. 14, p. 5.

    William Girling; Ch., 15 Eliz., No. 142.

    William Girling; W. and L., 26-29 Eliz., vol. 21, p. 133.

    William Girlinge; Ch., 28 Eliz., No. 87.

    William Girlinge; Ch., 29 Eliz., No. 180.

    William Gurlinge alias Gurlyn; Ch., 2 Jas. I., pt. 2, No. 132;
    and 1-3 Jas. I., vol. 27, p. 224.

    Thomas Girlinge; Ch., 11 Jas. I., pt. 3, No. 159.

    Nathaniel Gurlinge; Ch., 14 Chas. I., bund. 63, No. 260;
    Ch., 16 Chas. I., pt. 3, No. 78.

Glaunville—Galf. de Glaunvile; Tower, 16 Edw. I., No. 31 (1, p. 96b).

Gleane—Peter Gleane, Knt.; Misc. Ch., 11 Chas. I., pt. 22, No. 30.

Glemsford—John Glemesford; Tower, 15 Hen. VI., No. 9 (4, p. 173b).

Glemham—John Glemham, Knt.; Exch., 29-30 Hen. VIII. (John Plandon, Esch.), No. 6.

    Edward Glemham, Esq.; Exch., 3 Eliz. (Edmd. Wright, Esch.), No. 6.

Gloucester, Duke of—Thomas, Duke of Gloucester; Tower, 21 Ric. II., No. 29 (3, p. 216a), and see 3, p. 224b.

Gloys—William Gloys; Ch., 13 Hen. VIII., No. 99.

Godbold—Robert Godbold; Exch., 34-35 Hen. VIII. (Robt. Downys, Esch.), No. 27.

    Richard Godbould, Gent.; Misc. Ch., 11 Jas. I., pt. 6, No. 131.

Goddard—Thomas Goddard; W. and L., 4 Chas. I., bund. 47, No. 110.

    Thomas Goddard; Ch., 5 Chas. I., pt. 2, No. 88.

Godfrey—Richard Godfrey; W. and L., 16 Jas. I., bund. 28, No. 167.

    Richard Godfrey; Ch., 16 Jas. I., pt. 1, No. 136.

Godsalve or Godsale (also see **Gowsell?**)—Thomas Godsale; Ch., 36 Hen. VIII., No. 4.

    Thomas Godsalve; W. and L., 36 Hen. VIII., vol. 1, p. 139.

    John Godsalve, Knt.; Ch., 3 and 4 Philip and Mary, pt. 1, No. 70.

    William Godsale; Ch., 4 Eliz., No. 79.

    Thomas Godsalve; W. and L., 30-34 Eliz., vol. 23, p. 42.

    Thomas Godsalve; Ch., 30 Eliz., pt. 2, No. 89.

Goffe—Edward Goffe; Misc. Ch., 10 Jas. I., pt. 6, No. 137.

    Thomas Goffe; W. and L., 14 Jas. I., bund. 60, No. 363.

    Thomas Goffe; Ch., 14 Chas. I., pt. 3, No. 44.

Gogges—John Gogges; Ch., v.o. 16 Jas. I., No. 8.

    John Gogges; W. and L., 16 Jas. I., bund. 28, No. 125.

Gogney—Edmund Gogney; W. and L., 37 Hen. VIII., vol. 2, p. 39.

    Edmund Gognye; Exch., 37-38 Hen. VIII. (John Spencer, Esch.), No. 8.

    Edward Gogney; Ch., 37 Hen. VIII., No. 51.

Goldsmith—Christopher Goldsmith; Ch., 38 Eliz., pt. 1, No. 49.

    Christopher Gouldsmith; Ch., 36 Eliz., pt. 2, No. 38.

Gonnor. See **Gunnor.**

Gonevill—Nicholas de Gonevill; Tower, 7 Edw. III. (1st Nos.), No. 25 (2, p. 55b).

Richard Gunville, Esq.; Exch., 1 Mary, 1 and 2 Philip and Mary (Edmd. Wright, Esch.), No. 18.

Gonshill (? Goushill or Godsell)—Robert Gonshill; Tower, 5 Hen. IV., No. 22 (3, p. 295a).

Gooch—John Gooch; W. and L., 21 Jas. I., bund. 37, No. 43.

John Gooche; Ch., 21 Jas. I., pt. 1, No. 50.

John Gooche; Ch., 3 Chas. I., pt. 2, No. 17.

John Gooche; W. and L., 3 Chas. I., bund. 68, No. 29.

Thomas Gooch, Gent.; Misc. Ch., 9 Chas. I., pt. 21, No. 170.

Goodwin—John Goodwyn; Exch., 1 Eliz. (James Bigott, Esch.), No. 37.

Theodore Goodwyn; W. and L., 16 Jas. I., bund. 26, No. 69.

Gording. See **Gurdon.**

Gorge—Walter Gorge; Tower, 6 Edw. IV., No. 33 (4, p. 334a).

Gorges—Edmund Gorges; Tower, 18 Edw. IV., No. 59 (4, p. 392b).

Gosenhall—Matthew Gosenhall; Ch., 23 Eliz., pt. 2, No. 109. See **Gosnold.**

Gosling. See **Gosslyn.**

Gosnold—Mathew Gosnold; W. and L., 20-24 Eliz., vol. 20, p. 121. See **Gosenhall.**

Gosslyn or Gosling—Roger Gosslyn; Exch., 2-3 Edw. VI. (John Flowerdew, Esch.), No. 15.

Roger Goslyn; Ch., 3 Edw. VI., pt. 1, No. 102.

Roger Gostlyn; W. and L., 3-5 Edw. VI., vol. 5, p. 30.

William Gosselyn; W. and L., 1-3 Eliz., vol. 8, p. 10.

William Gosselyn; Exch., 3 Eliz. (Edmund Wright, Esch.), No. 2.

William Goslinge; Ch., 3 Eliz., No. 163.

John Goslinge; Ch., v.o. Eliz., bund. 3, No. 179.

John Goseling; W. and L., 1-6 Jas. I., bund. 2, No. 185.

John Goselinge; Ch., 5 Jas. I., pt. 2, No. 62.

Robert Gostling, Gent.; Misc. Ch., 16 Chas. I., pt. 31, No. 186.

John Gostlyn, Gent.; Misc. Ch., 17 Chas. I., pt. 31, No. 115.

Gough. See **Goffe.**

Gowsell—Richard Gowsell; Ch., 31 Hen. VIII., No. 84.

Gourdenge. See **Gurdon.**

Grave—Thomas Grave; Ch., 31 Eliz., pt. 2, No. 44.

Grave—Katherine Grave ; Misc. Ch., 5 Jas. I., pt. 13, No. 56.

Gredley de—Thomas de Gredley ; Tower, 56 Hen. III., No. 60.

Green—Robert Greene ; Ch., 38 Hen. VIII., No. 17.

    Robert Grene ; W. and L., 38 Hen. VIII., and 1 Edw. VI., bund. 1a, No. 64.

    Robert Grene ; Exch., 37-38 Hen. VIII. (John Spencer, Esch.), No. 6.

    John Grene, Gent. ; Exch., 2 and 3, 3 and 4 Philip and Mary (Ralph Shelton, Esch.), No. 1.

    John Greene ; Ch., 3 and 4 Philip and Mary, pt. 1, No. 78.

    Thomas Grene ; W. and L., 5-7 Eliz., vol. 10, p. 110.

    Thomas Greene ; Ch., 7 Eliz., No. 28.

    Thomas Greene ; Exch., 7-8 Eliz. (Geo. Waller, Esch.), No. 1.

    Francis Greene ; Ch., 22 Eliz., pt. 2, No. 50.

    John Greene ; Ch., 42 Eliz., pt. 2, No. 56.

    John Grene (melius inquirendum) ; Ch., 44 Eliz., pt. 2, No. 85.

    Thomas Greene ; Misc. Ch., 13 Jas. I., pt. 6, No. 145.

    Thomas Grene ; Misc. Ch., 13 Jas. I., pt. 6, No. 143.

    Robert Greene ; W. and L., 16 Jas. I., bund. 30, No. 220.

    John Greene ; W. and L., 17 Jas. I., bund. 28, No. 111.

    John Greene ; Ch., 17 Jas. I., pt. 1, No. 94.

    Robert Greene ; Ch., 18 Jas. I., pt. 2, No. 126.

    John Greene, Gent. ; Misc. Ch., 22 Jas. I., pt. 5, No. 66.

Greengrace (Greengrass)—John Grenegrace ; Exch., 7-8 Eliz. (Geo. Waller, Esch.), No. 4.

Grelle—Robert Grelle ; Tower, 10 Edw. I., No. 20 (1, p. 74a).

Gres—John Gres ; Ch., 7 Edw. VI., pt. 1, No. 45.

Gresham—Richard Gresham, Knt. ; Exch., 3-4 Edw. VI. (Henry Minne, Esch.), No. 2.

    Richard Gresham, Knt. ; Ch., 4 Edw. VI., pt. 2, No. 56.

    Thomas Gresham, Knt. ; Ch., 23 Eliz., pt. 1, No. 11.

    Edward Gresham ; Ch., 29 Eliz., No. 47.

Greynvyle—Simon de Greynvyle ; Tower, 9 Edw. I., No. 32 (1, p. 72).

Griggs—Thomas Grygges ; Exch., 9-10 Hen. VII. (James Braybroke, Esch.), No. 11.

    Thomas Grygges ; Ch., 10 Hen. VII., No. 68.

    Averey Gregges ; W. and L., 37 Hen. VIII., vol. 2, p. 14.

Griggs—Avercy Gregges; Ch., 37 Hen. VIII., No. 45.

    Avrcy Gregges; Exch., 37-38 Hen. VIII. (John Spencer, Esch.), No. 9.

Grime—Thomas Gryme; W. and L., 30-34 Eliz., vol. 23, p. 151.

    Thomas Gryme; Ch., 34 Eliz., pt. 2, No. 101.

Grimston, de—Agnes de Grimeston; Tower, 16 Edw. I., No. 16 (1, p. 95b).

    Edward Grymston; Exch., 11-12 Hen. VIII. (Philip Bernard, Esch.), No. 2.

Groom—John Grome; Exch., 2-3 Edw. VI. (John Flowerdew, Esch.), No. 6.

    Roger Groome; Ch., 4 Eliz., No. 75.

Grice, Le, or Grys, Le—John Gryce, Gent.; Exch., 6-7 Hen. VIII. (John Eston, Esch.), No. 1.

    John Grise; Ch., 7 Hen. VIII., No. 49.

    Anthony Grice; Ch., 1 and 2 Philip and Mary, pt. 2, No. 65.

    Anthony Grice, Esq.; Exch., 1 Mary to 1 and 2 Philip and Mary (Edmund Wright, Esch.), No. 4.

    Christopher Gryce, Gent.; Exch., 1 Eliz. (James Bigott, Esch.), No. 12.

    Charles Le Grys; W. and L., 17-18 Eliz., vol. 16, p. 43.

    Christopher Gryce; Ch., 2 Eliz., pt. 2, No. 30.

    Susan Grys or Le Grys; Ch., 10 Eliz., No. 61.

    Susanna Grys; Exch., 10 Eliz. (George Chettinge, Esch.), No. 4.

    Charles le Gryce; Ch., 17 Eliz., No. 98.

    Charles le Grys, Esq.; Exch., 17-18 Eliz. (John Bacon, Esch.), No. 10.

    Charles le Grys; W. and L., 17 and 18 Eliz., vol. 16, p. 43.

    Robert Grice; Ch., 26 Eliz., No. 85.

    Christopher le Grice; Ch., 44 Eliz., pt. 2, No. 130.

Groos, le, or Grose—Le Groos; Tower, 40 Edw. III. (1st Nos.), No. 29 (2, p. 280a).

    John Groos; Tower, 41 Edw. III. (1st Nos.), No. 25 (2, p. 286a).

    William Groos, son and heir of Hugh; Tower, 5 Ric. II., No. 25 (3, p. 36b).

Groos, le, or Grose—John Groos; Exch., 3-4 Hen. VII. (Edward Clopton, Esch.), No. 3.

Gros, or Le Gros—John Gross; Ch., 4 Hen. VII., No. 8.

John Grose; Ch., 7 Hen. VIII., No. 86.

John Groose, Esq.; Exch., 6-7 Hen. VIII. (John Eston, Esch.), No. 5.

John Groos, Esq.; Exch., 7 Edw. VI. to 1 Mary (John Spencer, Esch.), No. 6.

Thomas le Groos; W. and L., 21 Jas. I., bund. 43, No. 169.

Thomas Groos; Ch., 2 Chas. I., pt. 2, No. 146; W. and L., 1 and 2 Chas. I., bund. 43, No. 169; and Ch., 2 Chas. I., pt. 2, No. 146.

Grudgefield—William Grudgefeilde; W. and L., 14 Jas. I., bund. 24, No. 156.

William Grudgefeilde; W. and L., 15 Jas. I., bund. 24, No. 51.

William Grudgefield; Ch., 14 Jas. I., pt. 3, No. 44.

William Grudgfeld; Ch., 15 Jas. I., pt. 2, No. 13.

Gungate, de—Richard de Gunnegate; Tower, 8 Edw. II., No. 29 (1, p. 257a).

Gunner or Gunnoy—Cecily Gunnore; Tower, 5 Edw. IV., No. 10 (4, p. 329b).

Simon Gunnor; Ch., 20 Hen. VIII., No. 93; and Exch., 20-1 Hen. VIII. (Hy. Rychers, Esch.), No. 20.

Gunville. See **Goneville.**

Gurdon (formerly **Gourdinge, Gordyng, or Gurden**)—Robert Gourdinge; Ch., 36 Eliz., pt. 2, No. 64.

Robert Gurden alias Gordyng; Ch., 43 Eliz., pt. 1, No. 22 *.

Beatrice Gurding; W. and L., 43 and 44 Eliz., vol. 26, p. 235.

Beatrice Gurdinge; Ch., 44 Eliz., pt. 2, No. 74.

Gurney—William Gurnay, Sen., Esq.; Exch., 12-13 Hen. VIII. (Leonard Spencer, Esch.), No. 6.

William Gourney; Ch., 13 Hen. VIII., No. 103.

Anthony Gurney; Ch., 2 and 3 Philip and Mary, pt. 2, No. 46.

Anthony Gurney, Esq.; Exch., 2 and 3, 3 and 4 Philip and Mary (Ralph Shelton, Esch.), No. 6.

Gurney—Anthony Gurnaye ; W. and L., 11 and 12 Eliz., vol. 12, p. 81.
Anthony Gurney, Esq. ; Ch., 12 Eliz., No. 67.
Thomas Gurney ; W. and L., 15 Jas. I., bund. 26, No. 80.
Thomas Gurnay ; Ch., 16 Jas. I., pt. 2, No. 10.
Thomas Gurnay ; Ch., 15 Jas. I., pt. 2, No. 126.
Edward Gornay ; Ch., 17 Chas. I., pt. 3, No. 60.
Guybon—Thomas Guybon, Esq. ; Exch., 29-30 Hen. VIII. (John
Plandon, Esch.), No. 9.
Humphrey Guybon ; Ch., 43 Eliz., pt. 2, No. 88.
Humphrey Guybon ; W. and L., 43 and 44 Eliz., vol. 26, p. 36.
Thomas Guibon ; W. and L., 1-4 Jas. I., bund. 1, No. 78.
William Guybon ; Ch., 11 Jas. I., pt. 2, No. 51.
Also see **Gebon** ? and **Gybons** ?
Hacon or Hagon—James Hacon ; Ch., 1 Eliz., pt. 3, No. 130.
James Hagon (?) ; Exch., 7-8 Eliz. (George Waller, Esch.),
No. 6.
Francis Hacon ; Ch., 25 Eliz., No. 188.
Hubert Hacon ; Ch., 41 Eliz., pt. 1, No. 41.
Hubert Hacon ; Ch., 41 Eliz., pt. 2, No. 46.
William Hagon ; Exch., 1 Mary to 1 and 2 Philip and Mary
(Edmund Wright, Esch.), No. 1.
Haddon—Walter Haddon ; Ch., 14 Eliz., No. 120.
Halcott—Robert Halcott, Gent.; Misc. Ch., 17 Chas. I., pt. 31,
No. 123.
Hale or Haile—Thomas Haile ; W. and L., 3 Chas. I., bund. 44,
No. 10.
Hales—William Hales ; Ch., 33 Hen. VIII., No. 182.
Hales als. White—John Hales alias White ; Ch., 39 Eliz., No. 67.
Hall—Francis Hall alias White ; Ch., 39 Eliz., pt. 1, No. 38.
Hall als. White*—Francis Hale alias White ; Ch., 38 Eliz., pt. 1,
No. 36.
Helena Hall alias White ; W. and L., 1-3 Jas. I., vol. 27,
p. 204.
James Hall ; Ch., 19 Jas. I., pt. 1, No. 19.
James Hall ; Ch., 20 Jas. I., pt. 1, No. 40.
James Hall ; W. and L., 20 Jas. I., bund. 36, No. 73.

---

* See Hales als. White, which seems to identify the names Hales and Hall.

Hall—Katherine Hall; Misc. Ch., 11 Chas. I., pt. 31, No. 103.

James Hall; W. and L., 19 Jas. I., bund. 32, No. 20.

Halley—John Halley; Ch., 7 Edw. VI., pt. 1, No. 42.

Hallez—John Hallez; Exch., 7 Edw. VI. to 1 Mary (John Spencer, Esch.), No. 9.

Halls—Henry Halls (lunatic); Ch., 2 Jas. I., pt. 2, No. 99.

Henry Halls; W. and L., 1-3 Jas. I., bund. 6, No. 45.

Halse—William Hals; Exch., 32-33 Hen. VIII. (John Tasburgh, Esch.), No. 6.

Thomas Halse, Esq.; Exch., 2-3 Edw. VI. (John Flowerdew, Esch.), No. 14.

William Halse; Ch., 3-4 Philip and Mary, pt. 1, No. 74.

Thomas Halse; Ch., 3 Edw. VI., pt. 1, No. 116.

Halsham—Jno. Halsham; Tower, 3 Hen. V., No. 38 (4, p. 13a).

Philippa ux. John Halsham; Tower, 19 Ric. II., No. 31 (3, p. 190a).

Hamond—John Hamond; W. and L., 19 Jas. I., bund. 33, No. 146.

John Hamond; Ch., 19 Jas. I., pt. 1, No. 5.

Richard Hamond; W. and L., 2 Chas. I., bund. 44, No. 77.

Richard Hamond; Ch., 2 Chas. I., pt. 3, No. 123.

John Hamond; Ch., 3 Chas. I., pt. 2, No. 30.

John Hamond; W. and L., 3 Chas. I., bund. 44, No. 8.

Thomas Hamond; W. and L., 7 Chas. I., bund. 49, No. 73.

Thomas Hamond; Ch., 7 Chas. I., pt. 3, No. 34.

John Hamond; Ch., 8 Chas. I., pt. 1, No. 34.

John Hamond; W. and L., 8 Chas. I., bund. 52, No. 235.

Hansard—Anthony Hansard; Exch., 11-12 Hen. VIII. (Philip Bernard, Esch.), No. 4.

Harborne—William Harborne, Esq.; Misc. Ch., 16 Jas. I., pt. 6, No. 118.

Harcourt—Katherine Harecourte; Ch., 10 Hen. VII., No. 132.

Hare—William Hare, Gent.; Exch., 32-33 Hen. VIII. (John Tasburgh, Esch.), No. 11.

William Hare, Gent.; Exch., 32-33 Hen. VIII. (John Tasburgh, Esch.), No. 25.

William Hare; Ch., 33 Hen. VIII., No. 126.

F

Hare—Nicholas Hare, Knt.; Exch., 4 and 5, 5 and 6 Philip and
    Mary (Andrew Revet, Esch.), No. 6.
    John Hare; Ch., 7 Eliz., No. 30.
    John Hare; Exch., 7-8 Eliz. (Geo. Waller, Esch.), No. 2.
    Nicholas Hare; Ch., 39 Eliz., pt. 2, No. 95.
    Michael Hare; W. and L., 8 and 9 Jas. I., bund. 5, No. 283.
    Michael Hare; Ch., 9 Jas. I., pt. 1, No. 151.
    John Hare; Ch., 12 Jas. I., pt. 1, No. 181.
    Ralph Hare; Ch., 22 Jas. I., pt. 2, No. 89.
    Ralph Hare; Ch., 43 Eliz., pt. 2, No. 86.
    Sir John Hare; W. and L., 13 Chas. I., bund. 59, No. 188.
    John Hare, Knt.; Ch., 13 Chas. I., pt. 4, No. 150.

Harleston—John Harleston; Tower, 36 Hen. VI., No. 13 (4, p. 276b).
    Elizabeth Harleston; Tower, 4 Edw. IV., No. 23 (4, p. 324a).
    Thomas Harleston; W. and L., 15 and 16 Eliz., vol. 14,
    p. 31.
    Thomas Harleston; Ch., 15 Eliz., No. 146.

Harman—Rose Harman; Exch., 37-38 Hen. VIII. (John Spencer,
    Esch.), No. 1.
    Rose Harman; W. and L., 38 Hen. VIII. and 1 Edw. VI.,
    bund. 1a, No. 38.
    Rose Harman; Ch., 38 Hen. VIII., No. 30.

Harmer—William Harmer, Gent.; Exch., 31-32 Hen. VIII. (Wm.
    Andrews, Esch.), No. 17.
    William Harmer; Ch., 32 Hen. VIII., No. 51.

Harpenden—Johanna Harpenden; Tower, 15 Hen. VI., No. 67 (4, p.
    181a).

Harrington—Richard Harrington; Ch., 6 Edw. VI., pt. 2, No. 56.
    Richard Harryngton; W. and L., 5 and 6 Edw. VI., vol. 6,
    p. 81.

Hart—John Harte, Sen.; Exch., 24-25 Hen. VIII. (John Stede, Esch.),
    No. 5.
    John Herte; Ch., 25 Hen. VIII., No. 105.
    Adam Harte; W. and L., 20-24 Eliz., vol. 20, p. 235.
    Adam Harte; Ch., 24 Eliz., pt. 1, No. 31.

Hartstrong—Francis Hartestrong; Ch., 10 Chas. I., pt. 3, No. 62.

Harvy—Isabella Harevy, widow; Ch., 5 Hen. VII., No. 85.

Harvy—Isabella Harevy; Exch., 5-6 Hen. VII. (John Falstolf, Esch.), No. 10.

Nichs. Harvye, Gent.; Exch., 33-34 Hen. VIII. (Thos. Halse, Esch.), No. 13.

Clement Harward; Exch., 1-2 Hen. VIII. (John Glemham, Esch.), No. 6.

Hast—William Hast; Exch., 33-34 Hen. VIII. (Thos. Halse, Esch.), No. 3.

William Hast; Ch., 34 Hen. VIII., No. 54.

Hastings, de—John de Hastynges, Sen.; Tower, 6 Edw. VI., No. 56 (1, p. 251a).

John de Hastings; Tower, 18 Edw. II., No. 83 (1, p. 322a, 323b).

Hugh de Hastynges; Tower, 21 Edw. III. (1st Nos.), No. 52 (2, p. 135b).

Jno. de Hastings, Comes Pembroc; Tower, 49 Edw. III. (1st pt.), No. 70 (2, p. 342a).

Anna ux. John de Hastings; Tower, 7 Ric. II., No. 67 (3, p. 61a).

Hugh de Hastings; Tower, 10 Ric. II., No. 21 (3, p. 84a).

Jno. de Hastinges; Tower, 13 Ric. II., No. 30 (3, p. 115b).

John fil' John Hastings; Tower, 14 Ric. II., No. 134 (3, p. 130a).

Philippa ux. John fil' John Hastings; Tower, 2 Hen. IV., No. 54 (3, p. 276a).

Anne Hastings, widow of —; Tower, 5 Hen. VI., No. 52 (4, p. 110b).

Jno. Hastings; Tower, 17 Edw. IV., No. 45 (4, p. 384b).

Hugh Hastynges, Knt.; Exch., 3-4 Hen. VII. (Edwd. Clopton, Esch.), No. 4.

Hugh Hastynges; Ch., 4 Hen. VII., No. 69.

John Hastyngs, Knt.; Ch., 20 Hen. VII., No. 63.

Geo. Hastynges; Exch., 2-3 Hen. VIII. (Geo. Bokenham, Esch.), No. 3.

Geo. Hastynges, Knt.; Exch., 3-4 Hen. VIII. (Anthony Hansart, Esch.), No. 1.

John Hastynges; Exch., 5-6 Hen. VIII. (Wm. Gryce, Esch.), No. 9.

Hastings, de—John Hastinges; Ch., 6 Hen. VIII., No. 83.

Hugh Hastinges, Knt.; Ch., 33 Hen. VIII., No. 155.

Hugh Hastynges, Knt.; Exch., 32-33 Hen. VIII. (John Tasburgh, Esch.), No. 16.

John Hastynges; Exch., 34-35 Hen. VIII. (Robt. Downys, Esch.), No. 43.

John Hastinges; Ch., 35 Hen. VIII., No. 13.

John Hastyngs; W. and L., 35 Hen. VIII., vol. 1, p. 85.

Thomas Hasteings; W. and L., 11 Jas. I., bund. 18, No. 34.

Thomas Hasteinges; Ch., 11 Jas. I, pt. 3, No. 171.

Hatton—John Haton, Gent.; Exch., 1 Eliz. (James Bigott, Esch.), No. 18.

Hauker, le—Peter le Hauker; Tower, 12 Ed. III. (1st Nos.), No. 14 (2, p. 83b).

Roger Haukers; Tower, 48 Edw. III. (1st Nos.), No. 38 (2, 333b).

Hauvill, de—Henry de Hauvile; Tower, 51 Hen. III., No. 34.

Thomas de Hauvill; Tower, 1 Edw. III. (2nd Nos.), No 25 (2, p. 10a).

Henry de Hauvill; Tower, 40 Hen. III., No. 32 (1, p. 15).

Thomas de Hauvill; Tower, 30 Edw. III., No. 51 (1, p. 175b).

Haversham—Jno. de Haversham; Tower (incert. temp.), Hen. III., p. 203.

Haward (see **Hayward** and **Howard**)—Sir John Haward; Tower, 5 Edw. III. (2nd Nos.), No. 80 (2, p. 43b).

Hawe—James Hawe, Esq.; Exch., 1 Mary to 1 and 2 Philip and Mary (Edmund Wright, Esch.), No. 7.

Henry Hawe; W. and L., 35-42 Eliz., vol. 24, p. 141.

Henry Hawe; Ch., 35 Eliz., No. 46.

James Hawe; Ch., 1 Mary, pt. 1, No. 90.

James Hawe, Gent.; Misc. Ch., 10 Chas. I., pt. 31, No. 100.

Hawes—Thomas Hawes, yeoman; Misc. Ch., 21 Jas. I., pt. 5, No. 60.

Hawley—Seath Hawley; W. and L., 1-3 Jas. I., vol. 27, p. 184.

Seth Hawley; Ch., v.o. 1 and 2 Jas. I., No. 20.

Hayle—Thomas Hayle; Ch., 3 Chas. I., pt. 2, No. 34.

Hayward—William Hayward; Ch., 7 Chas. I., pt. 3, No. 32.

Hayward—William Hayward; W. and L., 7 Chas. I., bund. 49, No. 72.
John Hayward; Ch., 13 Chas. I., pt. 1, No. 97.
John Hayward; W. and L., 13 Chas. I., bund. 58, No. 38.

Heath. See **Hethe, Haward,** and **Howard.**

Heigham—William Heigham, Esq.; Esch., 1 Eliz. (James Bigott, Esch.), No. 11.

Helme—Anne Helme, widow; W. and L., 5-6 Edw. VI., vol. 6, p. 58.
Anne Helme, widow; Ch., 6 Edw. VI., pt. 2, No. 40.

Hemenhale—Ralph de Hemenhale; Tower, 2 Edw. III. (1st Nos.), No. 38 (2, p. 146).
John de Hemenhale; Tower, 21 Edw. III. (1st Nos.), No. 22 (2, p. 134b).
Ralph de Hemenhale; Tower, 44 Edw. III. (2nd Nos.), No. 4 (2, p. 305b). See (2nd Nos.) No. 54 (2, p. 314a).
Robert Hemenhale; Tower, 15 Ric. II. (1st pt.), No. 32 (3, p. 136b).
Robert Hemenhale; Tower, 8 Hen. IV., No. 65 (3, p. 311b).

Hengham, de—Andrew de Hengham; Tower, 24 Edw. I., No. 92, in ad qd. (1, p. 130b).
William de Hengham; Tower, 25 Edw. I., No. 21 (1, p. 134a).

Hepham, de (Hexham?)—Joha. de Hepham; Tower, 33 Edw. I., No. 267.

Herling—John Herlyng; Tower, 6 Ric. II., No. 45 (3, p. 49a).

Herne. See **Hyrne.**

Heron—William Heron and Elizabeth ux. ej.; Tower, 6 Hen. IV., No. 21 (3, p. 399a).

Herring—Letitia ux. John Herring; Tower, 15 Ric. II. (1st pt.), No. 3 (3, p. 136b).
John Herring; Tower, 17 Ric. II., No. 28 (3, p. 175b).
Henry Herring; Tower, 4 Hen. V., No. 9 (4, p. 21a).
John Herring, Gent.; Misc. Ch., 8 Chas. I., pt. 22, No. 33.
Thomas Herringe; Misc. Ch., 9 Jas. I., pt. 6, No. 125.

Hervle (*sed ?* **Kervile**)—William Hervle; Tower (temp. incert.), Hen. III., No. 44.

Herward—Clement Herwade; Ch., 31 Eliz., pt. 2, No. 74.
Clement Herwade; Ch., 2 Hen. VIII., No. 69.

Hethe—Francis Heathe; Tower, 20 Edw. IV., No. 24 (4, p. 399b).

Heveningham, de—Philip de Heveningham; Tower, 14 Edw. I., No. 14.

> Johanne ux. Hy. Heveningham; Tower, 18 Ric. II., No. 23 (3, p. 181b).
>
> John Heveningham; Tower, 4 Hen. VI., No. 15 (4, p. 100a).
>
> John Heveningham; Tower, 31 Hen. VI., No. 7 (4, p. 253a).
>
> John Henyngham, Knt.; Ch., 15 Hen. VII., No. 65.
>
> John Hevenyngham, Knt.; Exch., 27-28 Hen. VIII. (Thos. Woodehouse, Esch.), No. 6.
>
> John Hevyngham, Knt.; Ch., 28 Hen. VIII., No. 51.
>
> Anthony Hevyngham, Knt.; Exch., 4 and 5, 5 and 6 Philip and Mary (Andrew Revet, Esch.), No. 23.
>
> Anthony Heveningham, Knt.; 5 and 6 Philip and Mary, pt. 1, No. 26.
>
> Henry Hevenyngham, Esq.; Ch., 13 Eliz., pt. 2, No. 12.
>
> Lady Mary Hevingham; Ch., 14 Eliz., No. 128.
>
> John Hevingham, Knt.; Ch., 10 Chas. I., pt. 3, No. 68.
>
> Sir John Heveningham; W. and L., 10 Chas. I., bund. 55, No. 202.

Hewar—Thomas Hewar; W. and L., 26-29 Eliz., vol. 21, p. 163.

> Thomas Hewer; Ch., 28 Eliz., No. 141.
>
> Thomas Hewar; Ch., 6 Chas. I., pt. 3, No. 80.
>
> Sir Thomas Hewar; W. and L., 6 Chas. 1, bund. 48, No. 152.

Hexham, de. See **Hepham, de.**

Heydon—John Heydon; Tower, 19 Edw. 4, No. 72 (4, p. 396a).

> Christopher Heydon, Knt.; Exch., 32-33 Hen. VIII. (John Tasburgh, Esch.), No. 13.
>
> Christopher Heydon, Knt.; Ch., 33 Henry VIII., No. 3.
>
> John Heydon, Knt.; Exch., 4-5 Edw. VI. (John Tirrell, Esch.), No. 4.
>
> John Heydon, Knt.; Ch., 5 Edw. VI., pt. 2, No. 31.
>
> Katherine Heydon, widow; Ch., 10 Eliz., No. 59.
>
> Katherine Heydon; Exch., 10 Eliz. (Geo. Chettinge, Esch.), No. 1.
>
> Christopher Heydon; Ch., 22 Eliz., pt. 2, No. 44.
>
> Henry Heydon; Ch., 23 Eliz., pt. 2, No. 107.

Heydon—William Heydon, Knt.; Ch., 41 Eliz., pt. 1, No. 32.

Christopher Haydon (*fatuus*); Ch., 2 Chas. I., pt. 3, No. 105.

Heyhowe—Thomas Heyhowe; Ch., 26 Eliz., No. 142.

William Heyhoo; W. and L., 8 Chas. I., bund. 52, No. 238.

William Heyhoo; Ch., 8 Chas. I., pt. 3, No. 156.

Heyle. See Hayle.

Heylett—William Heylett; Ch., 10 Jas. I., pt. 1, No. 35.

William Heylett; W. and L., 10 Jas. I., bund. 18, No. 126.

Heyn—Robert Hayne, Sen.; Tower, 15 Hen. VI., No. 26 (4, p. 174b).

Hickling—Thomas de Hicklingge; Tower, 16 Edw. II., No. 55 (1, p. 304a).

Hill—Edmund Hyll; Exch., 8-9 Hen. VIII. (John Stede, Esch.), No. 1.

Philip Hill, Gent.; Exch., 32-33 Hen. VIII. (John Tasburgh, Esch.), Nos. 23 or 24.

John Hill, yeoman; Misc. Ch., 22 Jas. I., pt. 5, No. 56.

Hills—Edmund Hills; W. and L., 5 Chas. I., bund. 56, No. 50.

Edmund Hills; Ch., 11 Chas. I., pt. 2, No. 41.

Hobart—James Hobert, Knt.; Exch., 8-9 Hen. VIII. (John Stede, Esch.), No. 6.

Walter Hobart, Knt.; Exch., 30-31 Hen. VIII. (Wm. Woodhouse, Exch.), No. 12.

Walter Hubert, Knt.; Ch., 30 Hen. VIII., No. 42.

Walter Hobart, Knt.; Exch., 32-33 Hen. VIII. (John Tasburgh, Exch.), No. 39.

Lady Anne Hobart; Exch., 7 Edw. VI. to 1 Mary (John Spencer, Exch.), No. 7.

Lady Anne Hoberde; Ch., 1 Mary, pt. 1, No. 89.

Miles Hubart; Ch., 4-5 Ph. and Mary, pt. 1, No. 117.

Thomas Hubart, Esq.; Exch., 1-3 Eliz. (Wm. Drake, Exch.), No. 9.

Thomas Hobarte; W. and L., 1-3 Eliz., vol. 8, p. 107.

Thomas Hubbard; 11 Eliz. (Wm. Attwood, Exch.), No. 7.

Thomas Hobart; Ch., 2 Eliz., pt. 1, No. 131.

Thomas Hobart, Esq.; Ch., 12 Eliz., No. 62.

Thomas Hobart; W. and L., 12-14 Eliz., vol. 13, p. 49.

Miles Hobard; Ch., 32 Eliz., No. 115.

Ewen Hubberd; Ch., 21 Eliz., pt. 2, No. 44.

Hobart—John Hobart; Ch., 41 Eliz., pt. 1, No. 22.

James Hobart; W. and L., 8-9 Jas. I., bund. 5, No. 287.

James Hobart; Ch., 9 Jas. I., pt. 1, No. 149.

William Hobart; W. and L., 10 Jas. I., bund. 16, No. 35.

William Hobart; Ch., 10 Jas. I., pt. 1, No. 30.

James Hobert; W. and L., 14 Jas. I., bund. 20, No. 94.

James Hobert; Ch., 14 Jas. I., pt. 3, No. 106.

Henry Hobart; Ch., 21 Jas. I., pt. 2, No. 70.

Henry Hobarte; W. and L., 21 Jas. I., bund. 36, No. 148.

Sir Thomas Hobarte; W. and L., 22 Jas. I., bund. 43, No. 86.

Thomas Hobart, Knt.; Ch., 1 Chas. I., pt. 1, No. 63.

Henry Hobart, Knt.; Ch., 3 Chas. I., pt. 2, No. 108.

Sir Henry Hobarte; W. and L., 3 Chas. I., bund. 45, No. 171.

John Hobart; Ch., 9 Chas. I., pt. 1, No. 73.

Miles Hobart; Ch., 16 Chas. I., pt. 3, No. 126.

James Hobart (lunatic); W. and L., 16 Chas. I., bund. 63, No. 104.

James Hobart; W. and L., 18 Chas. I., bund. 66, No. 67.

James Hobart (lunatic); Ch., 16 Chas. I., pt. 3, No. 22.

James Hobart; Ch., 19 Chas. I., No. 19.

Hogan—Robert Huggon; W. and L., 38 Hen. VIII. and 1 Edw. VI., bund. 1a, No. 114.

Robert Hogan; Ch., 1 Ed. VI., pt. 2, No. 14.

Anthony Huggan; Ch., 28 Eliz., No. 147.

Henry Hoogan; Ch., 34 Eliz., No. 81.

William Hogan; Ch., 1-2 Ph. and Mary, pt. 2, No. 59.

Robert Hoogan; W. and L., 10 Jas. I., bund. 21, No. 59.

Robert Hoogan; Ch., 13 Jas. I., pt. 1, No. 119.

Thomas Hogan; Ch., 29 Eliz., No. 248.

Holbeck—Beatrix, widow of Ralph de Holbeck; App., 9 Edw. III., No. 13 (4, p. 440a); 11 Edw. III. (1st. Nos.), No. 12 (2, p. 77a).

Holderness, Earl of—John, Earl of Holderness; Ch., 7 Chas. I., pt. 2, No. 17.

John, Earl of Holdernes; W. and L., 7 Chas. I., bund. 49, No. 91.

Holdich—Joan Holdich, widow; Ch., 5 Hen. VII., No. 104.

    Joan Holdyche; Exch., 5-6 Hen. VII. (John Falstolf, Exch.), No. 8.

    Henry Holdiche; W. and L., 36 Hen. VIII., vol. 1, p. 108.

    Henry Holdiche; Ch., 36 Hen. VIII., No. 51.

    Henry Holdich; W. and L., 16 Jas. I., bund. 36, No. 137.

    Henry Holdich; Ch., 21 Jas. I., pt. 2, No. 61.

    Robert Holdiche; Ch., 1 Eliz., pt. 1, No. 128.

    Richard Holdiche; W. and L., 5-7 Eliz., vol. 10, p. 37.

    Richard Holdiche; Ch., 6 Eliz., No. 143.

    John Holditche; Ch., 31 Eliz., pt. 1, No. 100.

    Robert Holdiche, Esq.; Exch., 1 Eliz. (James Bigott, Esch.), No. 30.

Holl—Thomas Holle, Gent.; Exch., 1 Eliz. (James Bigott, Exch.), No. 34.

    Thomas Holl; Ch., 1 Eliz., pt. 1, No. 133.

Holland—Hugh de Holland; Tower, 50 Edw. III. (2nd Nos.), No. 17 (2, p. 356b).

    Richard, son and heir of John de Holland; Tower, 4 Hen.V., No. 50 (4, p. 24a).

    John Hollonde, Gent.; Exch., 34-45 Hen. VIII. (Robt. Downys, Esch.), No. 1.

    John Holland; Ch., 35 Henry VIII., No. 105.

    John Holland; Ch., 10 Jas. I., pt. 1, No. 135.

    John Hollande; W. and L., 10 Jas. I., bund. 14, No. 87.

    Sir Thomas Holland; 2 Chas. I., bund. 44, No. 93.

    Thomas Holland, Knt.; Ch., 2 Chas. I., pt. 3, No. 129.

Holmes—James Holmes; Misc. Ch., 22 Jas. I., pt. 5, No. 62.

Homerston—John Homerston; Ch., 35 Eliz., pt. 2, No. 2.

Honeworth. See **Hunworth.**

Hoo—Anne Hoo; Exch., 7 Edw. VI. to 1 Mary (John Spencer, Esch.), No. 1.

    Anne Hoo; Ch., 7 Edw. VI., pt. 1, No. 53.

    Richard Hoo; W. and L., 9-11 Eliz., vol. 11, p. 109.

    Richard Hoo, Esq.; Ch., 11 Eliz., No. 97.

    Richard Hoo; Exch., 11 Eliz. (Wm. Attwood, Esch.), No. 11.

Hoo—Thomas Hoo; Ch., 13 Eliz., pt. 2, No. 26.

    Richard Hooe (proof of age); Ch., 24 Eliz., pt. 1, No. 35.

    John Hooe; Ch., 38 Eliz., pt. 1, No. 47.

    Richard Hoo; W. and L., 6 Ch. I., bund. 48, No. 170.

    Richard Hooe; Ch., 6 Ch. I., pt. 3, No. 84.

Hopton—Walter Hopton; Tower, 1 Edw. IV., No. 42 (4, p. 313a).

    George Hopton; Exch., 5-6 Hen. VII. (John Falstolf, Esch.), No. 3.

    John Hopton; Exch., 5-6 Hen. VII. (John Falstolf, Esch.), No. 4.

    Arthur Hopton, Knt.; Exch., 2 and 3, 3 and 4 Philip and Mary (Ralph Shelton, Esch.), No. 3.

Horford—William de Horford; Tower, 12 Edw. II., No. 35 (1, p. 290b).

Horsman—John Horsman; Ch., 33 Hen. VIII., No. —-

    George Horsman, Esq.; Ch., 1 Eliz., pt. 3, No. 124.

    John Horsman, Esq.; Exch., 32-33 Hen. VIII. (John Tasburgh, Esch.), No. 10.

    George Horseman, Esq.; Exch., 1 Eliz. (James Bigott, Esch.), No. 24.

Horton—Edward Horton; Ch., 4 Chas. I., pt. 4, No. 48.

    Edmund Horton; W. and L., 4 Chas. I., bund. 46, No. 134.

Houghton—Thomas Houghton, Clk.; Exch., 34-35 Hen. VIII. (Robt. Downys, Esch.), No. 31.

    Thomas Houghton; Ch., 35 Hen. VIII., No. 164.

    Thomas Houghton; W. and L., 35 Hen. VIII., vol. 1, p. 53.

    Francis Houghton; Ch., 5 Chas. I., pt. 2, No. 65.

    George Houghton; Ch., 38 Eliz., pt. 1, No. 44.

Hovell (Houell?)—Richard Hovell; W. and L., 9 and 10 Jas. I., bund. 4, No. 32.

    Richard Hovell; Ch., 10 Jas. I., pt. 1, No. 180.

Howard. See **Haward (Heyward)**—Margaret ux. Robert Howard; Tower, 12 Ric. II., No. 26 (3, p. 101a).

    Matilda ux. John Howard; Tower, 15 Ric. II. (1st pt.), No. 31 (3, p. 136b).

    Jno. Howard; Tower, 16 Hen. VI., No. 56 (4, p. 184b).

    Thomas Howard, Duke of Norfolk; Ch., 1 and 2 Philip and Mary, pt. 2, No. 56.

Howard—William Howarde; Tower, 9 Eliz. (Edmd. Ashefeld, Esch.), No. 4.

Robert Howard, Gent.; Misc. Ch., — Chas. I., pt. 31, No. 177.

Howes or Howse—Christopher Howse; W. and L., 3-7 Eliz., vol. 25, p. 56.

George Howse; Ch., 37 Eliz., pt. 2, No. 130.

William Howse, Gent.; Ch., 4 Jas. I., pt. 2, No. 109.

Christopher Howse; Ch., 7 Jas. I., pt. 1, No. 33.

William Howse; W. and L., 1-6 Jas. I., bund. 2, No. 107.

Nicholas Howes, yeoman; Misc. Ch., 15 Jas. I., pt. 6, No. 115.

Edmund Howse; W. and L., 18 Jas. I., bund. 30.

Edward Howse; Ch., v.o. 18 Jas. I., No. 20.

William Howes; W. and L., 3 Chas. I., bund. 46, No. 11.

William Howes; Ch., 4 Chas. I., pt. 4, No. 11.

William Howes; Ch., 4 Chas. I., pt. 4, No. 36.

William Howes *(melius inquirendum)*; W. and L., 4 Chas. I., bund. 46, No. 86.

Howlet—Thomas Howlet; Ch., 17 Jas. I., pt. 3, No. 22.

Hubbard and **Hubart.** See **Hobard.**

Huddleston—John Huddleston, Esq.; Exch., 22-23 Henry VIII. (Edmund Clere, Esch.), No. 1.

Huggan. See **Hogan.**

Hungerford—Alexander Hungerford; Tower, 33 Hen. VI., No. 35 (4, p. 267a).

Hunston—Henry Hunston; Exch., 26-27 Hen. VIII. (Philip Bedingfeld, Esch.), No. 6.

Richard Hunston; Ch., 1 Edw. VI., pt. 2, No. 24.

Richard Hunston; W. and L., 1 Edw. VI., vol. 3, p. 10.

William Hunston, Esq.; Exch., 9 Eliz. (Edmd. Ashefeld, Esch.), No. 8.

William Hunston; Ch., 9 Eliz., No. 47.

William Hunston; Ch., 25 Eliz., No. 38.

Hunt—Sir Thomas Hunt; W. and L., 15 Jas. I., bund. 24, No. 82.

Thomas Hunt; Ch., 15 Jas. I., pt. 2, No. 125.

Margaret Hunt (lunatic); W. and L., 20 Chas. I., bund. 68, No. 137.

Hunt—Margaret Hunt (lunatic); Ch., 20 Chas. I., No. 5.

Huntingdon, Countess of—Juliana, Countess of Huntingdon; Tower,
40 Edw. III. (1st Nos.), No. 34 (2, p. 280b).

Huntingfield, de—Roger Huntingfeld; Tower, 31 Edw. I., No. 31
(1, p. 180).

William de Huntingfield; Tower, 7 Edw. II., No. 47 (1, p.
255b).

Roger de Huntingfield; Tower, 3 Edw. III. (1st Nos.), No.
42 (2, p. 23a).

Roger de Huntingfeld; Tower, 11 Edw. III. (1st Nos.), No.
47 (2, p. 78b).

William de Huntingfield; Tower, 50 Edw. III. (1st pt.), No.
32 (2, p. 354b).

Hunworth—Roger de Huneworthe; Ch., 34 Edw. I., No. 21 (1, p.
206a).

John de Honeworth; Tower, App., 4 Edw. III., No. 6 (4, p.
438a).

John de Honeworth; Tower, 23 Edw. III. (2nd pt.), No. 34
(2, p. 155b).

William de Honeworth; Tower, 39 Edw. III. (1st pt.),
No. 15 (2, p. 270b).

John de Hunworth; Tower, 26 Edw. III. (1st Nos.), No. 17
(2, p. 173a).

John de Hunworth; Tower, 34 Edw. III. (1st Nos.), No. 8
(2, p. 218b).

Husband—Christopher Husband; Ch., 11 Chas. I., pt. 2, No. 38.

Christopher Husband; Ch., 11 Chas. I., pt. 2, No. 86.

Hyrne—Robert Hyrne; Ch., 3-4 Ph. and Mary, pt. 2, No. 130.

Robert Hirne, Gent.; Exch., 2-3, 3-4 Ph. and Mary (Ralph
Shelton, Esch.), No. 5.

Clement Herne; Ch., 38 Eliz., pt. 1, No. 101.

Michael Herne; Ch., 10 Jas. I., pt. 1, No. 136.

Nicholas Herne; W. and L., 10 Jas. I., bund. 14, No. 77.

Richard Herne; W. and L., 1 Chas. I., bund. 43, No. 81.

Richard Herne; Ch., 1 Chas. I., pt. 1, No. 84.

Sir Thomas Hyrne; W. and L., 14 Chas. I., bund. 66,
No. 69.

Hyrne—Sir Thomas Hyrne; Ch., 20 Chas. I., No. 66.

Ilketshale—Thomas Ilketeshale; Tower, 10 Hen. VI., No. 27 (4, p. 136a).

Ingham, de—Oliv. de Ingham; Tower, 10 Edw. I., No. 4 (1, p. 73).

John de Ingham; Tower, 3 Edw. II., No. 57.

Oliver de Ingham; Tower, 18 Edw. III. (1st Nos.), No. 49 (2, p. 117b).

Oliver de Ingham; Tower, 22 Edw. III. (1st Nos.), No. 50 (2, p. 146).

Inglose—Anna ux. Henry Ingelose; Tower, 18 Ric. II., No. 25 (3, p. 181b).

Henry Inglose; Tower, 31 Hen. VI., No. 48 (4, p. 257a).

Henry Inglos; Ch., 8 Hen. VIII., No. 28.

Henry Ingloose, Esq.; Exch., 8-9 Hen. VIII. (John Stede, Esch.), No. 13.

Ingoldesthorp, de—John de Ingoldesthorp; Tower, 11 Edw. I., No. 29.

Thomas de Ingoldesthorp; Tower, 1 Edw. III. (2nd Nos.), No. 83 (2, p. 11b).

John de Ingoldesthorp; Tower, 10 Edw. III. (1st Nos.), No. 41 (2, p. 72a).

Thomas de Ingoldesthorp; Tower, 12 Edw. III. (1st Nos.), No. 26 (2, p. 84a).

William de Ingelsthorp; Tower, 37 Edw. III. (1st pt.), No. 36 (2, p. 261a).

William de Ingelsthorp; Tower, 46 Edw. III. (1st Nos.), No. 33 (2, p. 318).

John Ingoldesthorp; Tower, 8 Hen. VI., No. 49 (4, p. 49a).

Thomas Inglesthorp; Tower, 10 Hen. V., No. 4 (4, p. 64b).

Elizabeth Inglesthorp; Tower, 10 Hen. V., No. 12 (4, p. 65a).

Elizabeth, widow of John Ingelthorp; Tower, 1 Hen. VI., No. 46 (4, p. 73a).

Margaret ux. Thomas Ingoldesthorpe; Tower, 5 Hen. VI., No. 23 (4, p. 107b).

Insula, de—Waren de Insula; Tower, 1 Edw. III., No. 15 (2, p. 1).

John de Insula and wife; Tower, 5 Edw. III. (2nd Nos.), No. 125 (2, p. 45a).

Insula, de—Robert de Insula; Tower, 41 Edw. III. (1st Nos.), No. 53
(2, p. 292a).

Ives—John Ives; W. and L., 9-11 Eliz., vol. 11, p. 45.

John Ives; Ch., 11 Eliz., No. 99.

John Ives; Ch., 8 Jas. I., pt. 2, No. 20.

John Ives; W. and L., 7 and 8 Jas. I., bund. 3, No. 123.

Thomas Ives; Ch., 9 Chas. I., pt. 1, No. 22.

Thomas Ives; W. and L., 9 Chas. I., bund. 53, No. 182.

Jakes (Jaques)—John Jakes; Ch., 40 Eliz., pt. 2, No. 55.

James—Sarah James, widow; W. and L., 3-7 Jas. I., vol. 25, p. 118.

Sarah James; Ch., v.o. 7 Jas. I., pt. 1, No. 35.

Samuel James; Misc. Ch., 5 Chas. I., pt. 24, No. 158.

Robert James; Ch., 10 Chas. I., pt. 3, No. 82.

Robert James; W. and L., 10 Chas. I., bund. 55, No. 199.

Jaques. See **Jakes.**

Jay—John Jaye; Ch., 16 Eliz., pt. 1, No. 66.

John Jay; W. and L., 16 Jas. I., bund. 38, No. 231b.

John Jay; Ch., 16 Jas. I., pt. 1, No. 66.

John Jaye, Esq.; Misc. Ch., 17 Jas. I., pt. 31, No. 89.

John Jaye; W. and L., 17 Jas. I., bund. 38, No. 67.

John Jaye; Ch., 21 Jas. I., pt. 1, No. 8.

John Jaye; Ch., 2 Chas. I., pt. 3, No. 70.

Jeggon—John Jegon; W. and L., 18 Jas. I., bund. 30, No. 209.

John Jegon; Ch., 18 Jas. I., pt. 2, No. 124.

Jenkinson—Richard Jenkinson; W. and L., 22 Jas. I., bund. 39, No. 156.

Richard Jenkinson; Ch., 22 Jas. I., pt. 2, No. 135.

Jenner alias **Joyner**—Thomas Jenner alias Joyner; Misc. Ch., 11
Jas. I., pt. 6, No. 133.

Jennison—Thomas Genyson; 37-38 Hen. VIII. (John Spencer, Esch.),
No. 14.

Thomas Genyson; W. and L., 37 Hen. VIII., vol. 2, p. 41.

Thomas Jenyson; Ch., 37 Hen. VIII., No. 52.

Robert Jenison; Ch., 25 Eliz., No. 107.

Jenny—John Jenny; Ch., 13 Hen. VII., No. 33.

William Jenny; Exch., 1-2 Hen. VIII. (John Glemham,
Esch.), No. 11.

William Jenney; Ch., 2 Hen. VIII., No. 68.

Jenny—Edward Jenney; Ch., 9 Hen. VIII., No. 92.

Edmund Jenney, Esq.; Exch., 9-10 Hen. VIII. (Henry Russell, Esch.), No. 11.

Edmund Jenney, Knt.; 14-15 Hen. VIII. (John Brampton, Esch.), No. 2.

Edward Jenny; Ch., 15 Hen. VIII., No. 58.

John Jenney, Sen.; 24-25 Hen. VIII. (John Stede, Esch.), No. 3.

George Jenney (lunatic); W. and L., 9-11 Eliz., vol. 11, p. 3.

George Jenney; Ch., 10 Eliz., No. 65.

Henry Jenney; W. and L., 7 and 8 Jas. I., bund. 3, No. 108.

Henry Jenny; Ch., 8 Jas. I., pt. 1, No. 24.

Henry Jenney; W. and L., 8 and 9 Jas. I., bund. 5, No. 253.

Henry Jenney; Ch., 9 Jas. I., pt. 1, No. 129.

Jermy—Edward Jermy; Ch., 1 Hen. VIII., No. 45.

John Jermy, Knt.; Exch., 3 Eliz. (Edmd. Wright, Esch.), No. 3.

Clement Jermy; W. and L., 3 Chas. I., bund. 68, No. 36.

Clement Jermy; Ch., 3 Chas. I., pt. 2, No. 11.

John Jermy; Ch., 7 Chas. I., pt. 3, No. 106.

John Jermy; W. and L., 7 Chas. I., bund. 50, No. 218.

Thomas Jermyn; Ch., 13 Hen. VII., No. 50.

Jermyn—Thomas Germyn; Ch., 21 Hen. VII., No. 96.

Ella Jermyn; Exch., 30-31 Hen. VIII. (Wm. Woodhouse, Esch.), No. 5.

Ele Jermyn; Ch., v.o. 5 Edw. VI., No. 66.

Thomas Jermyn, Knt.; Exch., 7 Edw. VI. to 1 Mary (John Spencer, Esch.), No. 14.

Edward Germyn, Esq.; Ch., 15 Eliz., No. 148.

Edmund Jermyn; Ch., 41 Eliz., pt. 2, No. 92.

Edmund Jermyn; W. and L., 33-44 Eliz., vol. 26, p. 65.

Edmund Jermyn (*melius inquirendum*); Ch., 44 Eliz., pt. 2, No. 66.

William Jermyn; W. and L., 4 Jas. I., bund. 0, No. 30.

William Jermyn; Ch., 6 Jas. I., pt. 2, No. 73.

John Jermyn; W. and L., 3 Chas. I., bund. 51, No. 43.

John Jermyn; Ch., 7 Chas. I., pt. 3, No. 56.

Jermyn—John Jermyn; W. and L., 8 Chas. I., bund. 52, No. 81.

John Jermyn, Esq.; Ch., 8 Chas. I., pt. 3, No. 47.

Jerningham—Edward Jerningham, Esq.; Exch., 6-7 Hen. VIII. (John Eston, Esch.), No. 4.

Henry Jerningham, Knt.; Ch., 15 Eliz., No. 145.

Henry Jerningham, Knt.; W. and L., 15-16 Eliz., vol. 14, p. 32.

John Jernyngham, Knt.; 1 Eliz. (James Bigott, Esch.), No. 9.

Jillett (see **Gillett**)—William Jillett; Ch., 22 Eliz., pt. 2, No. 60.

Johnson—John Johnson; Exch., 2-3 Edw. VI. (John Flowerdew, Esch.), No. 9.

John Johnson; W. and L., 3-5 Edw. VI., vol. 1, p. 5.

John Johnson; Ch., 3 Edw. VI., pt. 1, No. 114.

William Johnson; W. and L., 17 Jas. I., bund. 29, No. 53.

William Johnson; W. and L., 10 Jas. I., bund. 14, No. 76.

William Johnson; Ch., 10 Jas. I., pt. 1, No. 134.

William Johnson; W. and L., 17 Chas. I., bund. 64, No. 30.

William Johnson; Ch., 17 Jas. I., pt. 3, No. 70.

Jolly—Thomas Jolley; W. and L., 1-6 Jas. I., bund. 2, No. 159.

Thomas Jolly; Ch., v.o. 3-4 Jas. I., No. 1.

Jordan. See **Jurdan.**

Joyce—William Joyce; 1-2 Hen. VII. (Gregory Lovell, Esch.), No. 9.

Joyner. See **Jenner** alias **Joyner.**

Jurdan or Jordan—Humphrey Jurdan; W. and L., 5-7 Eliz., vol. 10, p. 73.

Humphrey Jurdan; Exch., 4-5 Eliz. (Augustine Curtes, Esch.), No. 3.

Humphrey Jurden; Ch., 5 Eliz., pt. 2, No. 37.

John Jordan; W. and L., 43-44 Eliz., vol. 26, p. 52.

John Jordan; Ch., 43 Eliz., pt. 2, No. 43.

Kateson. See **Cateson.**

Kaukewelle (? **Kaudewelle or Caldwell**)—Michael de Kaukewelle; Tower, 29 Edw. I., No. 20 (1, p. 166b).

Kelgett—William Kelgett; W. and L., 16-17 Eliz., vol. 15, p. 7.

Kemp—Robert Kempe; Ch., 17 Hen. VIII., No. 3.

Robert Kempe, Esq.; Exch., 18-19 Hen. VIII. (Wm. Gryce, Esch.), No. 1.

Kemp—Bartholomew Kempe; Exch., 1 Mary to 1-2 Ph. and M. (Edmd. Wright, Esch.), No. 9.

Bartholomew Kempe; Ch., 1-2 Ph. and Mary, pt. 2, No. 60.

Robert Kempe; Ch., 37 Eliz., pt. 2, No. 18.

Robert Kempe; W. and L., 10 Jas. I., bund. 15, No. 82.

Robert Kempe; Ch., 10 Jas. I., pt. 1, No. 148.

Robert Kempe; W. and L., 13 Jas. I., bund. 25, No. 90.

Robert Kempe; Ch., 15 Jas. I., pt. 2, No. 35.

Robert Kempe; W. and L., 15 Jas. I., bund. 25, No. 141.

Robert Kempe; Ch., 15 Jas. I., pt. 2, No. 106.

Kendall, alias Tyndall. See **Tindall.**

Henry Kendall, alias Tyndall; Misc. Ch., 14 Chas. I., pt. 22, No. 7.

Kent, Earl of—Edmund, Comes de Kent; Tower, 4 Edw. III. (1st Nos.), No. 38 (2, p. 31b).

John, Count of Kent; Tower, 26 Edw. III. (1st pt.), No. 54 (2, p. 176b).

Kerdiston—Roger de Kerdiston; Tower, 11 Edw. III. (1st Nos.), No. 45 (2, p. 78a).

William Kerdestone; Tower, 19 Edw. III. (2nd Nos.), No. 79 (2, p. 127b).

William de Kerdiston; Tower, 35 Edw. III. (1st Nos.), No. 106 (2, p. 233b).

Thomas Kerdeston; Tower, 29 Hen. VI., No. 31 (4, p. 249a).

Kervill or Chervill (? also see **Hervle**)—Frederick Chervill; Tower, 44 Edw. III. (1st pt.), No. 13 (2, p. 303b).

Humphrey Kervyle; Exch., 20-21 Hen. VIII. (Henry Rychers, Esch.), No. 14.

Humphrey Carvell; Ch., 36 Hen. VIII., No. 15.

Humphrey Kyrvyle; Misc. Ch., v.o. Hen. VIII., bund. 2, No. 94.

Thomas Karvile; Ch., 2 Eliz., pt. 1, No. 130.

Thomas Karvile; W. and L., 1-3 Eliz., vol. 8, p. 89.

Edward Korvile, Esq.; Ch., 18 Eliz., No. 20.

Henry Kervyll; W. and L., 13 Jas. I., bund. 21, No. 55.

Henry Kervill; Ch., 13 Jas. I., pt. 1, No. 141.

Henry Kirvill, Knt.; Ch., 6 Chas. I., pt. 2, No. 161.

Kett (? also see **Le Cath**), alias **Knight**—Robert Kett, alias Knight (attainted); Ch., v.o. 3 Edw. VI., pt. 1, No. 43.

    Edward Kett, alias Knight; W. and L., 8-9 Jas. I., bund. 5, No. 374a.

    Edward Kett, alias Knight; W. and L., 8-9 Jas. I., bund. 5, No. 250.

    Edward Kett, alias Knight; Ch., 9 Jas. I., pt. 2, No. 12.

    Edward Kett, alias Knight; Ch., 9 Jas. I., pt. 2, No. 16.

    Robert Kett; W. and L., 18 Jas. I., bund. 30, No. 174.

    Robert Kett; Ch., v.o. 18 Jas. I., No. 41.

    Robert Kett; Ch., 2 Chas. I., pt. 3, No. 162.

    Robert Kett; W. and L., 7 Chas. I., bund. 54, No. 50.

    Robert Kett; Ch., 10 Chas. I., pt. 3, No. 137.

Kettleborough—William Kettleborough; Misc. Ch., 1 Jas. I., pt. 6, No. 146.

King—John King, Gent.; Misc. Ch., 9 Jas. I., pt. 6, No. 130.

    John Kinge; Ch., 9 Chas. I., pt. 1, No. 53.

    John Kinge; W. and L., 9 Chas. I., bund. 54, No. 122.

Kingsfield—John de Kingsfield; Tower, 5 Ric. II., No. 31 (3, p. 37a).

Kitson—Thomas Kytson, Knt.; Exch., 31-32 Hen. VIII. (William Andrews, Esch.), No. 2.

    Thomas Kitson, Knt.; Exch., 32-33 Hen. VIII. (John Tasburgh, Esch.), No. 48.

Knapp—John Knapp; Ch., 4 Eliz., No. 71.

Knevett. See **Knyvett.**

Knight, alias Kett. See **Kett.**

Knightley—William Knyghtley; W. and L., 1 and 2 Edw. VI., vol. 3, p. 107.

    William Knightley; Ch., 2 Edw. VI., pt. 2, No. 46.

    Ursula Knightley; Ch., 2 Eliz., pt. 2, No. 34.

    Ursula Knightly, widow; W. and L., 1-3 Eliz., vol. 8, p. 124.

Knighton, alias Underhill—Thomas Knyghton, alias Underhyll, Gent.; Exch., 24-25 Hen. VIII. (John Stede, Esch.), No. 1.

Knipe—Peter Knipe; Ch., 10 Chas. I., pt. 3, No. 132.

Knolles—Robert de Knolles and Constance ux. ej.; Tower, 45 Edw. III. (1st Nos.), No. 36 (2, p. 309b).

Knyvett—John Knyvett, Esq.; Ch., 6 Hen. VII., No. 35.

Knyvett—John Kynvet; Exch., 5-6 Hen. VII. (John Falstolf, Esch.), No. 5.

Edward Knevett, Knt.; Exch., 20-21 Hen. VIII. (Henry Rychers, Esch.), No. 13.

William Knyvet, Knt.; Ch., 7 Hen. VIII., No. 9.

Edward Knyvett, Knt.; Ch., 20 Hen. VIII., No. 44.

Anne Knyvett; Ch., 21 Hen. VIII., No. 139.

Edward Knyvett, Knt.; W. and L., 3-5 Edw. VI., vol. 5, p. 152.

Edward Knyvett, Knt.; Ch., Edw. VI., pt. 1., No. 66.

Edmund Knyvett, Knt.; Exch., 4-5 Edw. VI. (John Tirrell, Esch.), No. 6.

Thomas Knyvett, Knt.; W. and L., 9-11 Eliz., vol. 11, p. 142.

Thomas Knyvett, Knt.; Ch., 12 Eliz., No. 68.

Thomas Knyvett, Knt.; Ch., 37 Eliz., pt. 2, No. 127.

Ambrose Knyvett, alias Nevyt; Ch., 40 Eliz., pt. 1, No. 15.

William Nevette; Ch., v.o. Eliz., bund. 1, No. 523.

Thomas Knyvett, Knt.; Ch., 16 Jas. I., pt. 1, No. 150.

Lady Elizabeth Knivet; W. and L., 9 Chas. I., bund. 53, No. 218.

Lady Elizabeth Knevett, widow; Ch., 9 Chas. I., pt. 1, No. 68.

Ladd, alias Baker—Awdley Ladd, alias Baker; W. and L., 4 Chas. I., bund. 45, No. 28.

Audley Ladd, alias Baker; Ch., 4 Chas. I., pt. 2, No. 1.

Lambe—William Lambe; Ch., 14 Hen. VII., No. 33.

Thomas Lambe, Gent.; Exch., 34-35 Hen. VIII. (Robert Downys, Esch.), No. 14.

Thomas Lambe; W. and L., 35 Hen. VIII., vol. 1, p. 41.

Thomas Lambe; Ch., 35 Hen. VIII., No. 89.

William Lambe, Gent.; Exch., 1 Eliz. (James Bigott, Esch.), No. 21.

Thomas Lambe, Esq.; Exch., 12 Eliz. (John Bull, Esch.), No. 5.

William Lambe, W. and L., 1 and 2 Jas. I., vol. 28, p. 151.

William Lambe; Ch., v.o. 1 and 2 Jas. I., No. 29.

Lancaster, Earl of—E . . . L . . . of Lancaster; Tower, 25 Edw. I., No. 51 (1, p. 136a).

Lancaster—William Lancaster; Ch., 8 Hen. VII., No. 59.

    Alianora Lancaster, widow; Ch., 16 Hen. VII., No. 73.

Lane—John Lane; Exch., 1-3 Eliz. (Wm. Drake, Esch.), No. 6.

Langholme—John Longholme; Ch., 20 Hen. VIII., No. 123.

Langton—Walter de Langton; Tower, 15 Edw. II., No. 44 (1, p. 300a).

Langwade—Robert Langwade, Gent.; Exch., 37-38 Hen. VIII. (John Spencer, Esch.), No. 12.

    Robert Langwade; Ch., 38 Hen. VIII., No. 20.

    Robert Langewade; W. and L., 38 Hen. VIII., vol. 2, p. 101.

Latham. See **Lethum?**

Lathe, atte—Tho. atte Lathe; Tower, App., 18 Edw. III., No. 7 (4, p. 444b).

Latimer—John Latimer; Tower, 5 Ric. II., No. 69 (3, p. 44a).

    Elizabeth ux. William Latimer; Tower, 7 Ric. II., No. 52 (3, p. 59b).

    George, Lord Latimer; Tower, 9 and 10 Edw. IV., No. 28 (4, p. 348b).

    Edward Latimer, Gent.; Exch., 32-33 Hen. VIII. (John Tasburgh, Esch.), No. 31.

Laverock—Robert Laverock; W. and L., 7 and 8 Jas. I., bund. 3, No. 120.

    Robert Laverack; Ch., 8 Jas. I., pt. 2, No. 16.

La Veylle. See **Veylle, la.**

Lawes—Alan Lawes; Exch., 10-11 Hen. VII. (Richard Hungerford, Esch.), No. 5.

    Alan Lawes; Ch., 10 Hen. VII., No. 119.

    Anne Lawes; Ch., 22 Eliz., pt. 2, No. 55.

Lawrence—Robert Laurence; Ch., 13 Chas. I., pt. 1, No. 101.

Lawson—Richard Lawson; Ch., 40 Eliz., pt. 2, No. 105.

Layer—Christopher Layer; W. and L., 1 Jas. I., bund. 7, No. 98.

    Christopher Layer; Ch., 43 Eliz., pt. 1, No. 26.

    Christopher Layer; Ch., 1 Jas. I., pt. 1, No. 35.

Leach or Leeche—William Leche; Tower, 1 Hen. IV., No. 29 (3, p. 261b).

    William Leeche; Tower, 7 Hen. IV., No. 35 (3, p. 305b).

Leach or Leeche—Sibilla Leche ; Tower, 11 Hen. VI., No. 20 (4, p. 139a).

William fil. Nicholas Leche ; Tower, 12 Hen. VI., No. 45 (4, p. 157b).

Lee, Atte—William atte Lee and Johanna ux. ej.; Tower, 8 Ric. II., No. 83 (3, p. 71a).

Ella Lee ; Exch., 27-28 Hen. VIII. (Thomas Woodehouse, Esch.), No. 1.

Legh—William Legh ; Tower, 2 Ric. III., No. 15 (4, p. 420a).

Isabelle, wid. of William Legh ; Tower, App., 18 Hen. VI., No. 1 (4, p. 472c).

Le Gros. See **Gros, le.**

Le Grys. See **Grice, le.**

Leman—Sir John Leman ; W. and L., 10 Chas. I., bund. 55, No. 201.

Le Neve. See **Neve.**

Le Scrope. See **Scrope.**

Le Strange—John Lestrange ; Tower, 4 Edw. I., No. 38 (1, p. 58a).

John Lestrange ; Tower, 33 Edw. I., No. 63.

Peter Lestraunge ; Tower, 51 Edw. III. (2nd Nos.), No. 9 (2, p. 360b).

John (Le) Strange and Alice his (wife); Tower, 15 Hen. VI., No. 52 (4, p. 177b).

Henry Le Straunge ; Ch., 1 Hen. VII., No. 56.

Henry Straunge ; Exch., 1-2 Hen. VII. (Gregory Lovell, Esch.), No. 7.

Roger Le Straunge, Knt.; 21 Hen. VII., No. 103.

Robert Le Straunge ; Ch., 3 Hen. VIII., No. 106.

Robert Lestraunge, Esq. ; Exch., 3-4 Hen. VIII. (Anthony Hansart, Esch.), No. 10.

John Lestraunge ; Exch., 5-6 Hen. VIII. (Wm. Gryce, Esch.), No. 4.

John Le Straunge, Esq. ; Exch., 9-10 Hen. VIII. (Henry Russell, Esch.), No. 15.

John Le Straunge ; Ch., 10 Hen. VIII., No. 28.

Thomas Lestraunge, Knt. ; Ch., 36 Hen. VIII., No. 72.

Hamon Lestrange ; Ch., 12 Eliz., No. 72.

Thomas Lestrange ; W. and L., 20-24 Eliz., vol. 20, p. 272.

Le Strange—Thomas Lestrange; Ch., 24 Eliz., pt. 1, No. 24.

　　　　Hamond Lestrange; Ch., 24 Eliz., pt. 1, No. 20.

　　　　Nicholas Le Straunge; W. and L., 33 and 34 Eliz., vol. 23,
　　　　　　p. 146.

　　　　Nicholas Le Straunge; Exch., 30 and 34 Eliz., vol. 23, p. 146.

　　　　Nicholas Le Straunge; Ch., 34 Eliz., pt. 1, No. 53.

　　　　Nicholas Lestraunge, Knt.; Ch., 34 Eliz., pt. 1, No. 53.

Lethum—Robert Lethum; Tower, 19 Edw. IV., No. 53 (4, p. 395a).

Lewgore—Alice Lewgore; Exch., 15-16 Hen. VIII. (Christopher
　　　Harman, Esch.), No. 10.

Lewkenor. See Lukenor.

Lexham—William Lexam, Esq.; Ch., 15 Hen. VII., No. 111.

Leyham (Lexham ?)—John de Leyham; 27 Edw. I., No. 29 (1, p. 149a).

Leyre (? Le Eyre)—William Leyre; Exch., 32-33 Hen. VIII. (John
　　　Tasburgh, Esch.), No. 34.

Limesey—William Lymsey, Gent.; Misc., 3 Jas. I., pt. 6, No. 144.

Limmer (see also Lomnor ?)—Edmund Limmer, Esq.; Exch., 4 and 5,
　　　5 and 6 Ph. and Mary (Andrew Revel, Esch.), No. 24.

　　　　Edward Limmer; Ch., 5 and 6 Ph. and Mary, pt. 1, No. 17.

Lincoln, Earl of—John, Earl of Lincoln; Ch., v.o. Rich. III. and
　　　Hen. VII., Nos. 126 and 124.

　　　　John, late Earl of Lincoln; Exch., 8-9 Henry VII.
　　　　　(Richard Ferrour, Mayor and Esch.), No. 1.

Lincoln—Samuel Lyncolne, Gent.; Misc. Ch., 12 Chas. I., pt. 31,
　　　No. 107.

　　　　Samuel Lincolne; W. and L., 12 Chas. I., bund. 56, No.
　　　　　245.

　　　　Samuel Lincolne; Ch., 12 Chas. I., pt. 3, No. 19.

Linford—Bridget Linford; Ch., 17 Jas. I., pt. 3, No. 2.

Lingwood—Thomas Lingwood; W. and L., 4 Jas. I., bund. 12,
　　　No. 45.

　　　　Thomas Lingwood; Ch., 8 Jas. I., pt. 2, No. 41.

Linnicke—John Lynnycke; Misc. Ch., 10 Jas. I., pt. 6, No. 135.

Lisiniaco, de—Galfr. de Lisiniaco; Tower, 33 Edw. I., No. 249 (1,
　　　p. 205a).

Lisle. See Insula, de.

Lisney. See Lisiniaco, de.

Liston—Robert Liston; Tower, 18 Edw. IV., No. 24 (4, p. 388a).

Isabella Lyston; Ch., 7 Hen. VII., No. 22.

Lock—Anthony Lock; W. and L., 18 Chas. I., bund. 66, No. 57.

Anthony Locke; 18 Chas. I., pt. 1, No. 15.

Anthony Locke; Ch., 18 Chas. I., pt. 1, No. 15.

Lomnor (see also **Limmer?**)—Thomas Lomnor, Gent.; Exch., 33-34 Hen. VIII. (Thos. Halse, Esch.), No. 5.

Thomas Lomnor; Ch., 34 Hen. VIII., pt. 2, No. 52.

London—William London; Ch., 9 Hen. VII., No. 45.

James London; Exch., 6-7 Hen. VIII. (John Eston, Esch.), No. 15.

James London; Ch., 7 Hen. VIII., No. 97.

Robert London, Gent.; Misc. Ch., 4 Chas. I., pt. 24, No. 143.

Long—John Longe; W. and L., Jas. I., bund. 38, No. 117.

John Longe; Ch., 21 Jas. I., pt. 2, No. 113.

Losse—Thomas Losse; Misc. Ch., v.o. Eliz., bund. 1, No. 1.

Thomas Losse; Exch., 1 Eliz. (James Bigott, Esch.), No. 31.

Loudham, de (see also **Leidham, de?**)—Thomas de Loudham and Margaret ux. ej.; Tower, 9 Ric. II., No. 33 (3, p. 75b).

Bartholomew de Loudham; Tower, 31 Edw. III. (1st Nos.), No. 37 (2, p. 202b).

John Loudham; Tower, 2 Hen. VI., No. 24 (4, p. 79a).

Joha. ux. John de Loudham; Tower, 46 Edw. III. (1st Nos.), No. 35 (2, p. 318b).

John de Loudham; Tower, 48 Edw. III. (1st Nos.), No. 43 (2, p. 334a).

John de Loudham; Tower, 1 Ric. II., No. 148 (3, p. 10a).

Lovell—John Lovell; Tower, 37 Hen. III., No. 22 (1, p. 11).

Thomas Lovell; Tower, App., 4 Edw. III., No. 8 (4, p. 438a).

Gilbert de Lovell; Tower, 10 Edw. III. (1st Nos.), No. 9 (2, p. 70b).

John Lovel; Tower, 21 Edw. III. (1st Nos.), No. 49 (2, p. 135a).

Isabella ux. John Lovel; Tower, 25 Edw. III. (1st Nos.), No. 62b (2, p. 170b).

John Lovell; Tower, 9 Hen. IV., No. 29 (3, p. 316b).

Margaret Lovell; Tower, 26 Hen. VI., No. 18 (4, p. 235b).

Lovell—William Lovell; Tower, 16 Edw. IV., No. 73 (4, p. 381a).

Thomas Lovell; Tower, 19 Edw. IV., No. 14 (4, p. 393a).

Henry Lovell, Lord Morley; Exch., 4-5 Hen. VII. (John Rodon, Esch.), No. 4.

Anne Lovell; Ch., 5 Hen. VII., No. 6.

Henry Lovell, Lord Morley; Ch., 5 Hen. VII., No. 47.

Alianora Lovell; Ch., 13 Hen. VIII., No. 101.

Robert Lovell, Knt.; Ch., 14 Hen. VIII., No. 54.

Thomas Lovell, Knt.; Exch., 15-16 Hen. VIII. (Christopher Harman, Esch.), No. 4.

Thomas Lovell; Ch., 16 Hen. VIII., No. 62.

Francis Lovell, Knt.; W. and L., 5 and 6 Edw. VI., vol. 6, p. 43.

Francis Lovell, Knt.; Ch., 6 Edw. VI., pt. 2, No. 41.

Thomas Lovell, Knt. ; Exch., 9 Eliz. (Edmund Ashefeld, Esch.), No. 13.

Thomas Lovell, Knt.; Ch., 9 Eliz., No. 44.

Thomas Lovell; Ch., 3 Jas. I., pt. 1, No. 142.

Philip Lovell; W. and L., 15 Jas. I., bund. 26, No. 132.

Philip Lovell ; Ch., 15 Jas. I., pt. 1, No. 6.

George Lovell ; Ch., 3 Chas. I., pt. 2, No. 24.

George Lovell ; W. and L., 3 Chas. I., bund. 69, No. 143.

Francis Lovell, Knt.; Misc. Ch., 1 Chas. I., pt. 5, No. 73.

Charles Lovell, Esq.; Misc. Ch., 17 Chas. I., pt. 31, No. 85.

Lucas—Jasper Lucas ; Exch., 21-22 Hen. VIII. (Anthony Thwaytys, Esch.), No. 3.

Thomas Lucas, Esq.; 22-23 Hen. VIII. (Edmund Clere, Esch.), No. 4.

Richard Lucas; W. and L., 17 and 18 Eliz., vol. 16, p, 93.

Richard Lucas; Ch., 18 Eliz., pt. 2, No. 42.

Ludham, de (see also **Loudham, de** ?)—John de Ludham; Tower, 30 Edw. III. (1st Nos.), No. 19 (2, p. 196b).

Ludkin—Robert Ludkin ; W. and L., 16 Chas. I., bund. 63, No. 87.

Robert Ludkin ; Ch., 16 Chas. I., pt. 3, No. 19.

Lukenor—John Lukenor ; Tower, 37 Hen. VI., No. 4 (4, p. 281a).

Lutterell—Hugh Luterel ; Tower, 6 Hen. VI., No. 32 (4, p. 115b).

Hugh Lutterell, Knt.; Exch., 12-13 Hen. VIII. (Leonard Spencer, Esch.), No. 5.

Lye—Thomas Lye; Exch., 9-10 Hen. VII. (James Braybroke, Esch.), No. 15.

Thomas Lye; 10 Hen. VII., No. 61.

Mainwaring—Warin de Menwarin; Tower, 18 Edw. I., No. 32.

Manfield—Andrew Manfild, Gent.; Exch., 1 Mary to 1 and 2 Philip and Mary (Edmund Wright, Esch.), No. 8.

Andrew Manfeld; Ch., 1 Mary, pt. 1, No. 81.

Jane Manfield; Ch., 31 Eliz., pt. 2, No. 54.

Manning—Robert Mannyng, jun., Gent.; Exch., 4-5 Edw. VI. (John Tirrell, Esch.), No. 13.

Mannock—William Mannock, Esq.; Exch., 4-5, 5-6 Ph. and Mary (Andrew Revet, Esch.), No. 13.

Manny—Walter de Manny; Tower, 46 Edw. III. (1st Nos.), No. 38 (2, p. 318b).

Manser—Thomas Manser, Gent.; Exch., 32-33 Hen. VIII. (John Tasburgh, Esch.), No. 38.

Richard Mansver; Ch., 41 Eliz., pt. 2, No. 85.

Mapes—Francis Mapes; Ch., 14 Chas. I., pt. 3, No. 100; and 14 Chas. I., bund. 61, No. 267.

March—William Marche; Tower, 4 Edw. III. (1st Nos.), No. 21 (2, p. 30a).

Walter March; Tower, 32 Edw. III. (1st Nos.), No. 16 (2, p. 206a).

William Marche; Tower, 21 Ric. II., No. 41 (3, p. 217b).

Thomas Marche; Tower, 2 Hen. IV., Nos. 38 and 38b (3, p. 274a).

Anna, wife of Edmund, Earl of March; Tower, 11 Hen. VI., No. 39 (4, p. 140b).

Marshall, le—Alina le Marischal; Tower, 1 and 3 (incert.), No. 77 (1, p. 42a).

John le Mareshall; Tower, 10 Edw. II., No. 79 (1, p. 287a).

John le Mareschal; Tower, 11 Edw. I., No. 27 (1, p. 79a).

John le Mareschall; Tower, 26 Edw. I., No. 73.

William de Maroochal; Tower, 0 Edw. II., No. 51 (1, p. 258b).

Constantia, Countess Marshall; Tower, 16 Hen. VI., No. 60 (4, p. 185b).

Marshall, le—Margery Marchall, widow ; Ch., 9 Hen. VII., No. 70.

    Margery Marchall; Exch., 9-10 Hen. VII. (James Braybroke, Esch.), No. 10.

Mareys—John Mareys ; Misc. Ch., v.o. Hen. VIII., bund. 2, No. 111.

Margery—Richard Margery, Gent. ; Misc. Ch., 8 Chas. I., pt. 25, No. 136.

Marsham—Robert Marsham ; Ch., 32 Eliz., No. 6.

    Robert Marsham, Gent.; Misc. Ch., 13 Jas. I., pt. 6, No. 141.

    Thomas Marsham ; Ch., 15 Chas. I., pt. 4, No. 45.

    Thomas Marsham ; W. and L., 15 Chas. I., bund. 62, No. 129.

Martin—Roger Martin, Esq. ; Exch., 34-35 Hen. VIII. (Robert Downys, Esch.), No. 35.

Martindale—Edward Martingdale ; Ch., 4 Eliz., No. 78.

Maryet (Mariot)—William Maryet; Tower (divers years), 6 Hen. VI. (4, p. 304a).

Mason—Paul Mason ; Misc. Ch., 15 Jas. I., pt. 32, No. 75. See **Miller, alias Mason.**

Maunsel—John Maunsel ; Tower, 35 Edw. III. (2nd Nos.), No. 3 (2, p. 238b).

    Walter Maunsel; Tower, 35 Edw. III. (1st pt.), No. 29 (2, p. 266b).

    Henry Maunsel and Beatrix his wife; Tower, 14 Edw. III. (1st Nos.), No. 5 (2, p. 92b).

Maupas—William Maupas and Agnes ux. ej.; Tower, 40 Edw. III. (2nd Nos.), No. 16 (2, p. 276b).

Mauteby—John de Mautby; Tower, 12 Hen. VI., No. 47 (4, p. 158a).

Mautravers—Agnes, ux. John Mautravers; Tower, 49 Edw. III. (2nd pt.), No. 17 (2, p. 347a).

Mayhew—Thomas Mayheu ; Ch., 17 Jas. I., pt. 3, No. 49.

    Thomas Mayhewe ; W. and L., 17 Jas. I., bund. 29, No. 63.

    Sarah Mayhew, widow ; Misc. Ch., 22 Jas. I., pt. 5, No. 67.

Maxtide—Edmund Maxtide ; Ch., 13 Chas. I., pt. 1, No. 179.

Meauling or Meling—William de Meauling; Tower, 20 Ric. II., No. 57 (3, p. 210a).

    Peter Melinge ; Tower, 1 Edw. I., No. 34 (1, p. 50a).

Melle—Robert Melle, Gent.; Exch., 32-33 Hen. VIII. (John Tasburgh, Esch.), No. 29.

Merlawe—Drogo de Merlawe; Tower, 11 Edw. II., No. 45 (1, p. 288b).

Messinger—Augustine Messinger; Ch., 2 Chas. I., pt. 3, No. 104.

Roger Messenger; W. and L., 8 Chas. I., bund. 62, No. 52.

Roger Messinger; Ch., 15 Chas. I., pt. 4, No. 32.

Methwold—Richard Methwold; Ch., 1 Hen. VII., No. 105.

Richard Methwold; Exch., 1-2 Hen. VII. (Gregory Lovell, Esch.), No. 13.

Richard Methewold; Exch., 3-4 Hen. VIII. (Anth. Hansart, Esch.), No. 7.

William Metwold, Esq.; Exch., 30-31 Hen. VIII. (William Woodhouse, Esch.), No. 1.

William Metwold; Ch., 32 Hen. VIII., No. 35.

John Methold; Ch., 2 Edw. VI., pt. 2, No. 38.

Thomas Methwold; W. and L., 14 Chas. I., bund. 60, No. 300.

Thomas Methwold, Esq.; Ch., 14 Chas. I., pt. 3, No. 74.

Michel—John Michel; Tower, 47 Edw. III. (2nd Nos.), No. 52 (2, p. 330b).

Might—Geoffrey Might; Ch., 38 Eliz., pt. 1, No. 127.

Thomas Mighte; W. and L., 1 and 2 Jas. I., vol. 28, p. 69.

Thomas Myght; Ch., 43 Eliz., pt. 2, No. 89.

Thomas Might; Ch., 2 Jas. I., pt. 2, No. 93.

Thomas Might; W. and L., 5 Jas. I., bund. 8, No. 67.

Thomas Might; Ch., 5 Jas. I., pt. 1, No. 158.

Mileham—Thomas de Mileham; Tower, 8 Edw. III. (1st Nos.), No. 34 (2, p. 59b).

Beatrix, ux. Thomas Mileham; Tower, 13 Edw. III. (1st Nos.), No. 12 (2, p. 89a).

Geo. de Mileham; Tower, 50 Edw. III. (1st pt.), No. 41 (2, p. 355a).

Gregory Myleham, Gent.; Misc. Ch., 15 Jas. I., pt. 13, No. 80; Ch., 17 Jas. I., pt. 2, No. 104.

Miller—John Miller; W. and L., 2 Edw. VI., vol. 3, p. 110.

John Myller; Ch., 2 Edw. VI., pt. 2, No. 45.

Thomas Myller; Exch., 4-5 Eliz. (Augustine Curtes, Esch.), No. 9.

Miller, alias Mason—Paul Miller, alias Mason; W. and L., 15 Jas. I.,
bund. 40, No. 98.

Miller, alias Threvell—Thomas Myller, alias Threvell; W. and L.,
1-3 Jas. I., vol. 27, p. 203; and Ch., v.o. 1 and 2 Jas. I.,
No. 30.

 Richard Miller, alias Mason; Misc. Ch., 21 Chas. I., pt. 32,
No. 125.

 Richard Miller, alias Mason; Misc. Ch., 21 Chas. I., pt. 32,
No. 90.

Miller, alias Milner. See **Milner, alias Miller.**

Milner, alias Miller—Thomas Milner, alias Miller; Misc. Ch., 15
Chas. I., pt. 31, No. 184.

Min. See **Mynne.**

Mingay—John Mingay; Misc. Ch., 2 Chas. I., pt. 26, No. 125.

 John Mingay; Ch., 8 Chas. I., pt. 3, No. 124.

 Henry Mingaye; W. and L., 9 Chas. I., bund. 61, No. 258.

 Henry Mingaye, Esq.; Misc. Ch., 15 Chas. I., pt. 31, No. 110.

 Henry Myngay, Esq.; Ch., 14 Chas. I., pt. 3, No. 110.

Minsterchamber—John Minsterchamber, Gent.; Exch., 34-35 Hen.
VIII. (Robt. Downys, Esch.), No. 21.

Moigne (le) (? see **Money**)—Thomas Moigne; Tower, 37 Edw. III.
(1st pt.), No. 51 (2, p. 261b).

Moleyns—William Molyns; Tower, 4 Rich. II., No. 38 (3, p. 31a).

Monceux (? see **Monoux**)—Thomas Monceux; Tower, 29 Hen. VI,
No. 4 (4, p. 246a).

Money—William Money; Ch., 43 Eliz., pt. 2, No. 23.

 William Money; W. and L., 43 and 44 Eliz., vol. 26, p. 109.

Monk, le—John le Monck; Tower, 2 Edw. III. (1st Nos.), No. 33
(2, p. 14b).

 Jno. le Monk; Tower, App., 3 Edw. III., No. 7 (4, p. 437b).

Monoux (? see **Monceux**)—Thomas Monoux; Exch., 29-30 Hen.
VIII. (John Plandon, Esch.), No. 8.

 Thomas Monoux; Ch., 30 Hen. VIII., No. 6.

Montagu—William, fil. William Montagu; Tower, 6 Ric. II., No. 56
(3, p. 50a).

 Isabella, Marchioness Montague; Ch., 2 Hen. VII., No.
52.

Monte Acuto, de—William de Monte Acuto and Elizabeth his wife; Tower, 13 Edw. II., No. 31 (1, p. 293b).

Edward de Monte Acuto; Tower, 35 Edw. III. (2nd pt.), No. 7 (2, p. 239a).

Edward de Monte Acuto; Tower, 40 Edw. III. (1st pt.), No. 26 (2, p. 274b).

Monte Alto, de—Robert de Monte Alto; Tower, temp. incert. Hen. III., No. 83 (1, p. 43a).

Robert de Monte Alto; 3 Edw. I., No. 29 (1, p. 55b).

Monte Caniso—William de Monte Caniso; App., Hen. III., No. 11 (4, p. 423a).

Monchenesy—William de Monchenesy; Tower, 14 Edw. I., No. 27.

Dionisea de Monte Caniso; Tower, 7 Edw. II., No. 51 (1, p. 256a).

Monteny or Mounteny—Robert de Monteny; Tower, 15 Edw. I., No. 26 (1, p. 93b).

Thomas Mountney; Ch., 10 Hen. VII., No. 173.

Christopher Mounteney; Ch., 5 Edw. VI., pt. 2, No. 100.

Monye or Moigne? q.v.—Robert Monye; Exch., Eliz. (James Bigott, Esch.), No. 22.

Mooll—Henry Mooll; Misc. Ch., 14 Chas. I., pt. 31, No. 65.

Moore—Thomas Moore; W. and L., 17 Jas. I., bund. 43, No. 161.

Thomas Moore; Ch., 2 Chas. I., pt. 2, No. 121.

Thomas Moore; Ch., 2 Chas. I., pt. 3, No. 60.

Thomas Moore; Ch., 5 Chas. I., pt. 2, No. 18.

Thomas Moore, Gent.; Misc. Ch., 6 Chas. I., pt. 31, No. 88.

Moptide—Humphrey Moptide, yeoman; Exch., 4-5 Eliz. (Augustine Curtes, Esch.), No. 7.

Mordaunte—Edward Mordaunte; Ch., 26 Eliz., No. 140.

Robert Mordaunt; W. and L., 20 Jas. I., bund. 35, No. 178.

Robert Mordaunt; Ch., 20 Jas. I., pt. 2, No. 141.

Lestrange Mordant; Ch., 15 Chas. I., pt. 4, No. 17.

Robert Mordaunt; Misc., 16 Chas. I., pt. 31, No. 181.

More—Edward More; Exch., 1 Eliz. (Jas. Bigott, Esch.), No. 2.

Thomas More, W. and L., 22 Jas. I., bund. 43, No. 135.

Moreff (?Morell)—John Moreff(?), Clerk; Exch., 31-32 Hen. VIII. (Wm. Andrews, Esch.), No. 8.

Moretofte—John Moretofte; Ch., 26 Hen. VIII., No. 62.

Morley, de—John de Morley, sen.; Tower, 3 Edw. III. (1st Nos.), No. 27 (2, p. 22b).

Alice de Morle; Tower, 23 Edw. III. (2nd Nos.), No. 4 (2, p. 161b).

Robert de Morley; Tower, 34 Edw. III. (1st Nos.), No. 82 (2, p. 222a).

Robert Morley; Tower, 36 Edw. III. (1st pt.), No. 117 (2, p. 252a).

Johanna, wife of Robert de Morley; Tower, 37 Edw. III. (1st pt.), No. 47 (2, p. 261b).

William de Morley; Tower, 2 Ric. II., No. 34 (3, p. 12b); 3 Ric. II., No. 47 (3, p. 22b). Place called Rey.

Cecilia, ux. William de Morley; Tower, 10 Ric. II., No. 27 (3, p. 84a).

Robert de Morley; 14 Ric. II., No. 38 (3, p. 126b).

Thomas de Morle; Tower, 4 Hen. V., No. 49 (4, p. 24a).

Robert Morle; Tower, 3 Hen. V., No. 23 (4, p. 12b).

Thomas Morley; Tower, 5 Hen. V., No. 57 (4, p. 32b).

Robert Morley; Tower, 6 Hen. V., No. 18 (4, p. 34b).

Anne, ux. Thomas de Morley; Tower, 5 Hen. VI., No. 52 (4, p. 110b).

Thomas Morley; Tower, 14 Hen. VI., No. 20 (4, p. 163b).

Robert Morley; Tower, 21 Hen. VI., No. 38 (4, p. 212).

Margaret Morley; (proof of age), Tower, 9 Hen. VI., No. 67 (4, p. 134b).

Lady Isabella Morley; Tower, 6 Edw. IV., No. 21 (4, p. 334b).

Lady Alice Morley; Exch., 10-11 Hen. VIII. (Geoffrey Cobbe, Esch.), No. 10.

Lady Alice Morley; Ch., 11 Hen. VIII., No. 11.

Lord Henry Morley; Ch., 3-4 P. and M., pt. 1, No. 87.

Morrell (? also see **Moreff**)—John Morrell; Ch., 29 Eliz., No. 5.

Mortimer—William de Mortimer; Tower, 25 Edw. I., No. 45 (1, p. 135a).

Edmund de Mortuomari; Tower, 5 Ric. II., No. 43 (3, p. 37b).

Thomas Mortimer; (see 3, p. 224 a and b), 21 Ric. II.

Mortimer—Roger de Mortimer ; Tower, 22 Ric. II., No. 34 (3, p. 231b).

Edmund de Mortimer, Earl of March ; Tower, 3 Hen. VI., No. 32 (4, p. 85b).

Mote, de la—William de la Mote ; Tower, 32 Edw. I., No. 161 (1, p. 194b).

Mowbray—John Mowbray ; Tower, 43 Edw. III. (2nd Nos.), No. 7 (2, p. 298a).

Thomas Mowbray ; Tower, 8 Hen. IV., No. 76 (3, p. 313b).

John de Mowbray, Duke of Norfolk ; Tower, 11 Hen. VI., No. 43 (4, p. 145b).

Mownteney—Christopher Mownteney, Gent. ; Exch., 4-5 Edw. VI. (John Tirroll, Esch.), No. 2.

Mowtyng—Thomas Mowtyng, Gent. ; Exch., 3-4 Edw. VI. (Henry Minne, Esch.), No. 1.

Thomas Mowting ; W. and L., 3-5 Edw. VI., vol. 5, p. 135.

Thomas Mowtynge ; Ch., 4 Edw. VI., pt. 2, No. 58.

Multon—Matilda de Multon ; Tower, 21 Edw. I., No. 25 (1, p. 114a).

Thomas de Multon ; Tower, 28 Edw. I., No. 32 (1, p. 155a).

Hubert de Multon ; Tower, 28 Edw. I., No. 586.

John Multon, jun., Gent. ; Exch., 37-38 Hen. VIII. (John Spencer, Esch.), No. 26.

Mundeford—Osbert de Mundeford ; Tower, 20 Ric. II., No. 38 (3, p. 207b).

Osbert de Mundeford ; Tower, App., 4 Hen. IV., No. 3 (4, p. 464a). Proof of age.

Osbert Mondford ; Tower, 20 Edw. IV., No. 19 (4, p. 399a).

Francis Mounfford, Esq. ; Exch., 32-33 Hen. VIII. (John Tasburgh, Esch.), No. 9.

Francis Moundford ; Ch., 33 Hen. VIII., No. 146.

Osbert Mounford ; Ch., 22 Eliz., pt. 2, No. 45.

Francis Moundford ; Ch., 33 Eliz., pt. 2, No. 41.

Edward Moundeford, Knt. ; Ch., 16 Jas. I., pt. 1, No. 166.

Edmund Moundforde, Knt. ; Misc. Ch., 19 Chas. I., pt. 19, No. 00.

Edmund Moundeford, Knt. ; Misc. Ch., 19 Chas. I., pt. 30, No. 54.

Mundes—Robert Mundes ; W. and L., 26-29 Eliz., vol. 21, p. 92.

Murrell—Agnes Murrell; W. and L., 16 Jas. I., bund. 26, No. 71.

    Agnes Murrell; Ch., v.o. 16 Jas. I., No. 47.

Mynne—Edward Mynne; Ch., 36 Hen. VIII., No. 6.

    Edward Mynne; W. and L., 1 Edw. VI., vol. 3, p. 32.

    Nicholas Mynne; Ch., 1 Edw. VI., pt. 2, No. 18.

    Henry Mynne; W. and L., 9-11 Edw. VI., vol. 11, p. 6.

    Henry Mynne, Esq.; Ch., 9 Eliz. No. 49.

    Henry Mynne, Esq.; Exch., 9 Eliz. (Edm. Ashefeld, Esch.), No. 7.

    Edward Myn; W. and L., 15 and 16 Eliz., vol. 14, p. 4.

    Edward Mynn; Ch., 15 Eliz., No. 147.

    Edward Myn; Ch., 10 Chas. I., pt. 3, No. 129.

    Edward Min; W. and L., 10 Chas. I., bund. 55, No. 93.

Narburgh—William Narburgh; Tower, 6 Hen. VI., No. 9 (4, p. 114b).

Neel—Thomas Neel; Tower, 50 Edw. III. (1st pt.), No. 45 (2, p. 355a).

Neffield—George Neffield; Tower, 9 Hen. VI., No. 39 (4, p. 130b).

Nerburgh. See **Narburgh?**

Nerford—Edmund de Nerford; Tower, 2 Edw. III. (2nd Nos.), No. 8 (2, p. 17b).

    Edmund de Nerford; Tower, 5 Edw. III. (1st Nos.), No. 39 (2, p. 38a).

    Thomas de Nerford; Tower, 5 Edw. III. (2nd Nos.), No. 76 (2, p. 43b).

    Thomas de Nerford; Tower, 18 Edw. III. (1st Nos.), No. 25 (2, p. 116a).

    John de Nerford; Tower, 38 Edw. III. (1st pt.), No. 31 (2, p. 266b).

    John de Nerford; Tower, 50 Edw. III. (1st pt.), No. 46 (2, p. 355a).

    Elizabeth, ux. Thomas Nerford; Tower, 17 Ric. II., No. 40 (3, p. 176a).

Neve—John Neve; Exch., 34-35 Hen. VIII. (Robt. Downys, Esch.), No. 37.

    Robert Neve; Ch., 26 Eliz., No. 94.

    William Neave; W. and L., 18 Jas. I., bund. 30, No. 205.

    William Neeve; Ch., 18 Jas. I., pt. 2, No. 69.

Nevill—Maria de Nevill; Tower, 13 Edw. II., No. 23 (1, p. 293a).

Nevill—Ralph de Nevill; Tower, 40 Edw. III. (1st Nos.), No. 47
(2, p. 281b).

John de Nevill; Tower, 12 Ric. II., No. 40 (3, p. 102a).

Elizabeth, wife of John Nevill; Tower, 1 Hen. VI., No. 45
(4, p. 72b).

George Nevile, Lord Latimer; Tower, 9-10 Edw. IV.,
No. 28 (4, p. 348b).

Edward Nevill; Tower, 16 Edw. IV., No. 66 (4, p. 378a).

Ralph Nevill, Earl of Westmoreland; Tower, 2 Ric. III.,
No. 14 (4, p. 419b).

Margaret Neville; Exch., 1-2 Hen. VII. (Gregory Lovell,
Esch.), No. 12.

Margaret Nevill; Ch., 1 Hen. VII., No. 3.

Ralph Nevill, Earl of Westmoreland; Ch., 15 Hen. VII.,
No. 10.

Isabella Nevill; Ch., 9 Hen. VIII., No. 95.

Lady Isabella Nevell; Exch., 8-9 Hen. VIII. (John Stede,
Esch.), No. 11.

John Nevell; Ch., v.o. Eliz., bund. 1, No. 504.

Nevette (see also **Knevett** ?)—William Nevette; Ch., v.o. Eliz., bund.
1, No. 523.

Ambrose Newytt, alias Knyvitt; Ch., 40 Eliz., pt. 1, No. 15.

Newgate—William Newgate (outlaw); Ch., 15 Hen. VII., No. 122.

Newton—Alexandra Newtone, Esq.; Exch., 12 Eliz. (John Bull, Esch.),
No. 3.

Nicholls—Humphrey Nicholls; W. and L., 1 and 2 Edw. VI., vol. 4, p. 52.

Richard Nicolls; W. and L., 16 and 17 Eliz., vol. 15, p. 59.

Humphrey Nycolles; Ch., 2 Edw. VI., pt. 2, No. 53.

Richard Nicholles; Ch., 16 Eliz., pt. 1, No. 60.

Richard Nicholles, Esq.; Exch., 16-17 Eliz. (John Dowbes,
Esch.), No. 5.

Nix—Richard Nix; Exch., 29-30 Hen. VIII. (John Plandon, Esch.),
No. 10.

Noion, de, or Nuion (see **Nowne** or **Nunne**)—John de Nuioun; Tower,
18 Edw. II., No. 1 (1, p. 317a).

John de Noioun; Tower, 15 Edw. III. (1st Nos.), No. 29
(2, p. 99b).

Noion, de, or Nuion (see **Nowne or Nunne**)—Beatrix, ux. John Noioun; Tower, 23 Edw. III. (2nd pt.), No. 132 (2, p. 158b).

Beatrix, ux. John Noiun; Tower, 25 Edw. III. (1st Nos.), No. 52 (2, p. 170a).

Noloth—Geoffrey Noloth; Tower, 2-3 Edw. VI. (John Flowerdew, Esch.), No. 2.

Norburghe, de (Nerburgh?)—Cecilia, daughter of William Norburgh; Tower, 17 Edw. IV., No. 67 (4, p. 387b).

Norfolk (see **Howard**)—Thomas, Duke of Norfolk; Tower, 22 Ric. II., No. 101b (3, p. 255b).

Thomas, Duke of Norfolk; Tower, 1 Hen. IV., No. 71b (3, p. 267a).

Duchess of Norfolk; Tower, 1 Hen. IV., No. 72a (3, p. 270a).

John, Duke of Norfolk; Tower, 1 Edw. IV., No. 46 (4, p. 313b).

Jno., Duke of Norfolk; Tower, 17 Edw. IV., No. 58 (4, p. 386a).

John, Duke of Norfolk; Tower, 19 Edw. IV., No. 73 (4, p. 396b).

John, Duke of Norfolk; Ch., 21 Hen. VII., No. 104.

Thomas, Duke of Norfolk; Ch., 1 and 2 Ph. and Mary, pt. 2, No. 56.

Norris—Thomas Norrys; W. and L., 5 Jas. I., bund. 10, No. 201.

Thomas Norris; Ch., 6 Jas. I., pt. 2, No. 71.

Thomas Norrys, Esq.; Misc. Ch., 8 Jas. I., pt. 6, No. 129.

Cuthbert Norris, S.T.P.; Misc. Ch., 20 Jas. I., pt. 5, No. 68.

Robert Norris; Ch., 15 Chas. I., pt. 4, No. 72.

Robert Norris; W. and L., 15 Chas. I., bund. 62, No. 294.

Northampton—Henry, Earl of Northampton; Ch., 18 Jas. I., pt. 2, No. 161.

Henry, Earl of Northampton; W. and L., 18 Jas. I., bund. 30, No. 224.

Norton—Richard Norton; Ch., 14 Hen. VII., No. 43.

John Norton; Exch., 6-7 Hen. VIII. (John Eston, Esch.), No. 16.

John Norton, Gent.; Exch., 37-38 Hen. VIII. (John Spencer, Esch.), No. 11.

Norton—John Norton; Ch., 38 Hen. VIII., No. 18.

> Robert Norton, Gent.; Exch., 3 Eliz. (Edmd. Wright, Esch.), No. 4.

Norwich—Geoffrey de Norwich; Tower, 28 Edw. I., No. 51 (1, p. 163b).

> Walter de Norwico; Tower, 3 Edw. III. (1st Nos.), No. 58 (2, p. 23b).

> John de Norwico; Tower, 36 Edw. III. (2nd pt.), No. 6 (2, p. 252b).

> John de Norwico; Tower, App., 36 Edw. III., No. 9 (4, p. 450b).

> Margeria, ux. John do Norwico; Tower, 40 Edw. III. (1st pt.), No. 28 (2, p. 274b).

> Roger de Norwico; Tower, 45 Edw. III. (1st Nos.), No. 44 (2, p. 310a).

> John de Norwico; Tower, 48 Edw. III. (1st Nos.), No. 52 (2, p. 334b).

> Richard, Bishop of Norwich; Ch., 21 Hen. VII., No. 104.

Noth—Jno. Noth; Tower, 12 Edw. I., No. 36.

Nowne alias Noon (Noion, q.v.)—Henry Nowne, alias Noon; Ch., 3 Hen. VII., No. 71.

> John Nune; Exch., 32-33 Hen. VIII. (John Tasburgh, Esch.), No. 45.

> Simon Nunne, Gent.; Exch., 37-38 Hen. VIII. (John Spencer, Esch.), No. 17.

> Simon Nunne; W. and L., 38 Hen. VIII., vol. 2, p. 135.

> Simon Nune; Ch., 38 Hen. VIII., pt. 2, No. 19.

> George Nunne; Ch., 24 Eliz., pt. 1, No. 26.

> George Nonne; W. and L., 15 Jas. I., bund. 26, No. 153.

> George Nonne; Ch., 15 Jas. I., pt. 1, No. 169.

> John Nonne; W. and L., 14 Jas. I., bund. 28, No. 137.

> John Noune; Ch., 16 Jas. I., pt. 1, No. 40.

> George Nonne; Ch., 9 Chas. I., pt. 1, No. 86.

> George Nonne; Ch., 10 Chas. I., pt. 3, No. 72.

> James Nonne; W. and L., 10 Chas. I., bund. 55, No. 204.

Ogard—Andrew Ogard; Tower, 33 Hen. VI., No. 25 (4, p. 263b), see 4, p. 287b.

Oldcastle—Jno. Oldcastle and Johanna ux. ej.; Tower, 6 Hen. V.,
No. 45 (4, p. 38a).

Oliver—John Olyver; Exch., 1 Eliz. (James Bigott, Esch.), No. 23.
John Oliver; Ch., 1 Eliz., pt. 3, No. 131.

Ormesby—Elene, ux. William de Ormesby; Tower, 7 Edw. II., No. 33
(1, p. 254a).
Roger de Ormesby; Tower, 16 Edw. III. (1st Nos.), No. 42
(2, p. 104b).
John de Ormesby; Tower, 24 Edw. III. (1st Nos.), No. 48
(2, p. 164a).
Juliana de Ormesby; Tower, 13 Ric. III., No. 36 (3, p. 117a).

Orreby—John de Orreby; Tower, 27 Edw. III. (1st Nos.), No. 57
(2, p. 182b).
Margaret, ux. John de Orreby; Tower, 43 Edw. III. (2nd
Nos.), No. 12 (2, p. 298b).

Osante—William Osannte; W. and L., 1-3 Eliz., vol. 8, p. 8.
William Osenante; Exch., 3 Eliz. (Edmd. Wright, Esch.),
No. 5.
William Osant; Ch., 4 Eliz., No. 77.
Thomas Ossant; W. and L., 22 Jas. I., bund. 41, No. 26.
Thomas Ossant; Ch., 22 Jas. I., pt. 2, No. 46.
Richard Ossant; Ch., 33 Eliz., pt. 2, No. 10.
Nicholas Ossant; W. and L., 4 Chas. I., bund. 16, No. 64.
Nicholas Ossant; Ch., 4 Chas. I., pt. 4, No. 50.
Mary Ossant; Ch., 16 Chas. I., pt. 3, No. 110.
Nicholas Ossant; Ch., 16 Chas. I., pt. 3, No. 94.

Osbert, fil.—Katherine, ux. Robert fil. Peter Osbert; Tower, 12
Edw. III. (1st Nos.), No. 83 (2, p. 83b).

Osborne—John Osborne; Ch., 3 Chas. I., pt. 2, No. 51.
Nicholas Osborne, Gent.; Misc. Ch., 17 Chas. I., pt. 31,
No. 114.

Ovedale, de—John de Ovedale; Tower, 15 Edw. II., No. 26 (1,
p. 298a).

Overend—William Overend; Exch., 1 Eliz. (James Bigott, Esch.), No. 16.
William Overend; Ch., 1 Eliz., pt. 1, No. 134.

Oxborough, Oxburgh—Thomas Oxburgh; W. and L., 22 Jas. I., bund.
41, No. 42.

Oxborough, Oxburgh—Thomas Oxburough; W. and L., 22 Jas. I., bund. 41, No. 11.

Thomas Oxburgh; Ch., 22 Jas I., pt. 2, No. 39.

Thomas Oxburgh; Ch., 22 Jas. I., pt. 2, No. 108.

Thomas Oxborough; Ch. 22 Jas. I., pt. 2, No. 26.

John Oxburghe; W. and L., 1 Chas. I., bund. 42, No. 25.

John Oxburgh; Ch., 1 Chas. I., pt. 1, No. 61.

Hewar Oxburgh; W. and L., 4 Chas. I., bund. 47, No. 73.

Hewar Oxburgh; Ch., 5 Chas. I., pt. 2, No. 48.

Oxford, Earl of—John, Earl of Oxford; Exch., 4-5 Hen. VIII. (John Turges or Sturges, Esch.), No. 1.

John, Earl of Oxford; Ch., 5 Hen. VIII. No. 88.

Page alias Baxter—John Page, alias Baxter, Gent.; Exch., 32-33 Hen. VIII. (John Tasburgh, Esch.), No. 32.

John Page, Gent.; Exch., 34-35 Hen. VIII. (Robt. Downys, Esch.), No. 33.

Anthony Page; W. and L., 18 Jas. I., bund. 30, No. 169.

Anthony Page; Ch., 18 Jas. I., pt. 2, No. 58.

Richard Page; Ch., 19 Chas. I., No. 26.

Pagrave—Henry Pagrave; Exch., 34-35 Hen. VIII. (Robt. Downys, Esch.), No. 16.

Henry Pagrave; Ch., 35 Hen. VIII., No. 30.

Henry Pagrave; W. and L., 35 Hen. VIII., vol. 1, p. 41.

Clement Pagrave; Ch., 25 Eliz., No. 122.

Clement Pagrave; Ch., 28 Eliz., No. 110.

Gregory Pagrave, sen., Gent.; Misc. Ch., 20 Jas. I., pt. 6, No. 110.

Pakenham—William de Pakenham; Tower, 33 Edw. I., No. 46.

Edmund de Pakenham; Tower, 25 Edw. III. (1st Nos.), No. 36 (2, p. 169b).

Rocsia, ux. Edmund de Pakenham; Tower, 27 Edw. III. (1st Nos.), No. 64 (2, p. 183a).

Maria de Pakenham; Tower, 33 Edw. III. (2nd pt.), No. 19, (2, p. 240b).

Richard de Pakenham; Tower, 51 Edw. III. (2nd pt.), No. 43.

Henry Pakenham; Tower, 10 Hen. IV., No. 24 (3, p. 322a).

Pakenham—Henry Pakenham; Tower, 24 Hen. VI., No. 11 (4, p. 225a).

Robert Pakenham; Tower, 4 Edw. IV., No. 1 (4, p. 323a).

Henry Pakenham; Tower, 21 Edw. IV., No. 61 (4, p. 408a).

Henry Pakenham; Tower, 8 Edw. IV., No. 71 (4, p. 346b).

Anne Pakenham; Ch., 13 Hen. No. VII., 38.

Henry Pakenham; Tower, 1 Ric. III., No. 34 (4, p. 416b).

Henry Pakenham; Ch., v.o. Ric. III. and Hen. VII., No. 5.

Palgrave (? see **Pagrave**)—John Palgrave; Ch., 9 Jas. I., pt. 1, No. 127.

John Palgrave; W. and L, 9 and 10 Jas. I., bund. 4, No. 148.

Parke, alias Sparke—William Parke, alias Sparke; Ch., 43 Eliz., pt. 1, No. 23*.

Francis Parke; Ch., 10 Chas. I., pt. 3, No. 57.

Francis Parke; W. and L., 10 Chas. I., bund. 55, No. 86.

Parker—Henry Parker, Knt., Lord Morley; Ch., 3 and 4 Ph. and Mary, pt. 1, No. 87.

Henry Parker, Knt.; W. and L., 5 and 6 Edw. VI., vol. 6, p. 15.

Henry Parker, Knt.; Ch., 6 Edw. VI., pt. 2, No. 34.

John Parker, Gent.; Exch., 17-18 Eliz. (John Bacon, Esch.), No. 2.

Eleanor Parker; W. and L., 35-42 Eliz., vol. 24, p. 169.

Gilbert Parker, Gent.; W. and L., 1-5 Jas. I., vol. 30, p. 10.

Gilbert Parker; Ch., 9 Jas. I., pt. 2, No. 15.

Gilbert Parker, Gent.; Ch., 4 Jas. I., pt. 2, No. 101.

Gilbert Parker; W. and L., 8 and 9 Jas. I., bund. 5, No. 246.

Lady Dorothy Parker; Misc. Ch., 16 Chas. I., pt. 31, No. 174.

Parmenter—Thomas Parmenter; Ch., 9 Chas. I., pt. 2, No. 61.

Parseley—Adam Parseley; Misc. Ch., 9 Chas. I., pt. 22, No. 25.

Partington—Thomas Partington; W. and L., 18 Chas. I., bund. 65, No. 26.

Thomas Partington; Ch., 18 Chas. I., pt. 1, No. 7.

Paston—Jno. Paston; Tower, 6 Edw. IV., No. 44 (4, p. 336b).

William Paston, Knt.; Exch., 1 Mary to 1-2 Ph. and Mary (Edmd. Wright, Esch.), No. 11.

William Paston, Knt.; Ch., 1-2 Ph. and Mary, pt. 2, No. 61.

Paston—Christopher Paston; W. and L., 8-9 Jas. I., bund. 5, No. 248.

Sir William Paston; W. and L., 8-9 Jas. I., bund. 5, No. 290.

Christopher Paston; Ch., 9 Jas. I., pt. 2, No. 5.

William Paston; Ch., 9 Jas. I., pt. 1, No. 157.

Thomas Paston; Ch., 10 Chas. I., pt. 3, No. 117.

Thomas Paston; W. and L., 10 Chas. I., bund. 55, No. 163.

Pattesley—Jno. Pattesley; Tower, 29 Hen. VI., No. 1 (4, p. 246a).

Hamo de Pattesley; Tower, 18 Hen. VI., No. 4 (4, p. 196a).

Paunton—Jno. Paunton; Tower, 17 Ric. II., No. 44 (3, p. 176a).

Payn—Jno. Payn; Tower, App., 9 Edw. IV., No. 1.

William Payn; Exch., 2-3 Hen. VIII. (Geo. Bokenham, Esch.), No. 6.

William Payne; Ch., 3 Hen. VIII., No. 38.

Alice Payne, widow; W. and L., 1-2 Edw. VI., vol. 4, p. 42.

Alice Payne; Ch., 2 Edw. VI., pt. 2, No. 54.

Henry Payne, Esq.; Exch., 10 Eliz. (George Chettinge, Esch.), No. 3.

John Payne; Ch., 9 Jas. I., pt. 2, No. 34.

John Payne; W. and L., 8-9 Jas. I., bund. 5, No. 269.

Paynell—Henry Paynell; W. and L., Chas. I., bund. 69, No. 169.

Henry Paynell; Ch., 20 Chas. I., No. 55.

Payton (see **Peyton**)—Dorothy Payton; W. and L., 1-3 Jas. I., vol. 27, p. 221.

Dorothy Payton; Ch., 2 Jas. I., pt. 2, No. 151.

Pearse—William Pearse; W. and L., 17 Chas. I., bund. 64, No. 133.

William Pearse; Ch., 17 Chas. I., pt. 3, No. 103.

Pecche—Margaret Pecche; Tower, 13 Edw. I., No. 39 (1, p. 57a).

Almarie Pecche; Ch., 16 Edw. I., No. 31.

William Pecche; Ch., 30 Edw. I., No. 96, and Ch., 31 Edw. I., No. 112.

William Peech; Ch., 31 Edw. I., No. 62 (1, p. 182a).

John Pcche, Knt.; Exch., 13-14 Hen. VIII. (John Cusshyn, Esch.), No. 1.

John Peache, Knt.; Ch., 14 Hen. VIII., No. 41.

Pecke—Thomas Pecke; Ch., 34 Eliz., pt. 2, No. 107.

John Pecke; Ch., 38 Eliz., pt. 1, No. 45.

William Pecke; Ch., 11 Chas. I., pt. 2, No. 125.

William Peck, Esq.; Ch., 14 Chas. I., pt. 3, No. 86.

William Peck, Esq. ; Ch., 14 Chas. I., pt. 3, No. 87.

William Peeke; W. and L., 13 Chas. I., bund. 61, No. 179.

William Peeke; W. and L., 14 Chas. I., bund. 61, No. 209.

Peirce—Thomas Peirce (lunatic); Ch., 11 Chas. I., pt. 2, No. 46.

Pelerin—Godfrey Pelerin; Tower, 25 Edw. I., No. 92.

Pell—John Pell; W. and L., 1-3 Ph. and Mary, vol. 7, p. 53.

John Pell, Gent. ; Misc. Ch., 16 Jas. I., pt. 6, No. 113.

Ralph Pell, Clerk; Misc. Ch., 11 Chas. I., pt. 31, No. 104.

Ralph Pell ; Ch., 11 Chas. I., pt. 2, No. 82.

William Pell, Esq. ; Misc. Ch., 13 Chas. I., pt. 31, No. 185.

Pelles—John Pelles ; Ch., 2-3 Ph. and Mary, pt. 2, No. 48.

Pembroke, Countess of—Anna, Countess of Pembroke; Tower, 7 Ric. II., No. 67 (3, p. 61a).

Pennington—Robert Pennington, Esq. ; Misc. Ch., 4 Chas I., pt. 25, No. 24.

Penton—Richard Penton; Misc. Ch., v.o. Eliz., bund. 3, No. 5.

Pepes or Pepys—John Pepes ; Exch., 33-34 Hen. VIII. (Thos. Halse, Esch.), No. 8.

John Pepys ; Ch., 34 Hen. VIII.

Thomas Pepes; W. and L., 12-14 Eliz., vol. 13, p. 27.

Thomas Pepes, Esq. ; Ch., 13 Eliz., pt. 2, No. 17.

Percy—Henry de Percy; Tower, 41 Edw. III. (1st Nos.), No. 48 (2, p. 290a).

Pereres—Elizabeth Pereres ; Tower, 17 Ric. II., No. 210 (3, p. 176a).

Petitt—Temperance Petitt; Ch., 2 Chas. I., pt. 3, No. 108.

Pettys or Pettus—Thomas Pettys ; Ch., 40 Eliz., pt. 2, No. 166.

Augustino Pettus ; Ch., 11 Jas. I., pt. 2, No. 3.

Sir Augustine Pettus; W. and L., 11 Jas. I., bund. 18, No. 120.

Mary Pettus ; Ch., 13 Jas. I., pt. 2, No. 150.

John Pettus, Knt. ; Ch., 13 Jas. I., pt. 2, No. 151.

Thomas Pettus, Esq.; Misc. Ch., 19 Jas. I., pt. 31, No. 94.

Mary Pettus ; Ch., 20 Jas. I., pt. 2, No. 29.

Pettys or Pettus—Mary Pettus; Ch., 20 Jas. I., pt. 2, No. 138.

Mary Pettus; W. and L., 20 Jas. I., bund. 35, No. 180.

Mary Pettus; W. and L., 20 Jas. I., bund. 32, No. 80.

Peverel—Hugh Peverel; Tower, 27 Edw. I., No. 21 (1, p. 149a).

John Peverell and Johanna ux. ej.; Tower, 8 Edw. II., No. 59 (1, p. 259b).

Edmund Peverel and Elizabeth his wife; Tower, 5 Edw. III. (1st Nos.), No. 46 (2, p. 38b).

Peyton—Robert Peyton, Knt.; Exch., 9-10 Hen. VIII. (Henry Russell, Esch.), No. 10.

Phelips or Philips—William Phelips; Tower, 19 Hen. VI., No. 30 (4, p. 203b).

Robert Phillipps; W. and L., 22 Jas. I., bund. 44, No. 109.

Robert Phillippes; Ch., 2 Chas. I., pt. 3, No. 157.

William Phillips; W. and L., 8 Chas. I., bund. 52, No. 233.

William Phillippes; Ch., 8 Chas. I., pt. 1, No. 41.

Picot or Pigot—Thomas Pycote; Ch., 3 Hen. VIII., No. 51.

John Pygott; Ch., 1 Edw. VI., pt. 2, No. 13.

John Pigott; Ch., 38 Eliz., pt. 1, No. 38.

Thomas Pygotte; Exch., 2-3 Hen. VIII. (Geo. Bokenham, Esch.), No. 5.

Rosa Pigot; Tower, 11 Hen. VI., No. 9 (4, p. 138b).

Pigeon—Thomas Pigeon; Exch., 1 Eliz. (James Bigott, Esch.), No. 32.

Thomas Pigeon; Ch., 1 Eliz., pt. 1, No. 132.

John Pigeon; Misc. Ch., v.o. Eliz., bund. 1, No. 501.

Pilkington—Margaret Pilkington; Tower, 15 Hen. VI., No. 61 (4, p. 180a).

Pincerna. See **le Butiler.**

Pinkeny—Hamund de Pynkeny; Tower, 33 Edw. I., No. 71 (1, p. 198b).

Plaiz or Playz, de—Richard de Playz; Tower, 53 Hen. III., No. 24.

Richard de Playz; Tower, 53 Hen. III., No. 24 (1, p. 32).

Giles de Plays; Tower, 31 Edw. I., No. 37.

Richard de Plaiz; Tower, 1 Edw. III., No. 55 (2, p. 3a and 3b).

Richard de Plays; Tower, 34 Edw. III. (1st Nos.), No. 43 (2, p. 219b).

Plaiz or Playz, de—Richard de Plays; Tower, 35 Edw. III. (2nd pt.), No. 27 (2, p. 241a).

Jno. Playz; Tower, 12 Ric. II., No. 44 (3, p. 104b).

Playter—Thomas Playter; Tower, 19 Edw. IV., No. 62 (4, p. 395b).

William Playter, Esq.; Exch., 8-9 Hen. VIII. (John Stede, Esch.), No. 8.

Playters—William Drake Platers, Esq.; Misc. Ch., 10 Chas. I., pt. 31, No. 175.

Pleasaunce—John Pleasaunce; Exch., 1 Eliz. (James Bigott, Esch.), No. 5.

Plume—John Plume; Ch., 1 Eliz., pt. 3, No. 136.

John Plume; W. and L., 1-3 Eliz., vol. 8, p. 67.

John Plumme, Gent.; Exch., 1 Eliz. (James Bigott, Esch.), No. 39.

John Plume; Ch., 3 Eliz., No. 161.

John Plume, Gent.; Exch., 3 Eliz. (Edmd. Wright, Esch.), No. 1.

Pole, de la—Michael de la Pole and Katharine his wife; Tower, 13 Ric. II., No. 41 (3, p. 117).

Michael de la Pole, Earl of Suffolk; Tower, 3 Hen. V., No. 48a and b (4, p. 15b).

Michael de la Pole, jun.; Tower, 3 Hen. V., No. 48b (4, p. 17a).

Elizabeth de la Pole; Tower, 1 Hen. VI., No. 26 (4, p. 70a).

Edward de la Pole, Earl of Suffolk; Ch., v.o. Hen. VIII., bund. 1, No. 201.

Poley—Edmund Poley, Esq.; Exch., 2-3 Edw. VI. (John Flowerdew, Esch.), No. 4.

William Poley, Esq.; Exch., 4-5, 5-6 Ph. and Mary (Andrew Revet, Esch.), No. 10.

Poninges, de—Michael de Ponynges; Tower, 43 Edw. III. (2nd Nos.), No. 14 (2, p. 298a).

John de Ponynges; Tower, 43 Edw. III. (2nd Nos.), No. 15 (2, p. 298a).

Thomas de Ponyngges; Tower, 49 Edw. III. (2nd pt.), No. 27 (2, p. 348a).

Richard Poyninges; Tower, 11 Ric. II., No. 43 (3, p. 95b).

Poninges, de—Richard Ponynges; Tower, 15 Ric. II., 1st pt., No. 53 (3, p. 138a).

    Isabel, ux. Richard Ponynges (proof of age); Tower, 5 Hen. IV., No. 41 (3, p. 298a).

    Robert Ponynges; Tower, 25 Hen. VI., No. 24 (4, p. 232b).

Poringland. (? See **Porland**).

Porter—Richard Porter; Ch., v.o. Eliz., bund. 3, No. 420.

    Richard Porter; W. and L., 1-3 Jas. I., bund. 6, No. 35.

    Richard Porter; Ch., 2 Jas. I., pt. 2, No. 78.

    Gareth Porter; W. and L, 1-3 Jas. I., bund. 6, No. 60.

    Gareth Porter; Ch., 2 Jas. I., pt. 2, No. 104.

Powditch (Bowditch)—Thomas Powdiche; Ch., 42 Eliz., pt. 2, No. 138.

Pratis, de—Robert de Pratis; Tower, 10 Rich. II., No. 31 (3, p. 84b).

Pratt—Edmund Pratte; Exch., 33-34 Hen. VIII. (Thos. Halse, Esch.), No. 1.

    Edward Pratte; Ch., 34 Hen. VIII., No. —

    Gregory Pratt; W. and L., 3-7 Jas. I., vol. 25, p. 89.

    George Pratt; Ch., 7 Jas. I., part 1, No. 169.

    Francis Pratt; W. and L., 10 Jas. I., part 1, No. 133.

    Francis Pratt; W. and L., 10 Jas. I., bund. 14, No. 51.

    Francis Pratt; W. and L., 12 Jas. I., bund. 21, No. 48.

    Francis Pratt; Ch., 13 Jas. I., pt. 1, No. 120.

Pratiman or Prettyman—William Pratiman, sen.; Exch., 33-34 Hen. VIII. (Thos. Halse, Esch.), No. 11.

    John Pretyman; Exch., 1 Eliz. (James Bigott, Esch.), No. 10.

    Thomas Pratyman; Exch., 9 Eliz. (Edmd. Ashefeld, Esch.), No. 2.

Prentise—Thomas Prentise; W. and L., 1 and 2 Ed. VI., vol. 4, p. 53.

    Thomas Prenteyse; Ch, 2 Ed. VI., pt. 2, No. 47.

Prettyman. See **Pratiman**.

Pulham—Christopher Pulham; Exch., 1-3 Eliz. (Wm. Drake, Esch.), No. 8.

    Richard Pullum (*fatuus*); Ch., 10 Jas. I., pt. 6, No. 180.

Punder—Robert Punder; Ch., 18 Jas. I., pt. 2, No. 77.

    Robert Punder; W. and L., 18 Jas. I., bund. 30, No. 178.

Purland (Poringland?)—Robert Purland; W. and L., 14 Jas. I., bund. 20, No. 178.

Purland (Poringland?)—Robert Purland; Ch., 14 Jas. I., pt. 3, No. 9.

Robert Purland; Ch., 8 Chas. I., pt. 3, No. 167.

Purpett—John Purpett; Exch., 33-34 Hen. VIII. (Thos. Halse, Esch.), No. 14.

Puttock—Stephen Puttocke; W. and L., 12 Chas. I., bund. 57, No. 78.

Stephen Puttock; Ch., 12 Chas. I., pt. 3, No. 101.

Pye—Richard Pye; Ch., 12 Jas. I., pt. 1, No. 86.

Quodyngton—Richard Quodyngton; Exch., 9 Eliz. (Edmd. Ashefeld, Esch.), No. 5.

Radcliff or Ratcliff—John Radcliff; Tower, 19 Hen. VI., No. 33 (4, p. 204a).

John Radclyffe; Tower, 1 Edw. IV., No. 19 (4, p. 308b).

Thomas Radclyff; Exch., 3-4 Hen. VII. (Edw. Clopton, Esch.), No. 7.

Raine—Ralph Raine, yeoman; Misc. Ch., 7 Jas. I., pt. 5, No. 106.

Rainsford—Laurence Raynsford; Ch., 7 Hen. VII., No. 66.

Rake or Rakke (Rackheath?)—William Rakke; W. and L., 1 and 2 Edw. VI., vol. 4, p. 43.

William Rake; Ch., 2 Edw. VI., pt. 2, No. 49.

Rames. See **Reymes.**

Ramsey—Ralph Ramsey; Tower, 7 Hen. V., No. 24 (4, p. 40a).

Edward Ramsey; W. and L., 8 Chas. I., bund. 51, No. 75.

Edward Ramsey, Esq.; Ch., 8 Chas. I., pt. 1, No. 2.

Roger Ramsey; Ch., 9 Chas. I., pt. 2, No. 40.

John Ramsey, Gent.; Misc. Ch., 10 Chas. I., pt. 31, No. 173.

Rant—Roger Raunte; W. and L., 21 Jas. I., bund. 37, No. 9.

Roger Rante; Ch., 21 Jas. I., pt. 1, No. 115.

William Rant; W. and L., 3 Chas. I., bund. 46, No. 73.

William Rant; Ch., 4 Chas. I., pt. 4, No. 76.

Rapkin—Thomas Rapkin; Ch., 1 Eliz., pt. 3, No. 138.

Ratcliff (see Radcliff)—Geoffrey Ratcliff; Ch., v.o. Ric. III. and Hen. VII., No. 304.

Thomas Ratcliff; Ch., 3 Hen. VII., No. 18.

Geoffrey Ratcliff; Ch., 7 Hen. VIII., No. 33.

Geoffrey Radclyf; Exch., 6-7 Hen. VIII. (John Eston, Esch.), No. 11.

Rattlesden—John fil. John de Rattlesden; Tower, 36 Edw. III. (2nd pt.), No. 25 (2, p. 254b).

Raven—John Ravyn; Exch., 1 Mary to 1-2 Philip and Mary (Edmd. Wright, Esch.), No. 13.

John Raven; W. and L., 13 Chas. I., bund. 62, No. 72.

John Raven; Ch., 15 Chas. I., pt. 3, No. 42.

Ray—John Raye; Exch., 34-35 Hen. VIII. (Robt. Downys, Esch.), No. 39.

Raynbald—Robert Raynbald; Exch., 1 Eliz. (James Bigott, Esch.), No. 17.

Robert Raynebald; Misc. Ch., v.o. Eliz., bund. 1, No. 22.

Read, Rede, or Reed—William Rede; Exch., 34-35 Hen. VIII. (Robt. Downys, Esch.), No. 41.

Edward Rede; Exch., 37-38 Hen. VIII. (John Spencer, Esch.), No. 3.

Thomas Rede, clerk; Exch., 37-38 Hen. VIII. (John Spencer, Esch.), No. 27.

John Rede; Misc. Ch., v.o. Hen. VIII., bund. 2, No. 111.

William Rede, merchant; Ch., 35 Hen. VIII., No. 21.

Edward Reade; Ch., 38 Hen. VIII., No. 29.

Edward Reede (lunatic); Misc. Ch., v.o. Hen. VIII., bund. 1, No. 205.

Robert Rede; W. and L., 1-2 Edw. VI., vol. 4, p. 10.

Robert Reade; Ch., 1 Edw. VI., pt. 2, No. 17.

Thomas Reade; Ch., 23 Eliz., pt. 2, No. 110.

Robert Reade; Ch., 37 Eliz., pt. 2, No. 84.

Christopher Reade; W. and L., 11 Jas. I., bund. 22, No. 269.

Christopher Read; Ch., 13 Jas. I., pt. 1, No. 85.

Redell—Jno. Redell; Tower, 36 Hen. VI., No. 12 (4, p. 276b).

Thomas Redell; Ch., 4-5 Ph. and Mary, pt. 1, No. 129.

John Redgell; Misc. Ch., 14 Jas. I., pt. 5, No. 123.

Redenhall, de—Warin de Redenhal; Tower, 30 Hen. III., No. 46.

Thomas Rydnale; Exch., 11-12 Hen. VIII. (Philip Bernard, Esch.), No. 14.

Ree—Roger Ree; Tower, 15 Edw. IV., No. 33 (4, p. 371a).

Reedham—Bartholomew de Redham; Tower, 28 Edw. I., No. 153 (1, p. 166a).

William de Redham; Tower, 19 Edw. II., No. 55 (1, p. 325b).

Bartholomew Redham; Tower (proof of age), App., 1 Edw. III., No. 8 (4, p. 436a).

Remington—William Remington; W. and L., 1-3 Jas. I, bund. 6, No. 16.

William Remyngton; Ch., 2 Jas. I., pt. 2, No. 8.

Reppes, de—Laurence de Reppes; Tower, 16 Edw. II., No. 23 (1, p. 302a).

John de Reppes; Tower, 28 Edw. III. (2nd Nos.), No. 69 (2, p. 190a).

Robert de Reppes; Tower, 24 Hen. VI., No. 21 (4, p. 225b).

Henry Reppes, Esq.; Exch., 4-5, 5-6 Ph. and Mary (Andrew Revet, Esch.), No. 7.

Henry Reppes; Exch., 9 Eliz. (Edmund Ashefeld, Esch.), No. 14.

Henry Reppes; Ch., 9 Eliz., No. 43.

Henry Reppes; Ch., 21 Eliz., pt. 2, No. 41.

John Reppes; W. and L., 10 Jas. I., bund. 18, No. 22.

John Reppes; Ch., 11 Jas. I., pt. 3, No. 168.

Henry Reppes; Ch., 5 Chas. I., pt. 2, No. 29.

Henry Reppes; Ch., 5 Chas. I., pt. 2, No. 73.

Reve—Daniel Reve, S.T.D.; Misc. Ch., 4 Chas. I., pt. 24, No. 188.

Revesle, de—William de Revesle; Tower, 32 Ed. I., No. 188 (1, p. 195b).

Reymes—William Rames; W. and L., 1-6 Jas. I., bund. 2, No. 189.

William Reymes; Ch., 5 Jas. I., pt. 2, No. 14.

Robert Reynes (outlaw); Misc. Ch., v.o. Hen. VIII., bund. 1, No. 200.

Reyngham, de (? H)—William de Reyngham; Tower, App., 3 Hen. V., No. 7 (4, p. 467b.)

Richardson—Sir Thomas Richardson; W. and L., 13 Chas. I., bund. 58, No. 337.

Thomas Richardson, Knt.; Ch., 13 Chas. I., pt. 1, No. 6.

Thomas Richardson; W. and L., 19 Chas. I., bund. 68, No. 89.

Thomas Richardson; Ch., 20 Chas. I., No. 61.

Richers or Riches—John Richers; Ch., 18 Hen. VII., No. 49.

Henry Richers; W. and L., 36 Hen. VIII., vol. 1, p. 119.

Henry Rythers; Ch., 36 Hen. VIII., No. 109.

Henry Richers; Ch., 30 Eliz., pt. 1, No. 24.

Edmund Richers; Ch., 43 Eliz., pt. 2, No. 113.

John Richers; W. and L., 3-7 Jas. I., vol. 25, pt. 21.

John Rychers; Ch., 7 Jas. I., pt. 1, No. 24.

John Richars; W. and L., 7 Jas. I., bund. 12, No. 41.

John Rychers; Ch., 8 Jas. I., pt. 2, No. 141.

John Riches; Ch., 20 Jas. I., pt. 2, No. 106.

John Riches, Clerk; Misc. Ch., 1 Chas. I., pt. 5, No. 75.

Richman—John Richman; Ch., 16 Chas. I., pt. 3, No. 121.

Richmond, Earl of—Edmund, Earl of Richmond; Tower, 35 Hen. VI., No. 19 (4, p. 274a).

Richmond—John Richmond; Ch., 37 Eliz., pt. 2, No. 87.

Riddlesden—Sir Stephen Riddlesden (of London); W. and L., 10 Jas. I., bund. 18, No. 104.

Stephen Riddlesden; Ch., 10 Jas. I., pt. 1, No. 102.

Rightwise—John Ryhtwys (Rightwise?) (proof of age); Tower, 13 Hen. VI., No. 48 (4, p. 163a).

Rivers, Earl of—Elizabeth, widow of Anthony, Earl Rivers; Tower, 13 Edw. IV., No. 45 (4, p. 363b).

Anthony, Earl Rivers; Ch., 1 Hen. VII., No. 38.

Robell. See **Rokelle.**

Robartes—William Robartes; Ch., 34 Eliz., pt. 2, No. 69.

Robert fil. Ran.—Robert fil. Ran.; Tower, 38 Hen. III., No. 29 (1, p. 12).

Robsart—William Robsart, Esq.; Ch., 2 Hen. VII., No. 18.

Turunis Robyssert (?Terry); Ch., 13 Hen. VII., No. 56.

William Robesert; Exch., 6-7 Hen. VIII. (John Eston, Esch.), No. 6.

William Robsert; Ch., 7 Hen. VIII., No. 84.

Lady Elizabeth Robsert; Exch., 27-28 Hen. VIII. (Thos. Woodehouse, Esch.), No. 12.

Elizabeth Robsart; Ch., 28 Hen. VIII., No. 55.

John Robsarte, Knt.; Exch., 1 Mary to 1-2 Ph. and Mary (Edmd. Wright, Esch.), No. 2.

Robsart—John Robsart; Ch., 1-2 Ph. and Mary, pt. 2, No. 63.

Rocelyn—Joh., widow of William Rocelyn; Tower, 1 Edw. III.,
No. 45 (2, p. 2b).

Rochester, de—William de Roucestr'; Tower, 33 Hen. III., No. 52
(1, p. 6).

Rochester—Robert Rochester, Knt.; Exch., 4-5, 5-6 Ph. and Mary
(Andrew Revet, Esch.), No. 8.

William Rochester, Esq.; Exch., 1 Eliz. (James Bigott,
Esch.), No. 4.

Rochford—Matilda de Rockeford; Tower, 39 Hen. III., No. 10.

Roger, fil.—Robert fil. Roger; Tower, 3 Edw. II., No. 55.

Rogers—William Rogers; Ch., 1 Mary, pt. 1, No. 88.

William Rogers; Exch., 7 Edw. VI. to 1 Mary (John Spencer,
Esch.), No. 5.

Rokele, de la—Richard de la Rokele; Tower, 24 Edw. I., No. 48
(1, p. 128b).

Richard de la Rokele; Tower, 32 Edw. I., No. 36 (1, p. 187a).

Thomas Robell (Rokell?); Tower, 3 Hen. V., No. 16 (4,
p. 12a).

Robert Robell (Rokell?); Tower, 5 Hen. IV., No. 7 (3,
p. 294b).

Thomas Robell (Rokell?); Tower, 9 Hen. IV., No. 8 (3,
p. 315a).

Rokewood or Rookwood—Margaret Rokewoode; Ch., 9 Hen. VIII.,
No. 132.

Margaret Rokewood; Ch., 11 Hen. VIII., No. 120.

Margaret Rokwode; Exch., 10-11 Hen. VIII. (Geoffrey
Cobbe, Esq., Esch.), No. 9.

Thomas Rookwood; Exch., 11-12 Hen. VIII. (Philip
Bernard, Esch.), No. 3.

John Rokwood; Exch., 34-35 Hen. VIII. (Robt. Downys,
Esch.), No. 22.

Firmin Rockewood, Esq.; Exch., 1 Eliz. (James Bigott,
Esch.), No. 35.

Firmin Rockwood; Ch., 1 Eliz., pt. 3, No. 137.

Olive Rookewood; W. and L., 6 Eliz., bund. 9, No. 76.

Olive Rookewood; Ch., 6 Eliz., No. 148.

Roos, de (? also see **Rowse**)—John de Roos; Tower, 12 Edw. III. (1st Nos.), No. 41 (2, p. 85a).

William de Roos; Tower, 17 Edw. III. (1st Nos.), No. 60 (2, p. 112a).

Mageria, ux. William de Roos; Tower, 37 Edw. III. (1st pt.), No. 62 (2, p. 262).

Maria, ux. John de Roos; Tower, 18 Ric. II., No. 34 (3, p. 182b).

Thomas de Roos; Tower, 7 Ric. II., No. 68 (3, p. 61a).

Beatrix, ux. Thomas de Roos; Tower, 9 Ric. II., No. 44 (3, p. 76a).

Beatrix, ux. Thomas Roos; Tower, 3 Hen. V., No. 44 (4, p. 14a).

John, Lord Roos; Tower, 9 Hen. V., No. 58 (4, p. 62b).

Thomas Roos; Tower, 9 Hen. VI., No. 48 (4, p. 131a).

Rope (Rupe ?)—John Rope; Misc. Ch., 14 Chas. I., pt. 27, No. 183.

Roper—Thomas Rooper; Misc. Ch., 14 Jas. I., pt. 5, No. 121.

Ropkyn—Thomas Ropkyn, Gent.; Exch., 1 Eliz. (James Bigott, Esch.), No. 36.

Roscelyn—Thomas Roscelyn; Tower, App., 36 Edw. III., No. 5 (4, p. 447b).

Rothenale—John Rothenale; Tower, 7 Hen. V., No. 22 (4, p. 47b.)

Elizabeth Rothendale; Tower, 6 Hen. VI., No. 24 (4, p. 115a.)

John Rothenale; Tower, 9 Hen. VI., No. 57 (4, p. 134a.)

Rothinge—Henry de Rothinge; Tower, 30 Edw. I., No. 10.

Rowse (? see **Rous**)—Reginald Rowse; Exch., 32-33 Hen. VIII. (John Tasburgh, Esch.), No. 43.

Rugg—William Rugg, Esq.; Misc. Ch., 14 Jas. I., pt. 5, No. 124.

Rupe, de—Emeric de Rupe; Tower, 53 Hen. III., No. 36 (1, p. 32b).

Rus, le—William le Rus; Tower, 37 Hen. III., No. 49; 44 Hen. III., No. 15 (1, p. 19).

Richard le Rus; Tower, 16 Edw. I., No. 14; 20 Edw. I., No. 149 (1, p. 19a).

Rushall, de. ? See **Revesle**.

Rush—Arthur Russhe, Esq.; Exch., 28-29 Hen. VIII. (John Woodehouse, Esch.), No. 1.

Russell—Richard Russell; Misc. Ch., v.o. Eliz., bund. 3, No. 160.

William Russell; W. and L , 9-11 Eliz., vol. 11, p. 96.

William Russell, Gent.; Exch., 11 Eliz. (Wm. Attwood, Esch.), No. 3.

William Russell; Ch., 11 Eliz., No. 103.

Edward Russell; Ch., 32 Eliz., No. 71.

Henry Russell; W. and L,, 1-6 Jas. I., bund. —, No. 197.

Henry Russell; Ch., 5 Jas. I., pt. 2, No. 141.

Phillip Russell; W. and L., 16 Jas. I., bund. 26, No. 75.

Elizabeth Russell; Ch., v.o. 11 Jas. I., No. 52.

Elizabeth Russell; W. and L., 11 Jas. I., bund. 18, No. 151.

Philip Russell; Ch., 16 Jas. I., pt. 2, No. 125.

Edward Russell; Ch., 5 Chas. I., pt. 2, No. 39.

Katherine Russell; Ch., 16 Chas. I., pt. 3, No. 98.

Rust—Edward Rust, Gent.; Misc. Ch., 10 Jas. I., pt. 5, No. 130.

Ryde—Margaret, ux. John atte Ryde; Tower, 7 Rich. II., No. 2 (3, p. 56a.)

Rydnall—Thomas Rydnall. See **Redenhall, de.**

Sabaudia. See **Savaudia.**

Saborne or Sabin—William Sabyn, Gent.; Exch., 34-35 Hen. VIII. (Robt. Downye, Esch.), No. 44.

Thomas Saburne; Ch., 32 Eliz., No. 131.

Henry Saborne, alias Whitred; W. and L., 1-3 Jas. I., vol. 27, p. 187.

Thomas Saborne; W. and L., 1-3 Jas. I., vol. 27, p. 189.

Henry Saborn, alias Whitred; Ch., 2 Jas. I., pt. 2, No. 76.

Thomas Sabarne; W. and L., 2 Jas. I., pt. 2, No. 90.

Sadd—Robert Sadd; Misc. Ch., 14 Jas. I., pt. 6, No. 119.

Sagon (? Hagon)—James Sagon; Exch., 7-8 Eliz. (Geo. Waller, Esch.), No. 6.

Saham, de—William de Saham; Tower, 9 Edw. I., No. 63 (1, p. 72b).

St. Omer, de—Thomas de St. Omer; Tower, 40 Edw. III. (1st pt.), No. 36 (2, p. 274a).

St. Paul, de—Peter de St. Paul; Tower, 32 Edw. III. (2nd Nos.), No. 11 (2, p. 208a).

Maria de St. Paul, Comitessa de Pembroc; Tower, 51 Edw. III. (1st pt.), No. 28 (2, p. 359b).

St. Paul, de—Maria de St. Paul; Tower, 1 Ric. II., No. — (next
164), (3, p. 11a).

John de St. Philibert and Ada his wife; Tower, 7 Edw. III.
(1st Nos.), No. 35 (2, p. 53b).

Salhouse or Sallowes—Richard Sallowes; W. and L., 12 Jas. I.,
bund. 21, No. 80.

Richard Sallowes; Ch., 12 Jas. I., pt. 2, No. 98.

Salter—William Salter; Ch., 1 Edw. VI., pt. 2, No. 19.

William Salter; W. and L., 1 Edw. VI., vol. 3, p. 29.

Sampson—Thomas Sampson, Knt.; Exch., 3-4 Hen. VIII. (Anthy.
Hansart, Esch.), No. 4.

Simon Sampson, Esq.; Exch., 4-5 Eliz. (Augustine Curtes,
Esch.), No. 6.

Sares (Sayers?)—James Sares; W. and L., 16-17 Eliz., vol. 15, p. 7.

James Sares (idiot); Ch., 16 Eliz., pt. 1, No. 67.

Savaudia, de (Sabaudia?)—Peter de Savaudia; Tower, 10 Edw. I.,
No. 28 (1, p. 76b).

Saxham, de—Hugh de Saxham; Tower, 6 Edw. III. (2nd Nos.), No.
42 (2, p. 51b).

Saxlingham, de—Thomas de Saxlingham; Tower, 7 Ric. II., No. 72
(3, p. 62a).

Thomas de Saxlingham; Tower, 13 Ric. II., No. 45 (3, p. 118a).

Say, de—William de Say; Tower, 56 Hen. III., No. 37 (1, p. 40a).

Jno. Say; Tower, 18 Edw. IV., No. 43 (4, p. 390a).

Robert Saye, Gent.; Misc. Ch., 10 Chas. I., pt. 31, No. 96.

Sayer—William Sayer; W. and L., 43-44 Eliz., vol. 26, p. 218.

William Sayer; Ch., 44 Eliz., pt. 2, No. 55.

Thomas Sayer; W. and L., 1-2 Jas. I., vol. 28, p. 140.

Thomas Sayer; Ch., 2 Jas. I., pt. 2, No. 44.

William Sayer; W. and L., 10 Jas. I., bund. 14, No. 3.

William Sayer; W. and L., 10 Jas. I., bund. 14, No. 1.

William Sayer; Ch., 10 Jas. I., pt. 2, No. 10.

William Sayer; Ch., 10 Jas. I., pt. 2, No. 11.

Thomas Sayer; W. and L., 16 Jas. I., bund. 26, No. 79.

Thomas Sayer; Ch., 16 Jas. I., pt. 2, No. 121.

Thomas Sayer; Ch., 17 Jas. I., pt. 3, No. 45.

Sayers. ? See **Sares**.

Scalariis, de, or Scales, de—Thomas de Scalariis; Tower, 33 Edw. I.,
    No. 134 (1, p. 301b).

Robert de Scales; Tower, 33 Edw. I., No. 80 (1, p. 199b).

Robert de Scales and Emma his wife; Tower, 18 Edw. II.,
    No. 61 (1, p. 319b).

Robert de Scales; Tower, 6 Edw. III. (1st Nos.), No. 75
    (2, p. 50a).

Robert Scales; Tower, 43 Edw. III. (2nd Nos.), No. 22 (2,
    p. 299a).

Robert de Scales; Tower, 10 Ric. II., No. 50 (3, p. 88b).

Robert Scales; Tower, 4 Hen. IV., No. 20 (3, p. 284a).

Joh. ux. R. Scales; Tower, 2 Hen. V., No. 14 (4, p. 7a).

Robert fil. Robert Scales; Tower, 7 Hen. V., No. 48 (4,
    p. 42a).

Thomas Scales; Tower, 38-39 Hen. VI., No. 55 (4, p.
    288a).

Lord Thomas Scales; Exch., 1-2 Hen. VII. (Gregory Lovell,
    Esch.), No. 3.

Scamler—Edward Scamler, Esq.; Ch., 12 Chas. I., pt. 3, No. 64.

Edward Scamler; W. and L., 12 Chas. I., bund. 58, No.
    139.

Scarburgh—Henry Skarburghe, Gent.; Misc. Ch., 16 Jas. I., pt. 6,
    No. 116.

Scarlett—Henry Skarlett; Misc. Ch., 6 Jas. I., pt. 6, No. 105.

John Skarlett, Esq.; Misc. Ch., 13 Jas. I., pt. 6, No. 149.

Scarth—Robert Skarth; Ch., 18 Jas. I., pt. 2, No. 151.

Robert Skarthe; W. and L., 18 Jas. I., bund. 29, No. 269.

Schordich.   See **Bexwell alias Schordich.**

Scogan—John Scoggan; Tower, 15 Ric. II. (1st pt.), No. 57 (3,
    p. 138b).

Henry Scogan; Tower, 9 Hen. IV., No. 1 (3, p. 315a).

Robert Scogan; Tower, 11 Hen. IV. (proof of age), No. 53
    (3, p. 331b).

Scott—Jno. Scot; Tower, 13 Ric. II., No. 63 (3, p. 119a).

William Scotte; Ch., v.o. Eliz., bund. 2, No. 256.

John Scott; Ch., 19 Jas. I., pt. 1, No. 11.

John Scott; W. and L., 19 Jas. I., bund. 33, No. 166.

Scottow—Augustine Scottowe; W. and L., 12 Chas. I., bund. 57, No. 77.

Augustine Scottowe; Ch., 12 Chas. I., pt. 3, No. 102.

Scrop, le—Geoffrey le Scrop; Tower, 14 Edw. III. (1st Nos.), No. 35 (2, p. 95b).

Thomas le Scrope; Exch., 9-10 Hen. VII. (Jas. Braybrooke, Esch.), No. 6.

Anne Scrope; Ch., 14 Hen. VII., No. 3.

Seaman—William Seaman; Ch., 20 Jas. I., pt. 2, No. 149.

William Seaman; W. and L., 20 Jas. I., bund. 35, No. 211.

John Seaman; Ch., 14 Chas. I., pt. 3, No. 39.

John Seaman; W. and L., 14 Chas. I., bund. 60, No. 351.

Seckford or Sedgeford—Thomas Seckford, Esq.; Ch., 23 Hen. VII., No. 95.

Thomas Seckforde, Esq.; Exch., 17-18 Eliz. (John Bacon, Esch.), No. 4.

Sedley. See **Sydley.**

Segrave—Jno. de Segrave; Tower, 25 Edw. III. (1st Nos.), No. 16 (2, p. 169a).

John de Segrave and Margaret ux. ej.; Tower, 26 Edw. III. (2nd Nos.), No. 1 (2, p. 179a).

Jno. de Seagrave; Tower, 26 Edw. III. (2nd Nos.), No. 18 (2, p. 179b).

Michael de Segrave; Tower, 30 Edw. I., No. 86 (account of manor granted to, by Roger le Bygod).

John de Segrave, le uncle; Tower, 17 Edw. III. (1st Nos.), No. 52 (2, p. 110b).

John Segrave; Tower, 23 Edw. III. (2nd pt.), No. 44 (2, p. 156a).

John de Segrave; Tower, 27 Edw. III. (1st Nos.), No. 69 (2, p. 183a).

Semerycus—Judeus Semerycus; Tower, 25 Hen. III., No. 17, p. 1.

Sengylton—Edmund Sengylton, Gent.; Exch., 3-4 Hen. VIII. (Anthony Hansart, Esch.), No. 5.

Seyve—Richard Seyve; Ch., v.o. Ric. III. and Hen. VII., No. 192.

John Seyve; Ch., 9 Hen. VII., No. 35.

William Seyve; Ch., 22 Hen. VIII., No. 18.

Seyve—William Seyve, Esq.; Exch., 21-22 Hen. VIII. (Anthony Thwaytys, Esch.), No. 6.

Shakell—Thomas Shakell; Ch., 16 Jas. I., pt. 1, No. 62.

Shardelow—Jno. Shardelowe; Tower, 11 Hen. VI., No. 12 (4, p. 138b).

Bonaventure Shardelowe; Ch., 32 Eliz., No. 165.

Edmund Shardelowe, Gent.; Misc. Ch., 22 Jas. I, pt. 5, No. 64.

John de Shardelowe; Tower, 18 Edw. III. (1st Nos.), No. 37 (2, p. 117a).

Sharnborne or Sherborne—John Sharnbourn, Esq.; Ch., 3 Hen. VII., No. 62.

Thomas Shernburne; Ch., 4-5 Ph. and Mary, pt. 1, No. 128.

Christopher Sheareburne; W. and L., 17 and 18 Eliz., vol. 16, p. 113.

Christopher Sherborne; Ch., 18 Eliz., pt. 2, No. 49.

Francis Sharneborne; Misc. Ch., 7 Jas. I., pt. 6, No. 100.

Sharp—John Sharp, Knt.; Exch., 11-12 Hen. VIII. (Philip Bernard, Esch.), No. 15.

John Sharpe, Knt.; Ch., v.o. Hen. VIII., bund. 1, No. 219.

Sharrington—Giles Sherington; Ch., v.o. Ric. III. and Hen. VII., No. 278.

Thomas Sharyngton, Gent.; Ch., 11-12 Hen. VII., No. 66.

Thomas Sharyngton; Exch., 10-11 Hen. VII. (Rich. Hungerford, Esch.), No. 9.

Shaxton—John Shaxton; W. and L., 2 Edw. VI., vol. 3, p. 94.

Christopher Shaxton; W. and L., 8 Jas. I., bund. 13, No. 12.

Christopher Shaxton; Ch., 9 Jas. I., pt. 2, No. 47.

Leonard Shaxton, Gent.; Misc. Ch., 4 Chas. I., pt. 25, No. 86.

Sheldon—Mary Sheldon; Ch., 33 Hen. VIII., No. 54.

Shelton—Robert de Shelton; Tower, 34 Edw. I., No. 43 (1, 207a).

Alice, wife of John Shelton; Tower, 8 Edw. III. (1st Nos.), No. 33 (2, p. 59b).

Ralph Shelton; Tower, 2 Hen. V., No. 2 (4, p. 6b).

William Shelton; Tower, 9 Hen. V., No. 50b (4, p. 60b).

John Shelton (proof of age); Tower, 6 Hen. VI., No. 73 (4, p. 119a).

Shelton—John Shelton and Margaret ux. ej.; Tower, 9 Hen. VI., No. 43 (4, p. 131a).

Ralph Shelton, Knt.; Exch., 13-14 Hen. VII. (Philip Tilney, Esch.), No. 4.

Ralph Shelton, Knt.; Ch., 14 Hen. VII., No. 119.

Margaret Shelton; Ch., 18 Hen. VII., No. 82.

Mary Shelton, widow; Exch., 32-33 Hen. VIII. (John Tasburgh, Esch.), No. 5.

John Shelton, Knt.; Exch., 4-5 Ph. and Mary; 1 Eliz. (John Aldriche, Mayor and Esch.), No. 1.

Ralph Shelton, Knt.; W. and L., 20-24 Eliz., vol. 20, p. 251.

Ralph Shelton; Ch., 24 Eliz., pt. 1, No. 32.

Ralph Shelton, Knt.; Ch., 26 Eliz., No. 154.

William Shelton; Ch., 26 Eliz., No. 170.

Henry Shelton; Ch., 13 Chas. I., pt. 1, No. 124.

Sherman—Timothy Sherman, Gent.; Misc. Ch., 11 Chas. I., pt. 31, No. 102.

John Sherman; Ch., 40 Eliz., pt. 2, No. 143.

Sherwood—Nicholas Shirwodde; Ch., 29 Eliz., No. 226.

William Sherewood; Ch., 10 Jas. I, pt. 2, No. 13.

William Sherewoode; W. and L., 10 Jas. I., bund. 15, No. 71.

William Sherewood; W. and L., 10 Jas. I., bund. 15, No. 129.

William Sherewood (*mel. inq.*); Ch., 11 Jas. I., pt. 3, No. 119.

Shirley—Ralph Shurley; Exch., 8-9 Hen. VIII. (John Stode, Esch.), No. 3.

Shordiche. See **Bexwell alias Shordiche.**

Shouldham. See **Shuldham.**

Shovell—Nathaniel Shovell; Ch., 17 Chas. I., pt. 3, No. 7.

Nathanel Shovell; Ch., 17 Chas. I., pt. 3, No. 93.

Nathaniel Shovell; W. and L., 17 Chas. I., bund. 64, No. 28.

Shuldham—John Shuldham; Ch., 2-3 Edw. VI., pt. 2, No. 54.

John Shuldham; W. and L., 1-3 Ph. and Mary, vol. 7, p. 35.

Sidley (Sedley ?)—Martin Sydley; Ch., 9 Jas. I., pt. 1, No. 135.

Sidney—Thomas Sydney; Ch., 34 Hen. VIII., No. 39; and Exch., 34-35 Hen. VIII. (Robt. Downys, Esch.), No. 17.

Sidney—Thomas Sidney; Ch., 28 Eliz., No. 80.

Henry Sidney, Knt.; Ch., 12 Jas. I., pt. 1, No. 167.

Sir Henry Sydney; W. and L., Jas. I., bund. 22, No. 222.

Simonds—Ralph Symonds; Ch., 36 Hen. VIII., No. 155.

Ralph Symons; W. and L., 36 Hen. VIII., vol. 1, p. 106.

Ralph Symons; Ch., 3-4 Ph. and Mary, pt. 1, No. 75.

Giles Symonds; Ch., 39 Eliz., pt. 2, No. 91.

Singleton. See **Sengylton.**

Skerne—Bartholomew Skerne; Ch., 10 Eliz., No. 64.

Skippe—Thomas Skippe; W. and L. [Jas. I.], bund. 35, No. 7.

Thomas Skipp; W. and L., 14 Jas. I., bund. 33, No. 142.

Thomas Skypp; Ch., 19 Jas. I., pt. 1, No. 29.

Thomas Skypp; Ch., 20 Jas. I., pt. 1, No. 54.

Thomas Skipp, Esq.; Ch., 8 Chas. I., pt. 1, No. 46.

Skippon—Thomas Skippon; Ch., v.o. Eliz., bund. 3, No. 293.

William Skippon, Esq.; Misc. Ch., 11 Chas. I., pt. 22, No. 62.

Luke Skippon; Misc. Ch., 15 Chas. I., pt. 31, No. 171.

Skipwith—William Skipwith; Ch., 40 Eliz., pt. 2, No. 172.

Skryme, alias Cremer—John Skryme, alias Cremer; W. and L., 9-10 Jas. I., bund. 4, No. 146.

Smelt—Henry Smelt; Tower, 5 Ric. II., No. 68 (3, p. 44a).

Smith—Nicholas Smyth; Ch., 9 Hen. VII., No. 36.

John Smyth; Exch., 1 Mary to 1-2 Ph. and Mary (Edmd. Wright, Esch.), No. 12.

Nicholas Smyth, Gent.; Exch., 1 Eliz. (James Bigott, Esch.), No. 7.

George Smithe, Gent.; Exch., 1-3 Eliz. (Wm. Drake, Esch.), No. 4.

Smith—John Smythe; Ch., v.o. Eliz., bund. 2, No. 2.

George Smethe; Ch., 39 Eliz., pt. 2, No. 50.

William Smithe (proof of age); Ch., 42 Eliz., pt. 2, No. 36.

Robert Smythe; Ch., 43 Eliz., pt. 1, No. 24*.

Esdra Smith; W. and L., 1-5 Jas. I., vol. 29, p. 17.

Randle Smythe; W. and L., 1-6 Jas. I., bund. 2, No. 196.

Esdra Smithe; Ch., 3 Jas. I., pt. 1, No. 44.

Richard Smyth; Ch., 20 Jas. I., pt. 2, No. 68.

Richard Smithe; W. and L., 20 Jas. I., bund. 36, No. 90.

Smith—Richard Smyth, Gent.; Misc. Ch , 22 Jas. I., pt. 5, No. 58.

Richard Smyth; Ch., 3 Chas. I., pt. 2, No. 2.

Richard Smyth; Ch., 3 Chas. I., pt. 2, No. 43.

Richard Smith; W. and L , 3 Chas. I., bund. 19, No. 56.

Richard Smith; W. and L., 3 Chas. I., bund. 45, No. 125.

William Smith; W. and L., 5 Chas. I., bund. 48, No. 116.

William Smyth; Ch., 6 Chas. I., pt. 2, No. 39.

Owen Smyth, Knt.; Misc. Ch., 15 Chas. I., pt. 31, No. 57.

George Smyth; Misc. Ch., 15 Chas. I., pt. 31, No. 112.

Ralph Smyth, Gent.; Misc. Ch., 16 Chas. I., pt. 31, No. 113.

Snell—Robert Snell, Gent.; Misc. Ch., 21 Chas. I., pt. 32, No. 109.

Robert Snell; W. and L., 21 Chas. I., bund. 68, No. 151.

Soame—Thomas Some, Gent.; Exch., 11 Eliz. (Wm. Attwood, Esch.), No. 10.

John Soame ; W. and L. [Chas. I.], bund. 69, No. 123.

John Soame; Ch., 3 Chas. I., pt. 2, No. 127.

Somerset, Duke of—Jno., Duke of Somerset; Tower, 22 Hen. VI., No. 19 (4, p. 218a).

Sotherton—Nicholas Sotherton; Exch., 34-35 Hen. VIII. (Robt. Downys, Esch.), No. 10.

Nicholas Sotherton ; Ch., 35 Hen. VIII., No. 100.

Southwell—Robert Southwell, Knt.; Exch., 5-6 Hen. VIII. (Wm. Gryce, Esch.), No. 1.

Robert Southwell, Esq.; Exch., 6-7 Hen. VIII. (John Eston, Esch.), No. 26.

Elizabeth Southwell ; Exch., 9-10 Hen. VIII. (Henry Russell, Esch.), No. 12.

Francis Southwell; Ch., v.o. Hen. VIII., bund. 1, No. 183.

Robert Southwell, Knt.; Ch., 6 Hen. VIII., No. 15.

Richard Southwell, Knt.; Ch., 6 Eliz., No. 142.

Sir Richard Southwell; W. and L., 6 Eliz., bund. 9, No. 160.

Thomas Southwell, Esq.; Ch., 10 Eliz , No. 58.

Robert Southwell, Knt.; Ch., 41 Eliz., pt. 1, No. 33.

Elizabeth Suthwell ; Ch., 8 Hen. VIII., No. 48.

Spaney—Edward Spaney ; W. and L., 20 Eliz., vol. 19, p. 51.

Edward Spaney; Ch., 20 Eliz., pt. 2, No. 37.

Sparke, alias Parke—William Sparke, alias Parke; Ch., 43 Eliz., pt. 1, No. 23 *.

Spelman or Spilman—Henry Spylman; Ch., 11-12 Hen. VII., No. 17.

Thomas Spylman; Ch., 15 Hen. VII., No. 56.

Thomas Spylman; Ch., 19 Hen. VII., No. 55.

John Spelman; Exch., 3-4 Hen. VIII. (Anthony Hansart, Esch.), No. 12.

John Spelman; Ch., v.o. Hen. VIII., bund. 1, No. 203.

Elizabeth Spilman; Exch., 12-13 Hen. VIII. (Leonard Spencer, Esch.), No. 3.

Elizabeth Spilman; Ch., 13 Hen. VIII., No. 98.

Henry Spilman, Esq.; Exch., 15-16 Hen. VIII. (Christopher Harman, Esch.), No. 16.

Henry Spilman; Ch., 16 Hen. VIII., No. 65.

Elizabeth Spelman; Ch., 21 Hen. VIII., No. 140.

Elizabeth Spelman; Exch., 21-22 Hen. VIII. (Anthony Thwaytys, Esch.), Nos. 1 and 2.

John Spylman, Knt.; Exch., 37-38 Hen. VIII. (John Spencer, Esch.), No. 20.

John Spilman; Ch., 38 Hen. VIII., No. 14.

John Spylman, Knt.; W. and L., 38 Hen. VIII., vol. 2, p. 193.

Thomas Spelman, Esq.; Exch., 4-5 Eliz. (Augustine Curtes, Esch.), No. 12.

Thomas Spilman; Ch., 5 Eliz., pt. 2, No. 40.

Thomas Spelman; W. and L., 5-7 Eliz., vol. 10, p. 55.

John Spilman; Ch., 23 Eliz., pt. 2, No. 101.

Elizabeth Spilman; Ch., 3-4 Ph. and Mary, pt. 1, No. 86.

Sir Clement Spilman; W. and L., 5 Jas. I., bund. 8, No. 70.

Clement Spilman, Knt.; Ch., 5 Jas. I., pt. 1, No. 159.

Spencer (see **Despencer**)—Leonard Spencer, Esq.; Exch., 31-32 Hen. VIII. (Wm. Andrews, Esch.), No. 14.

John Spencer; Ch., 3 Eliz., No. 162.

James Spencer, Gent.; Exch., 11 Eliz. (Wm. Attwood, Esch.), No. 1.

Spencer (see **Despencer**)—Miles Spencer; W. and L., 11-12 Eliz., vol. 12, p. 10.

Miles Spencer?; W. and L., 12-14 Eliz., vol. 13, p. 109.

Miles Spencer, Doctor of Laws; Ch., 13 Eliz., pt. 2, No. 18.

Spice—Clement Spice; Tower, 1 Hen. VI., No. 14 (4, p. 69a).

Spilman. See **Spelman.**

Sponer or Spooner—John Sponer; Ch., v.o. Hen. VIII., bund. 2, No. 9.

Richard Sponer; Ch., 6 Hen. VIII., No. 140.

Richard Sponer; Exch., 5-6 Hen. VIII. (Wm. Gryce, Esch.), No. 10.

John Sponer; Exch., 12-13 Hen. VIII. (Leonard Spencer, Gent., Esch.), No. 1.

William Sponer; Ch., 34 Eliz., pt. 2, No. 115.

William Spooner; W. and L., 11 Jas. I., bund. 18, No. 23.

William Sponer; Ch., 11 Jas. I., pt. 3, No. 179.

Thomas Spooner, Esq.; Misc. Ch., 6 Chas. I., pt. 22, No. 34.

Sporle—William Sporle; W. and L., 10 Jas. I., bund. 16, No. 26.

William Sporle; Ch., 11 Jas. I., pt. 2, No. 66.

William Sporle; Ch., 12 Jas. I., pt. 2, No. 104.

John Sporle; Ch., v.o. 17 Jas. I., No. 26.

Spratt—Susan Spratt, widow; Misc. Ch., 19 Nov., 1658, pt. 32, No. 149.

Spring—Thomas Springe; Ch., 15 Hen. VIII., No. 13.

Robert Spryng, Esq.; Exch., 2-3 Edw. VI. (John Flowerdew, Esch.), No. 7.

Stafford—Walter de Stafford; Tower, 12 Edw. III. (1st Nos.), No. 21 (2, p. 84a).

Stafford, Earl of—Hugh, Earl of Stafford; Tower, 10 Ric. II., No. 38 (3, p. 84b).

Thomas, Earl of Stafford; Tower, 16 Ric. II. (1st pt.), No. 27 (3, p. 152b).

William, brother of Thomas, Earl of Stafford; Tower, 22 Ric. II., No. 46 (3, p. 245b).

Edward, Earl of Stafford; Tower, 4 Hen. IV., No. 41 (3, p. 288a).

Hugh Stafford; Tower, 1 Hen. VI., No. 33 (4, p. 71a).

Stalham—Matilda de Stalham; Tower, 20 Edw. I., No. 57 (1, p. 111a).

Stannowe—Roger Stannowe; Exch., 11 Eliz. (Wm. Attwood, Esch.), No. 8.

Roger Stannow; W. and L., 9-11 Eliz., vol. 11, p. 103.

Roger Stannowe; Ch., 11 Eliz., No. 98.

John Stanhaugh; W. and L., 9 Chas. I., bund. 55, No. 174.

John Stanhaugh; Ch., 10 Chas. I., pt. 3, No. 37.

William Stanhawe; Ch., 20 Chas. I., No. 37.

William Stanhawe; W. and L., 30 Chas. I., bund. 68, No. 97.

Stanton or Staunton— Isabella, ux. Galf. Stanton; Tower, 24 Edw. III. (1st Nos.), No. 51 (2, p. 164b).

Henry de Stanton (? Stanhow); Tower, 27 Edw. III. (1st Nos.), No. 32 (2, p. 181b).

William Staunton; Misc. Ch., 17 Jas. I., pt. 31, No. 86.

Stapleton—Miles Stapleton; Tower, 7 Hen. V., No. 47 (4, p. 41b).

Brian Stapleton; Tower, 17 Hen. VI., No. 34 (4, p. 188a).

Jno. Stapleton; Tower, 33 Hen. VI., No. 13 (4, p. 262b).

Miles Stapleton; Tower, 6 Edw. IV., No. 19 (4, p. 333b).

Brian Stapilton, Knt.; Exch., 9-10 Hen. VIII. (Henry Russell, Esch.), No. 3.

Starcolf—Richard Starcolf; Tower, 8 Edw. III. (1st Nos.), No. 14 (2, p. 58a).

Steede or Stede—John Stede; Exch., 32-33 Hen. VIII. (John Tasburgh, Esch.), No. 12.

John Stede; Ch., 33 Hen. VIII., No. 147.

William Stede; W. and L., 20-24 Eliz., vol. 20, p. 25.

William Stede; Ch., 21 Eliz., pt. 2, No. 39.

William Steede; W. and L., 11 Jas. I., bund. 18, No. 7.

William Steede; Ch., 11 Jas. I., pt. 3, No. 167.

Sterne—Thomas Sterne; Tower, 21 Edw. IV., No. 26 (4, p. 405a).

Thomas Sterne, Gent.; Exch., 28-29 Hen. VIII. (John Woodhouse, Esch.), No. 2.

Thomas Sterne; Ch., 29 Hen. VIII., No. 19.

Steward or Styward—Francis Styward; W. and L., 1-3 Eliz., vol. 8, p. 106.

Francis Steward; Ch., 2 Eliz., No. 35.

Alice Stuard; W. and L., 6 Eliz., bund. 9, No. 87.

Alice Steward; Ch., 6 Eliz., No. 145.

Steward or Styward—John Steward; W. and L., 1-4 Jas. I., bund. 1, No. 98.

John Steward; Ch., 3 Jas. I., pt. 1, No. 86.

William Steward, Esq.; Misc. Ch., 11 Jas. I., pt. 6, No. 138.

Stile—Anthony Style; Ch., v.o. Eliz., bund. 1, No. 512.

Stileman—Robert Styleman; W. and L., 10 Jas. I., bund. 14, No. 56.

Robert Stileman; Ch., 10 Jas. I., pt. 1, No. 103.

Stiles—Humphrey Stiles; W. and L., 42 Eliz., bund. 58, No. 28.

Humphrey Styles; Ch., v.o. 13 Chas. I., No. 35.

Stodhagh—John Stodhagh; Tower, 31 Hen. VI., No. 6, (4, p. 253b).

Stokes—Richard Stokes; Misc. Ch., 18 Jas. I., pt. 6, No. 111.

Stone—Robert Stone; Ch., 14 Jas. I., pt. 3, No. 91.

Robert Stone; W. and L., 14 Jas. I., bund. 20, No. 162.

Stonham—Robert Stonham; Tower, 9 Hen. V., No. 32a. (4, p. 58b).

Strabolgi, de—David de Strabolgi; Tower, 1 Edw. III. (1st Nos.), No. 85 (2, p. 5a).

David de Strabolgi; Tower, 9 Edw. III. (2nd Nos.), No. 63 (2, p. 70a).

David de Strabolgi; Tower, 11 Edw. III. (1st Nos.), No. 46 (2, p. 79b).

David de Strabolgi, Earl of Athol; Tower, 30 Edw. III. (2nd Nos.), No. 27 (2, p. 200a).

Elizabeth and Philippa, daus. and hrs. of David de Strabolgi; Tower, App., 49 Edw. III., No. 21 (4, p. 455b).

David de Strabolgi; Tower, 1 Ric. II., No. 164 (3, p. 10b).

Strange. See Le Strange.

Stratton—George Stratton; Exch., 13-14 Hen. VII. (Philip Tilney, Esch.), No. 6.

John Stratton, Esq.; Exch., 1-3 Eliz. (Wm. Drake, Esch.), No. 7.

Stubbe—Richard Stubbe; W. and L., 19 Jas. I., bund. 33, No. 200.

Francis Stubbe, Gent.; Misc. Ch., 22 Jas. I., pt. 5, No. 65.

Stubbs—Walter Stubbes, Gent.; Exch., 6-7 Hen. VIII. (John Eston, Esch.), No. 2.

Walter Stubbes; Ch., 7 Hen. VIII., No. 50.

Richard Stubbes; Ch., 19 Jas. I., pt. 1, No. 114.

Sturges—Elizabeth Sturges (proof of age); Ch., 10 Hen. VII., No. 171.

Francis Sturges; Ch., 17 Eliz., No. 100.

Sturges—Francis Sturges; W. and L., 17 and 18 Eliz., vol. 16, p. 53.

 Francis Sturgeis, Esq.; Exch., 17-18 Eliz. (John Bacon, Esch.), No. 9.

 Francis Sturges; Ch., 33 Eliz., pt. 2, No. 76.

Stuteville, de—Robert de Stutevill; Tower, 34 Edw. I., No. 33 (1, p. 206b).

 Thomas Stutevile; Exch., 6-7 Hen. VIII. (John Eston, Esch.), No. 25.

Suffolk, Duke of—William, Duke of Suffolk; Tower, 28 Hen. VI., No. 25 (4, p. 243b).

Suffolk, Earl of—Edward, Earl of Suffolk; Ch., v.o. Ric. III. and Hen. VII., No. 229.

 Edward, Earl of Suffolk; Ch., v.o. Ric. III. and Hen. VII., No. 317.

 Edward, Earl of Suffolk; Ch., v.o. Hen. VIII., bund. 1, Nos. 50, 64, 12.

Sulyard—John Sulyard, Knt.; W. and L., Exch., 3-4 Hen. VII. (Edw. Clopton, Esch.), No. 1.

 John Sulyard, Esq.; Exch., 31-32 Hen. VIII. (Wm. Andrews, Esch.), No. 10.

 John Sulyard, Knt.; Exch., 17-18 Eliz. (John Bacon, Esch.), No. 5.

Suncton (?)—Thomas Suncton [? Dunston or Hunston]; Ch., 43 Eliz., pt. 1, No. 25*.

Surrey, Earl and Countess of—Elizabeth, Countess of Surrey; Ch., 13 Hen. VII., No. 19.

 Thomas, Earl of Sussex; W. and L., 26-29 Eliz., vol. 21, p. 247.

 Thomas, Earl of Sussex; Ch., 28 Eliz., No. 84.

 Robert, Earl of Sussex; Exch., 34-35 Hen. VIII. (Robt. Dowyns, Esch.), No. 18.

 Henry, Earl of Sussex; Ch., 36 Eliz., pt. 2, No. 109.

 Robert, Earl of Sussex; Ch., 34 Hen. VIII., No. 38.

 Henry, Earl of Sussex; Ch., 3-4 Ph. and Mary, pt. 1, No. 77.

Sutton—Richard Sutton; Ch., 11 Chas. I., pt. 2, No. 9.

 Richard Sutton; Ch., 14 Chas. I., pt. 3, No. 83.

Sutton—Richard Sutton; W. and L., 14 Chas. I., bund. 61, No. 165.

Swillington—Roger Swillington; Tower, 5 Hen. V., No. 46 (4, p. 30b).

Jno. Swillington; Tower, 6 Hen. V., No. 24 (4, p. 34b).

Robert Swillington; Tower, 8 Hen. V., No. 71 (4, p. 50).

Joh., ux. Roger Swillington; Tower, 6 Hen. VI., No. 52 (4, p. 117b).

Sydney. See **Sidney.**

Talbot—Elizabeth, ux. Richard Talbot; Tower, 46 Edw. III. (1st Nos.), No. 66 (2, p. 323a).

Gilbert Talbot; Tower, 22 Ric. II., No. 47 (3, p. 251b).

Gilbert Talbot, Knt.; Exch., 9-10 Hen. VIII. (Henry Russell, Esch.), No. 6.

Gilbert Talbott, Knt.; Exch., 34-35 Hen. VIII. (Robt. Downys, Esch.), No. 23.

Gilbert, Talbott; W. and L., 35 Hen. VIII., vol. 1, p. 74.

Gilbert Talbott, Knt.; Ch., 35 Hen. VIII., No. 114.

Tateshale—Robert de Tateshale; Tower, 33 Hen. III., No. 39 (vol. 1, p. 6); 1 Edw. I., No. 4 (1, p. 48); 31 Edw. I., No. 40 (vol. 1, p. 147b).

Robert de Tateshale; Tower, 34 Edw. I., No. 57 (1, p. 209a) and (1, p. 181a).

Robert de Tateshale; Tower, 1 Edw. II., No. 55.

Johanna de Tatershale; Tower, 9 Edw. III. (1st Nos.), No. 46 (2, p. 66b).

Eva, ux. Robert Tateshale; Tower, 24 Edw. III. (1st Nos.), No. 97 (2, p. 165b).

Eva, ux. Robert Tateshale; Tower, 30 Edw. III. (1st Nos.), No. 44 (2, p. 198a).

Taverner—Thomas Taverner; W. and L., 1-5 Jas. I., vol. 29, p. 38.

Thomas Taverner; Ch., 2 Jas. I., pt. 2, No. 193.

Robert Taverner; W. and L., 16 Jas. I., bund. 28, No. 144.

Robert Taverner; Ch., 16 Jas. I., pt. 1, No. 67.

Anne Taverner; W. and L., 22 Jas. I., bund. 44, No. 78.

Anne Taverner; Ch., 2 Chas. I., pt. 3, No. 158.

Taylor—Thomas Taylor; Exch., 34-35 Hen. VIII. (Robert Downys, Esch.), No. 11.

Taylor alias Clarke. See Clarke alias Taylor.

Tempe—Thomas Tempe; Misc. Ch., 12 Jas. I., pt. 13, No. 118.

Tendring—William Tendring, Esq.; Ch., 15 Hen. VII., No. 7.

Terry—John Terry; Exch., 33-34 Hen. VIII. (Thos. Halse, Esch.)
    No. 6.

    John Terry, Ch., 34 Hen. VIII., No. 51.

Tesmond—Thomas Tesmond; W. and L., 12 Chas. I., bund. 58,
    No. 270.

    Thomas Tesmonde; Ch., 12 Chas. I., pt. 3, No. 67.

    Thomas Tesmond; Ch., 13 Chas. I., pt. 1, No. 182.

    Thomas Tesmond; W. and L., 14 Chas. I., bund. 61, No. 263.

    Thomas Tesmond; Ch., 14 Chas. I., pt. 3, No. 94.

Thaxter—Daniel Thaxter, Clerk; Misc. Ch., 10 Chas. I., pt. 31, No. 98.

Thimbleby—Richard Thymlyby; Exch., 3-4 Hen. VIII. (Anthony
    Hansart, Esch.), No. 11.

    Richard Thimylby; Ch., 4 Hen. VIII., No. 102.

    Thomas Thymylby; W. and L., 35 Hen. VIII., vol. 1, p. 35.

    Thomas Thimleby; Ch., 35 Hen. VIII., No. 158.

Thimblethorpe—Edmund Thymbylthorpe; Exch., 37-38 Hen. VIII.
    (John Spencer, Esch.), No. 13.

    Edmund Thymbelthorp; W. and L., 37 Hen. VIII., vol. 2,
    p. 55.

    Edward Thymbylthorpe; Ch., 37 Hen. VIII., No. 44.

    Barbara Themilthorpe; Ch., 17 Jas. I., pt. 3, No. 37.

    Sir Edmund Themilthorpe; W. and L., 11 Jas. I., bund. 18,
    No. 15.

    Edward Themilthorpe, Knt.; Ch., 11 Jas. I., pt. 3, No. 133.

Theobald—Anthony Theobald; W. and L., 19 Jas. I., bund. 53, No. 145.

    Anthony Theobald; Ch., 9 Chas. I., pt. 2, No. 44.

    Anthony Theobald, Gent.; Misc. Ch., 11 Chas. I., pt. 31,
    No. 176.

Thetford—John Thetford; Ch., 3-4 Ph. and Mary, pt. 1, No. 81.

    Robert Thetford; Ch., 34 Eliz., pt. 2, No. 36.

    Andrew Thetford; Ch., 37 Eliz., pt. 2, No. 53.

Thoresby—Robert Thoresby; Ch., 15 Hen. VII., No. 124.

    Thomas Thorysby; Exch., 2-3 Hen. VII. (Geo. Bokenham,
    Esch.), No. 4.

Thornton—William Thornton ; W. and L., 12-14 Eliz., vol. 13, p. 33.

William Thornton, Esq.; Ch., 13 Eliz., pt. 2, No. 15.

Robert Thornton ; Ch., 12 Jas. I., pt. 1, No. 145.

Thorp—John, fil. Robert de Thorp; Tower, 14 Edw. III. (1st Nos.), No. 16 (2, p. 92b).

John, fil. Robert de Thorp; Tower, 23 Edw. III. (2nd pt.), No. 164 (2, p. 159b).

Robert Thorpe; Ch., 16 Hen. VII., No. 68.

Robert Thorpe; Ch., 18 Hen. VII., No. 54.

Robert Thorpe; W. and L., 1-3 Jas. I., vol. 27, p. 191.

Robert Thorpe; Ch., v.o. 1 and 2 Jas. I., No. —

Threvell—Thomas Threvell ; Ch., v.o. 1 and 2 Jas. I., No. 30. See **Miller alias Threvell.**

Throgmerton—John Throgmerton; Exch., 1-2 Hen. VIII. (John Glemham, Esch.), No. 6.

Thurger—John Thurger ; W. and L., 16 Jas. I., bund. 28, No. 132.

John Thurger; Ch., 16 Jas. I., pt. 1, No. 39.

Thurlow—John Thurlowe; W. and L., 7 Chas. I., bund. 50, No. 199.

John Thurlowe; Ch., 7 Chas. I., pt. 3, No. 61.

Thursby—Henry Thursby ; Ch., 23 Hen. VII., No. 56.

Thomas Thursby ; Ch., 3 Hen. VIII., No. 97.

Thomas Thursbye, Esq.; Exch., 34-35 Hen. VIII. (Robt. Downys, Esch.), No. 2.

Thomas Thursby ; Ch., 35 Hen. VIII., No. 63.

Edmund Thursbie; W. and L., 1 and 2 Edw. VI., vol. 4, p. 24.

Edward Thursbie; Ch., 2 Edw. VI., pt. 2, No. 50.

Thomas Thursby; W. and L., 10 Chas. I., bund. 55, No. 22.

Thomas Thursby, Esq.; Ch., 10 Chas. I., pt. 3, No. 144.

Thwaytes—William Thwaytes; Exch., 24-25 Hen. VIII. (John Stede, Esch.), No. 6.

Thomas Thwaites; Ch., 36 Eliz., pt. 2, No. 91.

Richard Thwaite; W. and L., 15 Jas. I., bund. 25, No. 60.

Richard Thwaites; Ch., 15 Jas. I., pt. 1, No. 181.

Tilles—Robert Tylles; Exch., 3-4 Hen. VIII. (Anthy. Hansart, Esch.), No. 8.

Tilles—Robert Tyllys; Exch., 5-6 Hen. VIII. (Wm. Gryce, Esch.),
    No. 16.

    Robert Tillis; Ch., 4 Hen. VIII., No. 49.

    Robert Tyllis; Ch., 6 Hen. VIII., No. 66.

Tilney—Philip Tylney, Knt.; Ch., 16 Hen. VIII., No. 32.

    Robert Tylney; Ch., 43 Eliz., pt. 2, No. 41.

    Robert Tilney; W. and L., 43 and 44 Eliz., vol. 26, p. 111.

    Robert Tylney; Ch., 38 Eliz., pt. 1, No. 24.

    Francis Tilney; W. and L., 1-3 Jas. I., vol. 27, p. 202.

    Francis Tylney; Ch., 2 Jas. I., pt. 2, No. 9.

    Thomas Tylney; W. and L., 13 Jas. I., bund. 45, No. 13.

    Thomas Tylney; Ch., 4 Chas. I., pt. 4, No. 2.

Timpe. See **Tympe.**

Timperley—William Tymperley, Esq.; Exch., 20-21 Hen. VIII.
    (Henry Rychors, Esch.), No. 8.

Tindale—Richard Tindale; Tower, 3 Hen. V., No. 7 (4, p. 11b).

    William Tyndall, Knt.; Ch., 13 Hen. VII., No. 17.

    William Tyndale, Knt.; Exch., 13-14 Hen. VII. (Philip
        Tilney, Esch.), No. 2.

    Henry Tyndall; Ch., 36 Eliz., pt. 2, No. 28.

    Henry Tyndall; Ch., 40 Eliz., pt. 2, No. 107.

    Henry Tyndal, alias Kendell, Gent.; Misc. Ch., 14 Chas. I.,
        pt. 22, No. 8.

Tirell. See **Tyrrell.**

Tirry. See **Terry.**

Tite—Thomas Tyte; Ch., 19 Jas. I., pt. 13, No. 79.

Todenham. See **Tudenham.**

Toly—Robert Toli; Tower, 46 Hen. III., No. 7 (1, p. 21).

Tomlinson—Thomas Tomlinson; Ch., 14 Eliz., No. 121.

Tony—Robert de Tony and Matilda ux. ej.; Tower, 3 Edw. II., No. 33.

    Roger de Thony; Tower, 48 Hen. III., No. 28 (1, p. 27).

Topcliff—John Topcliffe, Gent.; Misc. Ch., 10 Chas. I., pt. 31, No. 97.

Toppesfield—Simon Toppesfeld, Gent.; Exch., 32-33 Hen. VIII. (John
    Tasburgh, Esch.), No. 1.

    William Toppesfeld, Gent.; Exch., 4 and 5, 5 and 6 P. and
        M. (Andrew Revet, Esch.), No. 5.

Touchet—William Touchet; Tower, 1 Edw. III., No. 47 (2, p. 3a).

Townsend—Adam atte Tounesend; Tower, 15 Edw. III. (2nd Nos.),
No. 1 (2, p. 100b).

Roger Touneshend, Knt.; Exch., 9-10 Hen. VII. (James
Braybroke, Esch.), No. 8.

Roger Townesende, Knt.; Ch., 10 Hen. VII., No. 170.

Roger Towneshende, Knt.; Ch., 11 and 12 Hen. VII., No. 1.

Eleanor Townesend; Ch., 17 Hen. VII., No. 1.

John Touneshend; Exch., 32-33 Hen. VIII. (John Tasburgh,
Esch.), No. 42.

Roger Towneshend, Knt.; W. and L., 5 and 6 Edw. VI., vol.
6, p. 68.

Roger Tounesend, Knt.; Ch., 6 Edw. VI., pt. 2, No. 32.

Lady Anne Towneshend; W. and L., 5 and 6 Edw. VI., vol.
6, p. 3.

Lady Anne Tounesend; Ch., 6 Edw. IV., pt. 2, No. 37.

Anne Touneshend; Exch., 7 Edw. VI. to 1 Mary (John
Spencer, Esch.), No. 16.

Robert Townesend, Knt.; Ch., 3 and 4 P. and M., pt. 1,
No. 69.

Roger Townesend; Ch., 7 Eliz., No. 137.

Thomas Townesend; W. and L., 15 and 16 Eliz., vol. 14,
p. 96.

Thomas Townshend; Ch., 16 Eliz., pt. 1, No. 55.

Thomas Townesende; Exch., 16-17 Eliz. (John Dowbes,
Esch.), No. 7.

Thomas Towneshend; W. and L., 20 Eliz., vol. 19, p. 168.

Thomas Townshend; Ch., 20 Eliz.. pt. 2, No. 39.

Thomas Towneshend; Ch., 33 Eliz., pt. 2, No. 71.

Thomas Towneshend; W. and L., 33 and 34 Eliz., vol. 23,
p. 99.

Roger Touneshend; Ch., 33 Eliz., pt. 2, No. 107.

John Towneshend, Knt.; W. and L., 1 and 2 Jas. I., vol. 28,
p. 122.

John Townesend; Ch., 1 Jas. I., pt. No. 42.

Roger Townesend, Bt.; Ch., 13 Chas. I., pt. 1, No. 26.

Trace (Tracy?)—Robert Trace; Exch., 11-12 Hen. VIII. (Philip
Bernard, Esch.), No. 9.

Trapps—Robert Trapps; Exch., 9 Eliz. (Edmd. Ashefeld, Esch.),
No. 9.

　　Robert Trapps; Ch., 9 Eliz., No. 50.

Tregoz—Galfs. Tregoz; Tower, 40 Hen. III., No. 7, (1, p. 15).

Trench—Thomas Trenche; Ch., 22 Jas I., pt. 2, No. 115.

Tresham—William Tresham, Bart.; Misc. Ch., 24 Chas. I., part 19,
No 5.

Trot—Thomas Trot; 6 Ric. II., No. 71 (3, p. 50b).

Trussell—William Trussell; 20 Edw. II., No. 83 (4, p. 402b).

　　Edward Trussell; Ch., 15 Henry VII., No. 118.

　　John Trussell; Ch.. 22 Henry VII., No. 70.

　　Edward Trussell; Ch., 22 Henry VII., No. 49.

Tuck—Richard Tucke; App., 12 Edw. III., No. I. (4, p. 441a).

Tudenham—Robert Tudenham; Tower, 1 Hen. V., No 56, proof of
age (4, p. 26b).

　　Thomas Tudenham; 5 Edw. IV., No. 34 (4, p. 332a).

Tumby (?)—Margaret Tumby, ux. Stephen; Tower, 23 Edw. III. (2nd
pt.), No. 42 (2, p. 136a).

　　Maria, ux. Stephen de Tumby; Tower, app., 28 Edw. III.,
No. 14 (4, p. 446a).

Turner—Henry Turnour, Esq.; Exch., 27-28 Henry VIII. (Thomas
Woodehouse, Esch.), No. 2.

　　Robert Turner; Ch., 9 Jas. I., pt. 2, No. 22.

　　Robert Turner; W. and L., 9 and 10 Jas. I., bund. 4, No.
134.

Tuthill—Henry Tuthill; W. and L., 8 Chas. I., bund. 52, No. 196.

　　Henry Tuthill; Ch., 8 Chas. I., pt. 3, No. 49.

　　Henry Tuthill; Ch., 9 Chas. I., pt. 2, No. 68.

Twyer—John Twyer; Tower, 21 Edw. IV., No. 47 (4, p. 406b).

Twytham—Alan de Twytham; Tower, 25 Edw. III. (1st Nos.), No.
22 (2, p. 169a).

Tympe—Thomas Tympe; W. and L., 14 Chas. I., bund. 60, No. 238.

　　Thomas Tympe; W. and L., 14 Chas. I., bund. 60, No. 231.

　　Thomas Tympe; Ch., 14 Chas. I., pt. 3, No. 19.

Tyrrell—James Tirell, Esq.; Exch., 31-32 Hen. VIII. (Wm. Andrews,
Esch.), No. 3.

　　Thomas Tirrill, Knt.; Ch., 5 Edw. VI., pt. 2, No. 37.

Tyrrell—John Tirrel, Knt.; Exch., 17-18 Eliz. (John Bacon, Esch.), No. 6.

Richard Tyrrell, Gent.; Misc., 17 Chas. I., pt. 31, No. 116.

Ufford—John de Ufford; Tower, 19 Edw. III. (2nd Nos.), No. 49 (2, p. 126b).

Robert de Ufford; Tower, 19 Edw. III. (2nd Nos.), No. 50 (2, p. 126b).

Cecilia de Ufford; Tower, 19 Edw. II., No. 74 (1, p. 326b).

John de Ufford; Tower, 35 Edw. III. (2nd pt.), No. 87 (2, p. 243a).

Margaret, ux. Robert Ufford; Tower, 41 Edw. III. (1st Nos.), No. 59 (2, p. 290a).

Robert de Ufford; Tower, 43 Edw. III. (2nd Nos.), No. 38 (2, p. 300a).

William de Ufford, Earl of Suffolk; Tower, 5 Ric. II., No. 57 (3, p. 40a).

Isabel, wife of William Ufford, Earl of Suffolk; Tower, 4 Hen. V., No. 48 (4, p. 24a).

Underhill. See **Knighton alias Underhill.**

Underwood—James Underwood; Exch., 4 and 5, 5 and 6 P. and M. (Andrew Revet, Esch.), No. 17.

James Underwood; Ch., 4 and 5 P. and M., pt. 3, No. 15.

John Underwood; W. and L., 9-11 Eliz., vol. 11, p. 93.

John Underwood; Exch., 11 Eliz. (Wm. Attwood, Esch.), No. 6.

John Underwood; Ch., 11 Eliz., No. 101.

Robert Underwood; (melius inquirendum), Ch., 44 Eliz., pt. 2, No. 60.

Robert Underwood; Ch., 42 Eliz., pt. 2, No. 38.

James Underwood; W. and L., 10 Chas. I., bund. 54, No. 77.

Urvyes—Nicholas Urvyes; Ch., 11 Chas. I., pt. 2, No. 7.

Utber—Bernard Utber; Misc. Ch., 4 Jas. I., pt. 6, No. 147.

Valencia, de—Adomar de Valencia and Maria ux. ej., Tower, 17 Edw. II., No. 76 (1, p. 312a, 315b).

Valeynes, de—Isabelle Valeynes; Tower, 37 Hen. III., No. 45 (1, p. 12).

Valeynes—Robert de Valeynes ; Tower, 21 Edw. I., No. 130.

Vallibus or Vaux—Jno. de Vallibus ; Tower, 15 Edw. I., No. 76; 16 Edw. I., No. 41, vol. — p. 97a.

> Joh., quond. ux. William de Vallibus ; Tower, 8 Ric. II., No. 83 (3, p. 71a).

Varley. See **Verley.**

Verdon—Elizabeth, ux. Theobald Verdon; Tower, 34 Ed. III. (1st Nos.), No. 83 (2, p. 222b).

> William Verden ; Ch., 39 Eliz., pt. 2, No. 68.

Vere—Dionisia, ux. Hugh de Veer; Tower, 7 Edw. II., No. 51 (1, p. 256a).

> Jno. de Vere ; Tower, 34 Edw. III. (1st. Nos.), No. 84 (2, p. 223a).

> Thomas de Vere, Comes Oxon.; Tower, 45 Edw. III. (1st Nos.), No. 45 (2, p. 310a).

> Alberic de Vere, Earl of Oxford ; Tower, 1 Hen. IV., No. 52 (3, p. 264b).

> Alice, wife of Alberic Vere ; Tower, 2 Hen. IV., No. 57 (3, p. 276a).

Verley—Hugh de Verle ; Tower, 8 Edw. I., No. 41 (1, p. 169).

Veylle, le—Thomas la Veylle ; Tower, incert., Hen. III., No. 190 (1, p. 345).

> Jno. le Veylle ; Tower, 7 Edw. I., No. 33 (1, p. 67) ; 23 Edw. I., No. 47b.

Ville—William la Ville ; Tower, 6 Hen. VI., No. 8 (4, p. 114b).

Ville, de la—John de la Ville ; (proof of age), 12 Hen. VI., No. 56 (4, p. 158a).

Vincent—Walter Vyncent; Exch., 1 Eliz. (James Bigott, Esch.), No. 15.

> Walter Vyncent; Ch., 1 Eliz., pt. 1, No. 124.

> Henry Vincent; Ch., 36 Eliz., pt. 2, No. 10.

> Thomas Vincent; W. and L., 10 Jas. I., bund. 16, No. 48.

> Thomas Vincent; Ch., 10 Jas. I., pt. 1, No. 142.

Violet—Grave Vilett, Gent.; Misc. Ch., 3 Chas. I., pt. 25, No. 21.

> Thomas Violett ; W. and L., 6 Chas. I., bund. 48, No. 154.

Wace—William Wace ; Tower, 29 Hen. VI., No. 37 (4, p. 250).

> William Wace, Yeoman ; Exch., 7-8 Eliz. (George Waller, Esch.), No 9.

Wachesham, de (Waxham)—Giles de Wachesham; Tower, 52 Hen. III., No. 14; and 1 Ed. I., No. 5.

Wade or Waite—William Wade, Gent.; Exch., 6-7 Hen. VIII. (John Eston, Esch.), No. 22.

William Wayte; Ch., 13 Hen. VII., No. 57.

Wake—John Wake; Tower, 22 Edw. III. (1st Nos.), No. 46 (2, p. 144a).

Thomas Wake; Ch., 23 Edw. III. (1st Nos.), No. 75 (2, p. 152a).

Walcote, de—Alexander de Walcote; Tower, 5 Edw. III. (2nd Nos.), No. 11 (2, p. 41b).

Alexander de Walcot; Tower, 6 Ed. III. (2nd Nos.), No. 2 (2, p. 50b).

William de Walcote; Tower, 29 Edw. III. (2nd Nos.), No. 37 (2, p. 195b).

Waldegrave—William Waldegrave, Knt.; Exch., 19-20 Hen. VIII. (Leonard Spencer, Esch.), No. 1.

Mary Walgrave; Exch., 4-5 Eliz. (Augustine Curtes, Esch.), No. 11.

Waleraund. See **Walraund.**

Wales, Prince and Princess of—Joan, Princess of Wales; Tower, 9 Ric. II., No. 54 (3, p. 77b).

Arthur, Prince of Wales; Ch., v.o. Ric. III. and Hen. VII., No. 281.

Walkfare—Richard Walkfare; Tower, 7 Ric. II., No. 81 (3, p. 62b).

Waller—William Waller, Esq., sen.; Exch., 2-3 Edw. VI. (John Flowerdew, Esch.), No. 8.

Wallis—John Wallys; Ch., v.o. Hen. VIII., bund. 2, No. 111.

Walpole—John Walpole; Exch., 9-10 Hen. VII. (James Braybroke, Esch.), No. 13.

John Walpole; Ch., 10 Hen. VII., No. 55.

Thomas Walpole; Ch., 5 Hen. VIII., No. 4.

Thomas Walpole; Ch., 6 Hen. VIII., No. 49.

Thomas Walpole; Exch., 5-6 Hen. VIII. (Wm. Gryce, Esch.), No. 14.

John Walpole; Ch., 4 and 5 P. and M., pt. 3, No. 2.

Edward Walpoole, Esq.; Ch., 1 Eliz., pt. 3, No. 132.

Walpole—Edward Walpole, Esq.; Exch., 1 Eliz. (James Bigott, Esch.),
No. 20.

Christopher Walpoole ; Ch., 38 Eliz., pt. 1, No. 51.

Walraund—John and Robert Walraund ; Tower, 2 Edw. II., No. 80.

Walter, fil.—Robert fil. Walter ; Tower, 2 Edw. III. (1st Nos.),
No. 59 (2, p. 16a).

Walter—William Walter ; Exch., 3-4 Edw. VI. (Henry Minne,
Esch.), No. 5.

William Walter ; W. and L., 3-5 Edw. VI., vol. 5, p. 58.

William Walter ; Ch., 4 Edw. VI., pt. 2, No. 62.

William Walter ; W. and L., 5 and 6 Edw. VI., vol. 6,
pp. 25, 79.

William Walter (proof of age) ; Ch., 7 Edw. VI., pt. 1,
No. 52.

Walton, de—Jno. de Walton ; Tower, 32 Edw. I., No. 33 (1, p. 187a).

Warblington, de—John de Warblyngton ; Tower, 6 Edw. III. (1st
Nos.), No. 72 (2, p. 50a).

Ward—Geoffrey Ward, Gent. ; Exch., 4 and 5, 5 and 6 P. and M.
(Andrew Revet, Esch.), No. 14.

Henry Warde ; Ch., 3 and 4 P. and M., pt. 1, No. 73.

Geoffrey Ward ; Ch., 5 and 6 P. and M., pt. 1, No. 28.

William Warde ; Ch., v.o. Eliz., bund. 2, No. 113.

Edward Warde ; Ch., 25 Eliz., No. 182.

Thomas Warde ; Ch., 27 Eliz., No. 155.

Thomas Warde ; W. and L., 8 and 9 Jas. I., bund. 5, No.
274.

Thomas Warde ; Ch., 9 Jas. I., pt. 1, No. 131.

Thomas Warde, Esq. ; Ch., 8 Chas. I., pt. 3, No. 168

Richard Ward, Gent. ; Misc. Ch., 8 Chas. I., pt. 31, No. 91.

Warmoll—Owen Warmoll ; W. and L., 2 Chas. I., bund. 44, No. 102.

Owen Warmoll ; Ch., 2 Chas. I., pt. 3, No. 73.

Owen Warmoll ; W. and L., 4 Chas. I., bund. 52, No. 174.

Owen Warmoll (melius inquirendum) ; Ch., 8 Chas. I., pt. 2,
No. 51.

Owen Warmol ; Ch., 8 Chas. I., pt. 2, No. 21.

Owen Warmoll ; Ch., 12 Chas. I., pt. 3, No. 35.

Owen Warmoll ; W. and L., 12 Chas. I., bund. 56, No. 24.

Warner—Robert Warner; Tower, 21 Edw. IV., No. 7 (4, p. 404b).

    Edward Warner, Knt.; Exch., 8-9 Eliz. (Thos. Dereham, Esch.), No. 3.

    John Warner, Gent.; Exch., 9-10 Hen. VIII. (Hen. Russell, Esch.), No. 13.

    Henry Warner; Exch., 10-11 Hen. VIII. (Geoffrey Cobbe, Esch.), No. 7.

    John Warner; Ch., 10 Hen. VIII., No. 96.

    Henry Warner; Ch., 11 Hen. VIII., No. 30.

    Robert Warner; Exch., 32-33 Hen. VIII. (John Tasburgh, Esch.), No. 40.

    Edward Warner; Ch., 8 Eliz., No. 67.

    Thomas Warner; Ch., 14 Eliz., No. 122.

    Robert Warner; W. and L., 17 and 18 Eliz., vol. 17, p. 44.

    Robert Warner; Ch., 18 Eliz., pt. 2, No. 41.

    John Warner; W. and L., 35-42 Eliz., vol. 24, p. 243.

    John Warner; Ch., 41 Eliz., pt. 2, No. 78.

    Henry Warner, Esq.; Misc. Ch., 21 Chas. I., pt. 32, No. 120.

    Henry Warner, Esq.; Ch., 21 Chas. I., pt. 32, No. 146.

Warren, de—William de Warrenne; Tower, 15 Edw. I., No. 23 (1, p. 93b).

    John de Warenne, Earl of Surrey; Tower, 21 Edw. III. (1st Nos.), No. 58.

Warren, alias Baker—John Waren, alias Baker; Exch., 32-33 Hen. VIII. (John Tasburgh, Esch.), No. 20.

Warwick, Earl of—Thomas, Earl of Warwick; Tower, 21 Ric. II. (see 3, p. 224a).

    Isabella, late Countess Warwick; Tower, 18 Hen. VI., No. 3 (4, p. 193b).

    Anna, dr. and hr. of the Duke of Warwick; Tower, 27 Hen. VI., No. 34 (4, p. 239a).

Waters—Edward Waters; W. and L., 15 and 16 Eliz., vol. 14, p. 95.

    Edward Waters; Ch., 16 Eliz., pt. 1, No. 64.

Watts—Laurence Wattes; Ch., 17 Jas. I., pt. 3, No. 89.

Waxham. See **Wachesham.**

Wauton (Walton ?)—Jno. de Wauton (daughter of); Tower, 33 Edw. I., No. 267.

Wayte. See **Wade.**

Welby—Thomas Welby; Ch., 6 Hen. VIII., No. 48.

Weld—John Weld; W. and L., 1-4 Jas. I., bund. 1, No. 106.

Welden—Hugh Welden, Esq.; Exch., 34-35 Hen. VIII. (Robt. Downys, Esch.), No. 32.

Welholm, de—Robert de Welholm; Tower, 2 Edw. III. (1st Nos.), No. 18 (2, p. 14a).

Wells—Jno. de Welles; Tower, Appx., 35 Edw. III., No. 5 (4, p. 450a).

    John Welles; Exch., 9-10 Hen. VII. (James Braybroke, Esch.), No. 1.

    John Wellys; Ch., 11 and 12 Hen. VII., No. 93.

    Thomas de Welles; Exch., 20-21 Hen. VIII. (Henry Rychers, Esch.), No. 11.

    Thomas Wellys; Ch., 21 Hen. VIII., No. 58.

Wensley—Thomas Wensley; Misc. Ch., 11 Chas. I., pt. 31, No. 105.

Went—Geoffrey Wente; Exch., 34-35 Hen. VIII. (Robt. Downys, Esch.), No. 12.

Wentworth—Henry Wentworth; Tower, 22 Edw. IV., No. 11 (4, p. 409a).

    Thomas Wentworthe, Knt.; Exch., 4-5 Edw. VI. (John Tirrel, Esch.), No 17.

    Richard Wentworth, Knt.; Exch., 20-21 Hen. VIII. (Henry Rychers, Esch.), No. 5.

    Michael Wentworth, Esq.; Exch., 1 Eliz. (James Bigott, Esch.), No. 6.

West—Thomas West, Gent.; Misc. Ch., 21 Jas. I., pt. 5, No. 61.

Westgate—William Westgate, yeoman; Exch., 1 Eliz. (James Bigott, Esch.), No. 13.

    William Westgate; Ch., 1 Eliz., pt. 1, No. 130.

    Robert Westgate; W. and L., 13 Jas. I., bund. 21, No. 43.

    Robert Westgate; Ch., 13 Jas. I., pt. 1, No. 5.

Westle, de—Burgia, ux. John de Westlee; Tower, 49 Edw. III. (2nd pt.), No. 53 (2, p. 350b).

    John de Westle; Tower, 50 Edw. III. (1st pt.), No. 66 (2, p. 356a).

Westmoreland, Earl of—Ralph Skarles, Earl of Westmoreland; Tower, 2 Ric. III., No. 14 (4, p. 419b).

Weston, de—Weston, Jno. de; Tower, 28 Edw. I., No. 80 (1, p. 164a).

Robert Weston; Misc. Ch., 13 Jas. I., pt. 6, No. 142.

Wetherby—Thomas Wetherby; Tower, 24 Hen. VI., No. 16 (4, p. 225a).

Weyland, de—Thomas de Weylond; Tower, 18 Edw. I., No. 51 (1, p. 102a).

William de Weyland; Tower, 1 Edw. III. (1st Nos.), No. 79 (2, p. 4b).

John de Waylaund; Tower, 1 Edw. III. (2nd Nos.), No. 83 (2, p. 11b).

Whall—Richard Whall; W. and L., 19 Jas. I., bund. 31, No. 43.

Richard Whall; W. and L., Ch., 19 Jas. I., pt. 1, No. 32.

Richard Whall; Ch., 15 Chas. I., pt. 4, No. 58.

Richard Whall; Ch., 15 Chas. I., pt. 3, No. 3.

Richard Whall; W. and L., 15 Chas. I., bund. 62, No. 280.

Wheatley—William Wheetley; Ch., 39 Eliz., pt. 1, No. 30.

Anthony Wheatley; Ch., 43 Eliz., pt. 2, No. 74.

Whipple—Thomas Whiple; W. and L., 10 Jas. I., bund. 16, No. 34.

Thomas Whipple; W. and L., 11 Jas. I., bund. 18, No. 160.

Thomas Whiple; Ch., 11 Jas. I., pt. 2, No. 38.

Thomas Whiple; Ch., 11 Jas. I., pt. 3, No. 153.

White—Bartholomew White; Ch., 10 Henry VII., No. 91.

Bartholomew White; Exch., 10-11 Hen. VII. (Richard Hungerford, Esch.), No. 1.

Robert Whight; Ch., v.o. Hen. VIII., bund. 2, No. 111.

Edward Whight [White]; Ch., 20 Hen. VIII., No. 43.

Edward White, Knt.; Exch., 20-21 Hen. VIII. (Henry Rychers, Esch.), No. 19.

George White, Esq.; Exch., 37-38 Hen. VIII. (John Spencer, Esch.), No. 18.

George White; W. and L., 38 Hen. VIII., vol. 2, p. 133.

George White; Ch., 38 Hen. VIII., No. 15.

Edmund White, Esq.; Exch., 4-5 Edw. VI. (John Tirrell, Esch.), No. 5.

Edward White; Ch., 5 Edw. VI., pt. 2, No. 34.

John White, alias Hales; Ch., 29 Eliz., No. 67.

White—Francis White, alias Hale; Ch., 39 Eliz., pt. 1, No. 38.

Blaise White, clerk; Ch., 39 Eliz., pt. 2, No. 46.

Blaise White, clerk; Ch., 40 Eliz., pt. 2, No. 103.

Helena White, alias Hall; W. and L., 1-3 Jas. I., vol. 27, p. 204.

Whitefoot—Michael Whitefoote; Misc. Ch., 18 Jas. I., pt. 31, No. 95.

Whiteman. See **Wightman.**

Whitewood or Witwood—William Wytewood; W. and L., 26-29 Eliz., vol. 21, p. 127.

William Witewoode; Ch., 28 Eliz., No. 103.

William Witwoode; Ch., 22 Eliz., pt. 2, No. 58.

Whitred, alias Saborne. See **Saborne**—Henry Whitred, alias Saborne; Ch., 2 Jas. I., pt. 2, No. 76.

Henry Whitred, alias Saborne; W. and L., 1-3 Jas. I., vol. 27, p. 187.

Whitwell, de—William de Whitwell; Tower, 22 Edw. I., No. 37 (1, p. 119a).

Jno. de Whitewell; Tower, 26 Edw. I., Nos. 26 and 27; Edw. I., No. 33 (1, p. 149b).

Thomas Whitwell; Tower, divers years, bef. Hen. VI. (4, p. 299b).

Jno. Whitewell; Tower, 7 Hen. VI., No. 47 (4, p. 121).

Richard Whitewell; Tower, 20 Edw. IV., No. 92 (4, p. 403b).

John Whitwell; W. and L., 36 Hen. VIII., vol. 1, p. 110.

John Whitwell; Ch., 36 Hen. VIII., No. 124.

Wichingham, de—William de Wichingham; Tower, 51 Edw. III. (2nd Nos.), No. 32.

Nicholas Wichingham and Elizabeth ux. ej.; Tower, 12 Hen. VI., No. 31 (4, p. 154a).

Robert Wichingham; Tower, 29 Hen. VI., No. 3 (4, p. 246a).

John Wichingham; Ch., v.o. Ric. III. and Hen. VII., No. 286.

John Wychyngham; Exch., 3-4 Hen. VII. (Edward Clopton, Esch.), No. 5.

John Wichingham; Ch., 4 Hen. VII., No. 65.

John Wichingham; Ch., 21 Hen. VII., No. 13.

Wigfall—William Wigfall, Clerk; Misc. Ch., 16 Chas. I., pt. 31, No. 22.

Wightman—Robert Wightman; Ch., 9 Jas. I., pt. 2, No. 18.

Robert Wightman; W. and L., 8 and 9 Jas. I., bund. 5, No. 239.

Wilby—Thomas Wylby, Gent.; Exch., 5-6 Hen. VIII. (Wm. Gryce, Esch.), No. 13.

William Wylby; Ch., 18 Hen. VII., No. 55.

Wilcock—Thomas Wilcock; W. and L., 44 Eliz., bund. 7, No. 160.

Thomas Wilcocke; Ch., 45 Eliz., No. 73.

Wild—Edward Wylde; Ch., 38 Eliz., pt. 1, No. 31.

Robert Wylde; Ch., 5 Jas. I., No. 27.

Robert Wyldo; W. and L., 1-6 Jas. I., bund. 2, No. 187.

Emma Wilde; Ch., 15 Jas. I., pt. 1, No. 32.

Emma Wilde; W. and L., 15 Jas. I., bund. 25, No. 120.

Stephen Wylde; Ch., v.o. 16 Chas. I., No. 29.

Wilkins—Thomas Wilkins; Misc. Ch., 4 Chas. I., pt. 24, No. 144.

Willoughby, de—John de Willoughby; Tower, 23 Edw. III. (1st Nos.), No. 59 (2, p. 151a).

Richard de Willoughby; Tower, 36 Edw. III. (2nd pt.), No. 81 (2, p. 256b).

John de Willoughby; Tower, 46 Edw. III. (1st Nos.), No. 78 (2, p. 323b).

Robert de Willoughby; Tower, 20 Ric. II., No. 54 (3, p. 208b).

William Willoughby, Lord D'Eresby; Tower, 11 Hen. IV., No. 29 (3, p. 329a).

John Willoughby; Tower, 15 Hen. VI., No. 3 (4, p. 173b).

Robert, Dnus de Willoughby; Tower, App., 37 Hen. VI., No. 1 (4, p. 473b).

Robert Willoughby; Tower, 5 Edw. IV., No. 35 (4, p. 332b).

Robert Willoughby; Tower, 7 Edw. IV., No. 37 (4, p. 340a).

Matilda Willoughby; v.o. Rich. III. and Hen. VII., No. 251.

Matilda Willoughby, widow; Ch., 13 Hen. VII., No. 15.

Matilda Willughby; Exch., 13-14 Hen. VII. (Philip Tilnoy, Esch.), No. 12.

Willoughby—Anne Willoughby, widow; Ch., 15 Hen. VII., No. 116.

Anne Willoughby; Ch., 19 Hen. VII., No. 54.

Lady Margery de Willoughby; Exch., 6-7 Hen. VIII. (John Eston, Esch.), No. 7.

Margery Willoughbie; Ch., 7 Hen. VIII., No. 20.

William Willughby; Exch., 18-19 Hen. VIII. (Wm. Gryce, Esch.), No. 3.

Margaret Willoughby; Exch., 34-35 Hen. VIII. (Robt. Downys, Esch.), No. 6.

Margaret Willoughby; W. and L., 35 Hen. VIII., vol. 1, p. 38.

Margaret Willoughby; Ch., 35 Hen. VIII., No. 90.

John Willoughby; Ch., 4 and 5 P. and M., pt. 1, No. 119.

John Willoughbie, Knt.; Ch., 4 Jas. I., pt. 2, No. 43.

Wilton—Arthur Wilton; W. and L., 42 Eliz., bund. 3, No. 115.

Arthur Wilton; Ch., 8 Jas. I., pt. 2, No. 191.

Richard Wilton; W. and L., 13 Chas. I., bund. 60, No. 365.

Richard Wilton; Ch., 14 Chas. I., pt. 3, No. 51.

Wilts, Earl of—James, Earl of Wilts; Tower, 1 Edw. IV., No. 29 (4, p. 309b).

Wincelawe—William Wincelawe; Tower, 12 Hen. IV. (proof of age), No. 48 (3, p. 335a).

Winde—Richard Wynde; W. and L., 11 and 12 Eliz., vol. 12, p. 22.

Thomas Winde; Ch., 1 and 2 Jas. I., vol. 28, p. 138.

Thomas Wynde, Esq.; Ch., 2 Jas. I., pt. 2, No. 120.

Windam. See **Wyndham.**

Wingfield—Elianor, ux. Jno. de Wingfield; Tower, 49 Edw. III. (2nd pt.), No. 54 (2, p. 351a).

Robert Wingfeld; Tower, 21 Edw. IV., No. 60 (4, p. 408a), and see No. 62.

William Wingfield; Tower, 6 Hen. V., No. 20 (4, p. 34b).

Anne Wingfeild; Ch., 3 Hen. VII., No. 96*.

Lady Anne Wyngfeld; Exch., 13-14 Hen. VII. (Philip Tilney, Esch.), No. 9.

Margaret Wingfeild; Ch., 21 Hen. VII., No. 17.

John Wyngfeld; Exch., 10-11 Hen. VIII. (Geoffrey Cobbe, Esch.), No. 4.

Wingfield—John Wingfeild; Ch., 11 Hen. VIII., No. 79.

 Anthony Wyngfeld, Knt.; Exch., 7 Edw. VI. to 1 Mary (John Spencer, Esch.), No. 12.

 Elizabeth Wyngfeld; Exch., 1 Eliz. (James Bigott, Esch.), No. 1.

 Mary Wingefeild; Ch., 42 Eliz., pt. 2, No. 107.

Winter—Edmund Winter; Tower, 26 Hen. VI., No. 4 (4, p. 234b).

 John Winter; Exch., 10-11 Hen. VII. (Richd. Hungerford, Esch.), No. 2.

 John Wynter; Ch., 10 Hen. VII., No. 71.

 John Wynter, Esq.; Ch., 1 Eliz., pt. 3, No. 127.

 John Wynter, Esq.; Exch., 1 Eliz. (James Bigott, Esch.), No. 38.

Wirham—Thomas de Wyrham; Tower, 29 Edw. III. (1st Nos.), No. 12 (2, p. 191b).

 Thomas de Wyrham; Tower, 12 Ric. II., No. 58 (3, p. 105b).

Wisham (Isham?)—Hawisia, ux. John de Wysham; Tower, 33 Edw. III. (1st Nos.), No. 22 (2, p. 212a).

Wiskard (Guiscard?)—Thomas Wyskard; Exch., 37-38 Hen. VIII. (John Spencer, Esch.), No. 15.

 Thomas Wyscard; W. and L., 37 Hen. VIII., vol. 2, p. 59.

 Thomas Wyskard; Ch., 37 Hen. VIII., No. 46.

 William Wyscard, yeoman; Misc. Ch., 1 Chas. I., pt. 5, No. 74.

Withe—Richard Wythe, Gent.; Misc. Ch., 8 Chas. I., pt. 31, No. 92.

Wolde—John Wolde; Ch., 30 Eliz., pt. 2, No. 102.

 John Wolde; Ch., 31 Eliz., pt. 2, No. 62.

 John Wolde; Ch., 32 Eliz., No. 49.

 John Wolde; Ch., 3 Jas. I., pt. 1, No. 91.

Wolferston—Thomas Wolferston, Esq.; Exch., 6-7 Hen. VIII. (John Eston, Esch.), No. 21.

Wolmer—John Wolmer; Ch., 41 Eliz., pt. 2, No. 81.

Wood—Edmund Woode; W. and L., 1 Edw. VI., vol. 3, p. 86.

 Edmund Wood; Exch., 2-3 Edw. VI. (John Flowordew, Esch.), No. 17.

 Edward Wood; Ch., 2 Edw. VI., pt. 2, No. 48.

 Robert Wood; Ch., 21 Jas. I., pt. 2, No. 60.

 Robert Wood, Knt.; Ch., 33 Eliz., pt. 1, No. 14

Woodcock—William Woodcok; Tower, 34-35 Hen. VIII. (Robt. Downys, Esch.), No. 40.

Woodhouse—John Woodhouse; Tower, 9 Hen. VI., No. 34 (4, p. 130a).

John Woodhouse; Tower, 6 Edw. IV., No. 6 (4, p. 333b).

John Woodhouse; W. and L., 5 and 6 Edw. VI., vol. 6, p. 80.

John Woodhouse; Ch., 6 Edw. VI., pt. 2, No. 38.

John Woodhouse; Ch., 7 Edw. VI., pt. 1, No. 44.

Lady Elizabeth Woodhouse; Ch., 6 Eliz., No. 149.

Elizabeth Woodhouse; W. and L., 6 Eliz., bund. 9, No. 96.

William Woodhouse; Ch., 8 Eliz., No. 64.

Edmund Woodhouse, Esq.; Exch., 8-9 Eliz. (Thomas Dereham, Esch.), No. 2.

Thomas Woodhouse; Ch., 14 Eliz., No. 116.

Thomas Woodhouse, Knt.; W. and L., 15 and 16 Eliz., vol. 14, p. 116.

Lady Elizabeth Woodhouse; Ch., 20-24 Eliz., vol. 20, p. 88.

Elizabeth Woodhouse; Ch., 21 Eliz., pt. 2, No. 49.

Sir Philip Woodhouse; W. and L., 22 Jas. I., bund. 39, No. 134.

Philip Woodhowse, Knt.; Ch., 22 Jas. I., pt. 2, No. 114.

Sir Henry Woodhouse; W. and L., 6 Chas. I., bund. 55, No. 162.

Henry Woodhouse; Ch., 10 Chas. I., pt. 3, No. 116.

William Woodhouse, Knt.; Misc. Ch., 16 Chas. I., pt. 31, No. 179.

Woods alias Atwoods—Joan Woodes alias Atwoodes; W. and L., 15 Jas. I., bund. 24, No. 45.

John Woods alias Atwood; Ch., 15 Jas. I., pt. 2, No. 4.

Worcester, Earl of—Edward, Earl of Worcester; Exch., 1-2 Hen. VII. (Gregory Lovell, Esch.), No. 11.

Charles, Earl of Worcester; Ch., 17 Hen. VIII., No. 41.

Wormall. See **Warmoll.**

Worship—William Worship; W. and L., 9 Chas. I., bund. 60, No. 264.

Worship—William Worshipp; Ch., 14 Chas. I., pt. 3, No. 21.

Worts—Thomas Wortes; Misc. Ch., 10 Chas. I., pt. 31, No. 99.

Wotton—Elizabeth Wotton; Ch., 28 Hen. VIII., No. 6.

Eliz. Wutton; Exch., 27-28, Hen. VIII. (Thomas Woodhouse, Esch.), No. 8.

John Wotton, Esq.; Exch., 37-38 Hen. VIII. (John Spencer, Esch.), No. 4.

John Wotton; W. and L., 38 Hen. VIII., and 1 Edw. VI., bund. 1a, No. 72.

John Wotton; Ch., 38 Hen. VIII., No. 31.

Elizabeth Wotton; C. of W., 38 Hen. VIII. and 1 Edw. VI., 1a, No. 85.

Elizabeth Wotton; Ch., 1 Edw. VI., pt. 2, No. 12.

Roger Wotton; W. and L., 1 Chas. I., bund. 54, No. 111.

Roger Wootton; Ch., 9 Chas. I., pt. 2, No. 63.

Wright—Thomas Wright; Ch., 41 Eliz., pt. 2, No. 55.

John Wright, Gent.; Misc. Ch., pt. 6, No. 104.

Wroth—John Wroth; Tower, 20 Edw. IV., No. 27 (4, p. 399b).

Wulferston—Robert Wulferston; Exch., 9-10 Hen. VII. (James Braybroke, Esch.), No. 2.

Richard Wulverston, Esq.; Exch., 30-31 Hen. VIII. (Wm. Woodhouse, Esch.), No. 14.

Wutton. See **Wotton.**

Wydevill—Richard Wydevill, Knt.; Ch., v.o. Rich. III. and Hen. VII., No. 11.

Wynde—Richard Wynde; Ch., 12 Eliz., No. 64.

Wyndham—John Wyndham; Tower, 16 Edw. IV., No. 24 (4, p. 375a).

Thomas Wyndham, Knt.; Ch., 14 Hen. VIII., No. 16.

Edward Wyndham, Knt.; W. and L., 9-11 Eliz., vol. 11, p. 10.

Edmund Wyndam; Exch., 11 Eliz. (Wm. Attwood, Esch.), No. 13; Ch., 11 Eliz., No. 96.

Francis Wyndham; Ch., 34 Eliz., pt. 1, No. 74.

Thomas Wyndham; Ch., 43 Eliz., pt. 2, No. 90.

Wythe—Jane Wythe; Exch., 4 and 5, 5 and 6 P. and M. (Andrew Revet, Esch.), No. 12.

Yarmouth—Richard Yarmouth; Tower, 12 Ric. II., No. 80 (3, p. 106a).

Yates—John Yates; Tower, 5 Edw. IV., No. 37 (4, p. 332b).

Yatingden, de—Nicholas de Yatingden; Tower, 2 Edw. I., No. 13 (1, p. 51).

Yaxley—John Yaxley; Ch., 21 Hen. VII., No. 3.

William Yaxley; Ch., 1 Mary, pt. 3, No. 14.

Richard Yaxley, Esq.; Exch., 4 and 5, 5 and 6 P. and M. (Andrew Revet, Esch.), No. 20.

William Yaxley; Ch., 31 Eliz., pt. 2, No. 21.

Yelverton—William Yelverton; Ch., 14 Hen. VII., No. 110.

William Yelverton, Esq.; Exch., 10-11 Hen. VIII. (Geoffrey Cobbe, Esch.), No. 8.

William Yelverton; Ch., 11 Hen. VIII., No. 32.

William Yelverton, sen., Esq.; Exch., 32-33 Hen. VIII. (John Tasburgh, Esch.), No. 2.

William Yelverton; Ch., 33 Hen. VIII., No. 34.

William Yelverton; Ch., 30 Eliz., pt. 2, No. 91.

William Yelverton; W. and L., 33 and 34 Eliz., vol. 23, p. 43.

Henry Yelverton; Ch., 43 Eliz., pt. 2, No. 94.

Sir William Yelverton; W. and L., 12 Chas. I., bund. 56, No. 149.

William Yelverton, Bart.; Ch., 12 Chas. I., pt. 3, No. 117.

York, Duke of—Edmund, Duke of York; Tower, 3 Hen. IV., No. 36 (3, p. 282a).

Philippa, Duchess of York; Tower, 10 Hen. VI., No. 45 (4, p. 137b).

Joh., ux. Edward, Duke of York; Tower, 3 Hen. V., No. 55 (4, p. 20a).

Zouche, le—William Le Zouche; Tower, 26 Edw. III. (1st Nos.), No. 51 (2, p. 174a).

William le Zouche; Tower, 5 Ric. II., No. 62 (3, p. 43b).

William le Zouche; Tower, 19 Ric. II., No. 52 (3, p. 192a).

Richard le Zouche; Tower, 20 Ric. II., No. 56 (3, p. 209b).

William le Zouch; Tower, 3 Hen. V., No. 46 (4, p. 15a).

Elizabeth, wife of William Zouche; Tower, 4 Hen. VI., No. 7 (4, p. 99b).

AGAS H. GOOSE, PRINTER, RAMPANT HORSE STREET, NORWICH.